JAMES BEARD'S MENUS FOR ENTERTAINING

Delacorte Press New York

CONTENTS

Introduction vii

I   *Breakfasts* 1

      Early 3
      Late 11

II   *Luncheons* 29

      Informal 32
      Formal 46
      Summer 53
      Ladies Only 64

III   *Dinners* 75

      Informal 77
      Formal 100
      Easy to Prepare 119
      Prepare in Advance 136
      Summer 164

IV   *Buffets* 177

      Luncheon 180
      Dinner 194
      Supper 215

V   *Cocktail Parties* 227

      Large 230
      Small 245

VI   *Entertaining Outdoors*   255

    Indoor–Outdoor Cooking .   257
    Picnics   288

VII   *Celebrations*   305

VIII   *Appendix*   341

    Basic Recipes   343
    A Guide to Wines   375
    A Guide to Apéritifs . . .   380
    A Guide to Liqueurs   382

IX   *Index*   385

INTRODUCTION

Entertaining is my main pleasure, my forte; and beyond that it is essential to my livelihood. I do it frequently with little help and often with none at all. It is not unusual for me to arrive home at 5:30 after a full day's work, with eight guests due for cocktails and dinner two hours later.

Whether you are entertaining at breakfast, luncheon, cocktails or dinner, you must plan carefully and make sure that most elementary chores are done in advance. Shop for food and liquor as far ahead as possible; check your linens or place mats, your silver and dishes a day or so before; get out any cooking equipment and serving dishes you will need. If you are lucky enough to have several hours before guests arrive, clean vegetables, set the table and arrange the centerpiece. If it is difficult, for one reason or another, to set the table in advance, try a serving method I often use. Simply put place mats and napkins on the dining table, and at the last minute put out plates and silver on a work area in the kitchen. Then invite your guests to come to the kitchen and dish up for themselves. Into a dirty kitchen, you say? You can keep it clear as you work if you stack all used utensils in the dishwasher or, as does one hostess I know, hide them in the cupboard under the sink. If you cook in handsome, decorative pots and pans, the food can be served right from the stove. One of the most popular restaurants near Wall Street in New York serves in just this manner. Patrons are ushered into the restaurant kitchen, where they select their meals from the array of delectable dishes on the stove. The men love it.

Choose menus that call for no more than one or two complicated jobs to be done at the last minute. Other dishes on the menu should be simple to prepare, or they should be the sort that can be made a day or so in advance. Most cooks, when they think of dishes in the latter category, automatically come up with beef bourguignon or coq au vin. I've become thoroughly tired of both dishes. There are fine terrines, cocottes, and other so-called casserole dishes available. But these must be cooked carefully and seasoned with discretion to achieve any kind of distinction. In the long run, such dishes take far more time and attention than a fine roast, a quick sauté, or a grill that is done at the last minute.

I find that American hostesses try to serve too many dishes at dinner. There is no need, for example, to have four or five complicated hors d'oeuvres with drinks. Such lavishness takes the edge off appetites. One or two items, not too rich, are enough—perhaps just olives, or radishes with sweet butter. The first course can sometimes be served in the living room with a chilled white wine in place of cocktails.

A first course isn't absolutely necessary, but if you have planned a grilled main course, it can prove a help. Most grilled meats cook quickly, and you should start them as guests sit down to their fish or soup, or whatever you have chosen. If there is a short wait between courses, no one will mind, particularly if you serve a pleasant wine that the guests can sip as they talk.

If you worry about timing and keeping foods hot, invest in an electric hot tray. With one of these you can hold a roast and vegetables for quite a few minutes at the right temperature. Also, there are many tasty dishes that can be prepared at the table in an electric skillet or chafing dish.

A sensible way to save yourself headaches in planning your menu is to take advantage of fine prepared foods available. If you live in a city of any size, investigate caterers and specialty shops that can supply you with first courses, such as pâtés, aspics, fish mousses and vol-au-vents with cream fillings, or desserts such as torten, pastries, and frozen sweets.

Entertaining is expensive, make no mistake, and this book is not dedicated to economy in the kitchen, although many menus presented here are relatively inexpensive to produce. It is dedicated to hosts and hostesses who want to provide the best for their guests, to achieve the finest in pleasures of the table effortlessly, graciously, and with flair. To entertain successfully one must create with the imagination of a playwright, plan with the skill of a director, and perform with the instincts of an actor. And, as any showman will tell you, there is no greater reward than pleasing your audience.

James A. Beard
New York

BREAKFASTS

EARLY BREAKFAST

Early breakfast usually means overnight guests—unless you happen to be catching a friend on the wing, between planes; or you happen to be one of those extraordinarily busy people who must do business or entertain from the crack of dawn on through the day. Actually, a business breakfast makes a nice change from the usual, hurried luncheon.

At no time are people's eating habits more fixed and less creative than in the early morning. Gauge your guests' appetites carefully: If you are faced with a "continental breakfast" appetite, at least find the best rolls and bread available and an interesting marmalade or preserve. If you think your guests might be afraid to stray too far from the bacon-and-eggs routine, try variations on these standards to give the meal a lift; offer a soufflé, or a quiche, or a good omelet.

Here is a range of menus for the early hours that are somewhat off-beat and quite un-American. There isn't an egg in the group—except in the orangeade!

 FOUR LIGHT BREAKFASTS
I

EGG ORANGEADE

HEATED FRENCH ROLLS

BUTTER   CHEESE

Egg Orangeade

For each person : 1 or 2 eggs, ¾ cup diluted frozen orange juice, and a dash of lemon juice. Whirl with a small amount of crushed ice in a blender.

 II

MELON WITH PROSCIUTTO

CRISPLY TOASTED FRENCH BREAD

BUTTER   MARMALADE

Melon with Prosciutto

Use any available ripe melon. Peel and cut into rather thin strips —3 or 4 to a portion. Arrange on a plate with 2 or 3 slices of prosciutto over the melon, and serve with a wedge of lime or lemon. Have the pepper grinder handy.

NOTE : Westphalian or Smithfield ham may be used instead of prosciutto.

III

HOT FRUIT COMPOTE — HEAVY CREAM

FRESHLY BAKED BRIOCHE

BUTTER

Hot Fruit Compote

Prepare a simple syrup, combining 1 part sugar, 2 parts water, and vanilla to taste. Boil 5 minutes. Add mixed fresh (or dried) fruits: apricots, prunes, figs, peaches or pears. Bring to a boil, lower heat, and simmer until tender. Serve with heavy cream.

Freshly Baked Brioche

See p. 356.

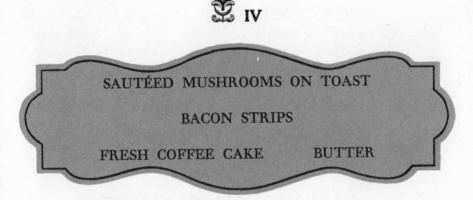

IV

SAUTÉED MUSHROOMS ON TOAST

BACON STRIPS

FRESH COFFEE CAKE   BUTTER

Sautéed Mushrooms on Toast

6 tablespoons butter
1½ pounds mushrooms (small caps)
1 teaspoon salt
½ teaspoon freshly ground black pepper
Dash Worcestershire
Buttered toast, as needed
Chopped chives and parsley
Bacon

Melt butter in a heavy skillet, add the mushrooms, and sauté over medium heat. Stir, and shake the pan from time to time. Cook until mushrooms are lightly browned and still crisp. Do not overcook. Add seasonings.

Serve on buttered toast with chopped herbs and crisp bacon.

Coffee Cake

You may use a coffee cake from a good bakery, if you wish, but if you prefer to do your own, try this quick version.

> *1½ cups less 2 tablespoons flour*
> *2 teaspoons double-action baking powder*
> *½ teaspoon salt*
> *½ teaspoon mace*
> *½ cup sugar*
> *1 egg, well beaten*
> *½ cup milk*
> *3 tablespoons melted butter*
> *Butter and sugar for topping*

Sift dry ingredients together. Combine with egg, milk and melted butter. Beat until smooth. Pour into a buttered 8- by 8-inch pan. Dot with butter that has been rolled in sugar, and sprinkle additional sugar over the top. Dust with mace or cinnamon. Bake at 400° for 25 minutes or until brown and puffy. Serve hot.

 FOUR HEARTY BREAKFASTS

I

STRAWBERRIES

TROUT SAUTÉ MEUNIÈRE   HASH BROWNS

THIN CRISP TOAST   LEMON MARMALADE

Strawberries

Choose ripe berries. There is only one sure way of getting sweet ones: sample one in the market. Wash the berries lightly, and drain. (One great food authority once said strawberries should never be washed with water—only wine!) Serve with the hulls on, with a mound of powdered sugar in each plate. Also pass heavy cream or sour cream for dipping.

Trout Sauté Meunière

For 4 trout, melt 4 tablespoons butter and 2 tablespoons oil in heavy skillet. Dust trout well with flour. Sauté gently, turning several times until fish is cooked through but not overcooked. Flesh should be moist but easily flaked with a fork or toothpick. Sprinkle with chopped parsley, and season with salt and pepper. Serve with lemon.

Serves 4.

Hash Browns

See p. 367.

II

SLICED RIPE TOMATOES

BROILED FLANK STEAK

CRISP PROTEIN TOAST   BUTTER

Sliced Ripe Tomatoes

Scald tomatoes, or sear over a gas flame, to loosen skin. Peel, and slice thin. Sprinkle with salt and freshly ground pepper.

Broiled Flank Steak

You will need a steak of top quality for this. Rub steak well with salt, ground black pepper and Tabasco. Broil steak close to broiling unit (allowing for shrinkage and thickening) 3 to 4 minutes on each side for rare. Carve into thin slices, holding the knife at an angle of 45° or less. The diagonal slicing is essential for tenderness.

A flank steak of medium size will serve 3 to 4 people.

III

GRAPEFRUIT SECTIONS

SAUTÉED SQUAB CHICKENS

FRIED CORNMEAL MUSH

BUTTER   HONEY   APPLE BUTTER

Grapefruit Sections

Peel grapefruit so that white skin is completely removed. With a sharp knife, a small pointed one preferably, remove sections in one piece. Dress with sugar. Add a little champagne or sherry if you wish.

Sautéed Squab Chickens

These generally weigh about 1 pound and are sold split. You decide whether you wish to serve a whole one or a half per person.

For 4 small chickens, heat 4 tablespoons butter and 1 table-spoon of oil in each of 2 large skillets. When the butter and oil are hot and bubbly, arrange the chickens, skin side down, in the pans, and brown nicely. Sprinkle with salt and freshly ground pepper, turn and continue cooking over medium heat for 12 to 15 minutes. Turn again, and test for tenderness. They should take 18 to 20 minutes. Remove to hot platter. Rinse the pan with ¼ cup cognac or Madeira, and add 2 tablespoons chopped parsley. Pour over chicken halves.

Serves 4 to 8.

Fried Cornmeal Mush

Follow directions on package for making cornmeal mush, noting quantity required for the number of guests you are serving. Pour into a loaf tin and cool. Slice in ½-inch slices, and brown well on both sides in butter. Serve hot with honey and apple butter.

IV

SHERRIED GRAPEFRUIT

STEAMED SMOKED BLACK COD OR SABLEFISH

RYE TOAST

BUTTER STEAMED POTATOES

CHERRY TOMATOES

Sherried Grapefruit

Peel grapefruit, and carefully slice into sections with a sharp knife, freeing the meat from the tough membrane that separates each section. Arrange in individual serving dishes. Sugar to taste, and add 2 tablespoons medium or sweet sherry to each dish. Chill.

Steamed Smoked Black Cod or Sablefish

This comes in plastic bags that may be heated in water. If purchased loose, wrap in foil and heat in a 375° oven. Serve with chopped parsley, melted butter, and lemon.

Butter Steamed Potatoes

Choose small new potatoes of uniform size. Steam them in about ½ inch butter in a heavy saucepan with a tight-fitting cover. Shake the pan several times during the cooking. Do not let potatoes overcook. Salt well with coarse salt and add freshly ground black pepper.

Cherry Tomatoes

Wash tomatoes but leave the hulls on. Allow some moisture to remain on the skins. Place in a bowl and sprinkle with salt (preferably coarse), or pass the salt separately, and pepper, if you wish.

LATE BREAKFAST

Entertaining at a late breakfast (or "brunch," to use a word I dislike) has become increasingly popular—especially on weekends and more especially on Sundays. To many hosts and hostesses it means entertaining without a great deal of fuss, for at this time of the day guests do not expect several courses of food. The hour also contributes to the general air of relaxation; no one needs to hurry back to work, or to bed, and there is plenty of time for the host and hostess to tidy up afterwards. Late breakfast can be served any time between 11 and 1. It is not the hour that makes it breakfast but, presumably, the fact that it is the first meal of the day. In content the menu for a late breakfast is hardly distinguishable from a light luncheon, and there are few types of food that cannot be considered breakfast fare. In the menus that follow, you will find such items as fettucine Alfredo and grilled porterhouse steaks.

Of course, one thing clearly distinguishes late from early breakfast: alcoholic drinks. Bloody Marys are good for such an occasion, and so also are various wine drinks. Champagne is perfection.

Breakfast can be as informal as you wish, but it can also be a rather sumptuous affair. I do a Christmas breakfast every year, to which I invite a dozen or so close friends. It is every bit as festive as a Christmas Eve supper.

A MINT JULEP BREAKFAST FOR 12

Serve perfectly made mint juleps before breakfast.

COLD SMITHFIELD HAM

RYE OR FRENCH BREAD

EGGS AND MUSHROOMS IN TARRAGON CREAM

RASPBERRY PRESERVE

TOASTED MUFFINS

POUND CAKE

Cold Smithfield Ham

Smithfield hams may be bought in many parts of the country already cooked. It will save you a great deal of preparation if you are able to find one or have time to order one through your butcher. Slice the ham very thin, and serve with thin rye or thin French bread and butter.

Eggs and Mushrooms in Tarragon Cream

14 hard-cooked eggs
2 pounds mushrooms
10 tablespoons butter
5 tablespoons flour
1½ cups chicken or mushroom broth
1½ cups cream
3 egg yolks

1 to 2 teaspoons dried tarragon or
1½ tablespoons finely chopped fresh tarragon

Slice the eggs. Sauté the mushrooms lightly in 6 tablespoons butter, and keep warm while you make a cream sauce : Heat 4 tablespoons butter in a saucepan, and add the flour. Cook over low heat for a minute, then add broth, stirring continuously, and the cream. Cook until sauce is slightly thickened, then add lightly beaten eggs yolks, first beating a bit of the sauce into the eggs. Do not allow the sauce to boil after eggs have been added. Add the tarragon and salt and pepper, if necessary (the broth may provide seasoning enough).

Place the eggs and mushrooms in the sauce, and serve in a chafing dish or tureen, garnished with chopped parsley.

Have quantities of buttered toasted muffins on hand and a good raspberry preserve. With coffee serve thinly sliced Pound Cake (*see* p. 360–361).

 ## CHAMPAGNE BREAKFAST FOR 8

Serve well-chilled champagne before and throughout the meal.

TINY CROUSTADES

SUPERB CHICKEN HASH

CHIPOLATAS

ASPARAGUS

TOASTED BRIOCHE

DAMSON PRESERVES

Tiny Croustades

1 loaf unsliced bread
Olive oil
Melted butter
6 hard-boiled eggs, finely chopped
Freshly ground pepper
2 tablespoons chopped parsley
4 anchovy fillets, chopped
12 to 16 anchovy fillets rolled with capers

Cut bread ½ inch thick. Remove crusts, and cut each slice in halves or thirds. With a sharp paring knife and a spoon, remove piece from center of one side, leaving a base and a frame of bread. Brush with olive oil and butter, and toast both sides to a delicate brown.

Combine eggs, a grind of pepper, parsley, chopped anchovies and 2 tablespoons melted butter. Spread into the small croustades. Dot with butter, and add a rolled anchovy to each. Heat for 3 to 4 minutes in a hot oven. Serve hot.

Superb Chicken Hash

1 large onion, finely chopped
2 green peppers, diced
5 tablespoons butter
2 tablespoons oil
4 cups or more cold chicken or turkey cut in wide dice
Salt and pepper
Tabasco
1½ teaspoons tarragon
½ cup chopped parsley
½ cup blanched almonds or ½ cup broken walnut meats
8 eggs, slightly beaten
¾ cup grated Parmesan cheese

Sauté the onion and green pepper in the butter and oil until just wilted. Add the chicken and mix well. Add seasonings and almonds and toss. Press the chicken down well in the skillet. Cover for just 2 or 3 minutes. When the chicken is thoroughly heated through pour in the beaten eggs, mixed with the grated cheese, and cook over low heat until set. If practicable, run the skillet under the broiler for just 2 or 3 minutes to brown the egg and cheese.

NOTE: If you are using turkey that has been stuffed, a little of the cold stuffing mixed with the turkey adds a pleasant flavor.

Chipolatas

These are small sausages. Broil according to instructions for Broiled Sausages (*see* p. 19).

Asparagus

Wash and trim 4 pounds of asparagus. Cook quickly, in boiling salted water to cover, until tender but still crisp. Serve with melted butter.

NOTE: If asparagus is out of season, serve a platter of radishes, celery and scallions instead.

Brioche

See p. 356.

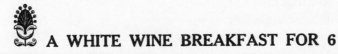 **A WHITE WINE BREAKFAST FOR 6**

Serve chilled Muscadet or Riesling.

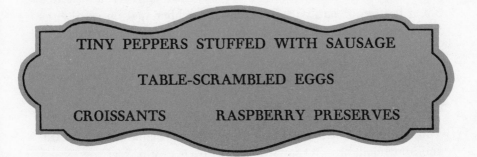

TINY PEPPERS STUFFED WITH SAUSAGE

TABLE-SCRAMBLED EGGS

CROISSANTS   RASPBERRY PRESERVES

Tiny Peppers Stuffed with Sausage

2 pounds ground pork, ¾ lean, ¼ fat
2 garlic cloves, finely chopped
1 teaspoon thyme
½ teaspoon ground cardamon
¼ teaspoon ground cumin
1½ teaspoons salt
½ teaspoon Tabasco
12 small green peppers or the lower halves of 12 large
*   ones*

Blend meat and seasonings well. Fry a small piece and taste. Correct the seasoning.

Parboil peppers 8 minutes in salted water. Drain. Fill with the sausage mixture. Arrange in a shallow, oiled baking pan. Bake at 350° for 25 to 30 minutes or till sausage is cooked and delicately browned.

Table-Scrambled Eggs

Use either a chafing dish or an electric skillet.

14 eggs
4 tablespoons water
1 teaspoon salt
2 or 3 dashes Tabasco
6 tablespoons or more of butter

Beat eggs lightly, together with water and seasonings. Melt butter over low heat, and add eggs. Increase heat slightly, and scrape along bottom of pan with a wooden or rubber spatula until eggs form large curds. Do not overcook. Add more butter if you wish.

Croissants

You may buy croissants if you have a good French bakery in the neighborhood, or you may make your own (*see* p. 357).

A VODKA OR ZUBROWKA BREAKFAST
FOR 12

The vodka or zubrowka should be served icy cold. (Zubrowka is vodka with a piece of sweet grass in it, which perfumes it delicately.)

SMOKED AND CURED FISH

SLICED TOMATOES AND ONIONS

PUMPERNICKEL SANDWICHES

CUCUMBER SANDWICHES

DANISH PASTRY

ROLLS AND BUTTER

MARMALADES

CHEESE

Smoked and Cured Fish

> *1 pound best smoked salmon, thinly sliced*
> *1 pound smoked sturgeon, thinly sliced*
> *2 pounds smoked eel, skinned and cut from bones in thin fillets*
> *2 or 3 whole smoked whitefish*
> *12 pieces herring in sour cream*
> *12 pieces herring in white-wine sauce*

Arrange smoked fish on a platter, together with lemon wedges and capers. Each type of herring should be on a separate platter, with chopped parsley for a garnish.

Arrange a plate of sliced tomatoes and thinly sliced onions, a plate of thin pumpernickel and butter sandwiches, and a plate of cucumber sandwiches on white bread. Also provide crisp rolls and butter, and have a cruet of oil on hand for the fish.

Follow with good Danish pastry and more rolls, with butter, cheese, and marmalades.

The vodka or zubrowka should be served throughout the fish course. Afterwards serve coffee and iced tea.

 A SHERRY BREAKFAST FOR 8

Offer a well-chilled fino sherry, a chilled medium sherry, and, if you wish, a cream sherry. With the sherry you might serve salted almonds and tiny green olives.

BROILED SAUSAGES

GALETTE POTATOES

BROILED KIDNEYS

WATERCRESS

TOASTED HOMEMADE BREAD

STRAWBERRY PRESERVES

Broiled Sausages

Choose 2½ pounds small pork sausages. Blanch in boiling water 5 minutes. Drain, and place under broiler, 4 to 5 inches from heat, and broil, turning once, till the sausages are golden brown and glazed. Remove to hot plate.

Galette Potatoes

See p. 367.

Broiled Kidneys

Remove most of the fat from 8 veal kidneys, and cut in half lengthwise. Remove the cord. Brush with butter or sausage fat (from the broiling pan), and broil quickly, turning once, for 5 to 6 minutes or to your taste. Salt and pepper.

Serve with a garnish of watercress.

Toasted Homemade Bread

See the recipe for Homemade Bread, p. 353. If you haven't the time or ambition to make your own, you can purchase frozen loaves of "homemade" bread ready to bake.

Slice bread fairly thick, toast well, butter, and keep hot.

A WHITE WINE AND CASSIS BREAKFAST
FOR 6

As an apéritif, serve chilled dry white wine with a touch of crème de cassis stirred in it.

SLICED ORANGES, MEXICAN

CODFISH PROVENCALE

CROISSANTS   STRAWBERRY JAM

Sliced Oranges, Mexican

Peel 6 or 7 oranges carefully, or slice off peel with a knife, so that no white skin remains. Slice thin, and arrange on a serving plate. Dust with 6 tablespoons confectioners' sugar, and sprinkle with cinnamon. Serve at once.

Codfish Provençale

The sauce on this fish dish is a favorite in the South of France. It is called *rayte* and is often used as a dip for crisp bread sticks or raw vegetables.

1½ pounds salt codfish
1 cup olive oil
¼ cup butter
3 cloves garlic, peeled
  and chopped
3 medium onions, peeled
  and chopped
1 large can solid-pack
  tomatoes

1 teaspoon rosemary
1 bay leaf
Touch of fennel
Pint of red wine
1 can tomato paste
½ cup pine nuts
¼ cup capers
1 cup black olives
Salt and pepper

First, put the salt cod to soak in cold water. It should soak at least 8 hours. Meanwhile, prepare the sauce. Sauté onion and garlic in the olive oil and butter. When they are just limp, add the can of tomatoes, the rosemary, bay leaf, fennel, red wine, and tomato paste. Blend thoroughly. Cook gently until slightly thickened. Add the nuts, capers, olives, and salt and pepper to taste, and continue cooking gently for about 30 minutes.

When the fish has soaked, drain it, and cut into square serving-size pieces. Roll in flour and sauté in olive oil until nicely browned. Pour the sauce over the fish and serve.

Croissants

See p. 357.

 ## A BLOODY MARY BREAKFAST FOR 12

Use either vodka or aquavit for the Bloody Marys.

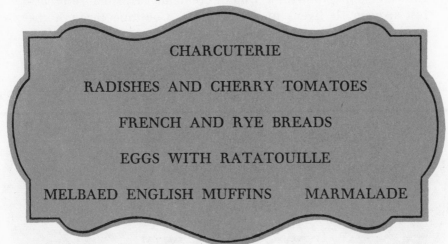

CHARCUTERIE

RADISHES AND CHERRY TOMATOES

FRENCH AND RYE BREADS

EGGS WITH RATATOUILLE

MELBAED ENGLISH MUFFINS   MARMALADE

Charcuterie

Place a selection of salami, summer sausage, liverwurst, and mortadella on a large cutting board, with sharp knives for slicing. Place French and rye breads on a bread board. Provide plenty of butter, and bowls of cherry tomatoes and radishes.

Eggs with Ratatouille

> *12 small casseroles of ratatouille* (see *p. 54–55*)
> *12 eggs*
> *1½ cups grated Gruyère cheese*

The ratatouille may be made the day before and reheated in individual casserole dishes. Top each dish with a poached egg, and cover with shredded Gruyère. Return to oven just long enough to melt cheese.

Serve with Melbaed English muffins (*see* p. 286).

 ## SUNDAY-NOON BREAKFAST FOR 6

Some of the California champagnes, such as Korbel, Almaden and Beaulieu, are delicious for summer drinking. Serve a briskly chilled champagne with a drop of crème de cassis before breakfast-at-noon. It livens up the appetite. Continue through the meal with plain champagne, well iced.

MELON WITH PORT

CHARCOAL-BROILED HAM STEAKS

ZUCCHINI FRITTATA

TOMATO SALAD

WARM BRIOCHE WITH

PRESERVES AND CREAM CHEESE

Melon with Port

Cantaloupe, honeydew or Cranshaw are all perfect for this dish. Be sure the melons are ripe and sweet. Cut them in halves or slices (depending on size) and make two or three gashes in the flesh of each piece with a spoon. Add 2 ounces of port to each serving, and let melon stand a half hour to mellow.

Charcoal-Broiled Ham Steaks

Do buy good ham. Country hams and the drier smoked hams are easy to find. Have your steaks cut about 1 to 1½ inches thick, and allow about 6 to 8 ounces per person. Slash the fat on the sides of the ham slices and broil slowly over medium coals, turning two or three times. The steaks will take about 12 to 15 minutes. If you like a glaze on ham steak, brush with a mixture of mustard and honey, and bring up the heat during the last few minutes. To serve, cut the ham into 2-inch strips.

Zucchini Frittata

> *6 to 8 small zucchini*
> *3 tablespoons olive oil*
> *2 tablespoons butter*
> *8 eggs*
> *1 teaspoon salt*
> *½ teaspoon freshly ground black pepper*
> *½ cup grated Parmesan cheese*

Wash but do not peel the zucchini. Cut into ¼-inch slices and cook slowly in oil and butter until just tender. Beat the eggs with the salt and pepper and pour gently over the zucchini. Cook until just set. Sprinkle the cheese on top and run under the broiler to brown lightly. Let the frittata stand for a minute or two, and then cut in wedges and serve.

Tomato Salad

Scald or singe the tomatoes quickly, and peel them. Cut into thin slices, and arrange on a serving plate. Salt and pepper to taste, and dribble a little oil over them. Add lemon juice or red-wine vinegar to taste, and garnish with chopped fresh basil, chopped chives, and chopped parsley.

Warm Brioche with Preserves and Cream Cheese

Many French bakeries make a specialty of fine brioche, and good frozen ones are now available. Or, you may make your own (*see* p. 356).

Offer a choice of several good preserves. Try black currant, ginger marmalade, pure apricot, damson plum, and raspberry; also, quince honey and pear butter. Serve with cream cheese.

 AN ELEGANTLY SIMPLE BREAKFAST FOR 6

PRUNES IN MADEIRA

SAUTÉED CALF'S LIVER   BACON

BOILED NEW POTATOES

TOASTED ROLLS   MARMALADE

Prunes in Madeira

These may be prepared in quantity and used when needed.

3 pounds choice prunes, pitted or unpitted
Madeira (or port or Marsala) to cover

Place the prunes in a large jar. Cover with the wine. Seal jar, and let prunes stand for 1 week before using. These will last indefinitely and will enhance many meals.

Sautéed Calf's Liver

12 thin slices calf's liver
Flour
5 tablespoons butter
4 tablespoons oil
Salt and pepper
¼ cup finely chopped shallots
¼ cup finely chopped parsley

Flour the liver lightly, and sauté very quickly on both sides in the oil and 4 tablespoons of the butter. Salt and pepper to taste, and remove to a hot platter. Add shallots and parsley to the sautéing pan with the remaining spoon of butter, and cook for 1 minute. Pour over the liver. Serve with sautéed or broiled bacon slices.

Boiled New Potatoes

See p. 365.

 ## A PIQUANT-FLAVORED BREAKFAST FOR 4

RHUBARB COMPOTE

KEDGEREE WITH CURRY SAUCE

TOAST   MARMALADE

Rhubarb Compote

Wash 1 to 2 pounds rhubarb. Cut in 3- to 4-inch lengths, and place in a casserole or baking dish. Add 1½ cups brown sugar. Cover, and bake at 350° for 25 minutes or until rhubarb is tender.

Serve hot or cold.

Kedgeree with Curry Sauce

May be made with fresh cooked, canned, or smoked salmon, although often made with other fish, such as cod, haddock, or finnan haddie.

> *1 pound salmon*
> *4 hard-cooked eggs*
> *1 or 2 tablespoons curry powder*
> *1½ cups Sauce Béchamel* (see p. *343*)
> *2 cups cooked rice*
> *¼ cup chopped parsley*

Flake the salmon, and slice the eggs. Mix curry powder with the sauce béchamel. Place alternate layers of rice, fish, eggs, parsley and béchamel in the top of a double boiler or in a mold. Place over hot water and heat thoroughly. Unmold on hot platter.

You may wish to serve additional curried béchamel.

AN ITALIAN BREAKFAST FOR 4

Pasta for breakfast?—why not? The incomparable fettucine Alfredo is rich with dairy products and gentle enough to begin the day. With it serve a good Italian white wine—perhaps a Soave or Verdicchio. And offer a bowl of crisp celery and some grissini (Italian bread sticks) to munch on.

FIGS AND PROSCIUTTO

FETTUCINE ALFREDO

CELERY   GRISSINI

ESPRESSO

Figs and Prosciutto

Buy either the white- or purple-skinned figs, making sure they are fully ripe but still firm. Allow 2 or 3 per person. Serve on a plate with a slice of prosciutto for each fig. Pass the pepper grinder.

Fettucine Alfredo

1 pound fettucine
6 tablespoons butter
½ cup grated Parmesan cheese
½ cup grated Switzerland Swiss or Gruyère cheese
½ cup heavy cream
Freshly ground black pepper

Cook fettucine to your favorite state of doneness. Drain. Melt butter over low heat or in chafing dish. Add the fettucine, and toss well. Then add the cheese, and toss gently until it is melted and blended. Last, add the cream and a generous sprinkling of pepper. When the cream is blended with the butter and cheese, remove pan from heat, and serve immediately.

 SPECIAL OMELETS FOR BREAKFAST

RED-CAVIAR AND SOUR-CREAM OMELETS

CRISP HOT ROLLS   BUTTER

CREAM CHEESE   STRAWBERRY PRESERVES

Serve Bloody Marys made with aquavit. You'll find that aquavit gives more flavor and will prime the palate for the unusual omelet to follow.

Red-Caviar and Sour-Cream Omelets

Prepare omelets in your usual fashion. Fill each omelet with about 2 tablespoons of chilled caviar, and serve with a dollop of sour cream on top.

LUNCHEONS

LUNCHEON

More and more Americans are adopting the French habit of inviting guests to luncheon at home. It is a pleasing, effortless way to entertain, and there is no worry about post prandial amusement, except on weekends. Guests are offered an apéritif or two, sit down to a two- or three-course luncheon, and linger a bit over coffee and brandies before leaving for their afternoon round of duties.

One busy woman of my acquaintance entertains six or so at luncheon in her handsome kitchen. These are friendly, informal occasions and a stimulating change from the ordinary cocktail or dinner event. One can do this sort of thing in an hour or two and be well rewarded. A simple menu such as sausage and an interesting omelet, cheese and fruit, or perhaps a fine chicken hash, is all that is necessary.

Although one thinks of luncheon fare in terms of light food, there are many hearty dinner dishes that are better consumed at midday. Cassoulet is one of these; feijoada is another. Both require long digestive periods. If eaten in the evening, these are apt to disturb one's sleep!

Six or eight is the ideal number for luncheon. Use your brightest, most informal table setting—unless it is a formal luncheon *d'affaire*. Ask guests to be prompt. Do not linger too long over the apéritif, and serve briskly. No cocktail hors d'oeuvres are necessary for a luncheon; menus should be appetizing but brief. In warm weather a cold plate, preceded or followed by a hot course, will suffice. Eschew heavier wines at lunch. Offer young, light wines that will not act as a sedative. Keep in mind the guest who has to return to the office or studio.

INFORMAL LUNCHEONS

 A MARSEILLAISE LUNCHEON FOR 6

It would be nice to start this luncheon with iced vodka and perhaps a few shrimp to dip in a little of the aïoli. With the bourride drink a Pouilly-Fumé, and after lunch, coffee and cognac.

BOURRIDE

FRENCH BREAD

PEACHES WITH RASPBERRY PUREE

Bourride

> 2 pounds fish (bass, haddock, or flounder)
> 1 medium onion, finely chopped
> Bouquet garni (thyme, bay leaf, fennel, peel of half
>   an orange)
> Salt and pepper
> Boiling water
> 12 slices bread
> Garlic
> 2 cups aïoli

Prepare the fish—fillets will do. Cut into small serving-size pieces. Place in the bottom of a saucepan, cover with the onion, add bouquet garni, and salt and pepper to taste. Add boiling water to a little more than cover, and let it boil for 10 minutes.

While the fish is cooking, toast the bread and rub well with garlic. Place in a large tureen or deep platter. Prepare the aïoli.

When the fish is cooked, remove it and keep warm. Strain the bouillon and combine 3 cups of it, little by little, with 1 cup of the aïoli. Mix well without letting it curdle. Put it in a saucepan over very low heat, or over hot water, and stir with a wooden spoon until the sauce just coats the spoon. *It must not boil.* Pour this sauce over the pieces of toast, and serve the fish separately with additional aïoli.

For the aïoli :

> *6 cloves garlic*
> *3 egg yolks*
> *Salt*
> *1 to 2 cups olive oil or peanut oil*
> *Lemon juice*

Chop the garlic very fine or put it through a garlic press. Add the egg yolks, and beat in the electric mixer or blender.

Gradually add the oil until thickened to the consistency of a mayonnaise, then add lemon juice and salt to taste. The garlic flavor should be dominant.

Have plenty of crusty, hot French bread to accompany the Bourride.

Peaches with Raspberry Puree

> *8 to 10 ripe peaches*
> *2 cups water*
> *1 cup sugar*
> *Dash vanilla*
> *2 packages frozen raspberries*
> *Candied violets*

Drop peaches into boiling water for 3 minutes. Remove, and peel as quickly as possible. Have ready a boiling syrup—the water and sugar cooked together for 5 minutes—and transfer the peaches to this immediately after peeling. Cook till just tender, then cool in syrup. Arrange in a serving dish.

Whirl raspberries in a blender and strain or put through a food mill. Spoon over peaches, and chill. Serve with whipped cream, if you wish, and garnish with candied violets.

 A GOOD, HEARTY LUNCHEON FOR 4

The only hard work here is in the preparation of the brioche. Serve Alsatian wine.

SAUSAGE EN BRIOCHE

HOT POTATO SALAD

TOASTED FRENCH ROLLS

ORANGE MARMALADE SOUFFLÉ

Sausage en Brioche

> *1 or 2 coteghino or kielbasy sausages*
> *Basic Brioche dough* (see *p. 356*)
> *2 eggs*
> *3 tablespoons heavy cream*

Poach the sausage for 20 to 25 minutes in boiling water. Peel off the skin, and cool.

Prepare the brioche dough and allow to rise. Punch down, and roll out ⅛ inch thick. Cut piece, or pieces, large enough to cover sausage. Place sausage in center of dough, and make a neat package, tucking in the ends and then bringing the sides together to overlap. Place seam side down on a buttered baking sheet, and let dough rise for 10 minutes. Beat the eggs and cream together. Brush the surface of the dough with this mixture. Bake at 375° till brioche is done and lightly browned—about 35 minutes.

Slice, and serve with a variety of mustards.

Hot Potato Salad

> *2½ pounds small new potatoes, scraped*
> *6 tablespoons chopped parsley*
> *3 tablespoons wine vinegar*
> *Salt and pepper*
> *⅓ cup finely chopped onion*
> *2 tablespoons chopped parsley*

Boil potatoes in salted water till just tender. Cut in halves or quarters, depending on size, and toss with oil, vinegar, salt, freshly ground pepper, onion and parsley. Return to heat for a moment. Serve at once.

Orange Marmalade Soufflé

> *6 egg whites*
> *1 cup orange marmalade*
> *Whipped cream, if desired*

Beat egg whites till stiff but not dry. Fold into orange marmalade, and pour into the buttered top of a 2-quart double boiler. Cover, place over hot water, and steam 45 to 50 minutes.

Unmold. Serve with whipped cream, if you wish.

A LIGHT, SIMPLE LUNCHEON FOR 6

SCALLOPS SAUTÉ, PROVENÇALE

POTATOES ANGLAISE

APPLE CHARLOTTE

Scallops Sauté, Provençale

> *2 pounds bay scallops*
> *Flour*
> *Oil*
> *Salt and pepper*
> *3 to 4 cloves garlic, finely chopped*
> *⅓ cup chopped parsley*

Flour the scallops lightly just before cooking. Add to hot oil in skillet. (You may have to use 2 skillets for this amount.) Toss scallops so they do not stick to pan. When they are just brown, lightly salt and pepper, and add garlic and parsley. Cook for a moment longer, shaking pan. Serve at once.

Potatoes Anglaise

These are simply plain boiled potatoes. Be sure to cook them so they are nice and floury.

Apple Charlotte

> *About 18 slices white bread*
> *Butter*
> *6 tart apples, peeled, and sautéed in butter*
> *1 teaspoon vanilla*
> *¼ cup sugar*
> *Whipped cream, flavored with sherry*

Trim the crusts from the bread. Sauté in butter until crisp and brown on both sides.

Place the apples in a heavy skillet with butter and vanilla. Cover and steam over medium heat till soft but not mushy. Sugar to taste.

Line a mold—a charlotte mold or bread tin—with overlapping pieces of bread on bottom and sides. Fill with apple mixture and top with bread.

Bake at 375° for 25 minutes or until golden brown. Unmold and serve with sherry-flavored whipped cream.

AN EASY, INFORMAL LUNCHEON FOR 6

OEUFS EN COCOTTE

BEEF SALAD PARISIENNE

ROLLS

TARTE AUX APRICOTS

Oeufs en Cocotte

> *12 eggs*
> *Salt and pepper*
> *6 tablespoons cream*

You will need 6 small individual soufflé dishes or "cocottes" for this. Butter the dishes well, and into each break 2 eggs. Salt and pepper to taste. Bake at 350° for 10 to 12 minutes, or until eggs are just set. Add a spoonful of heavy cream to each cocotte, and bake for another minute or so. Serve at once.

Beef Salad Parisienne

> *2 to 3 pounds cold pressed*   *Salad greens*
>   *boiled beef or beef*   *Vinaigrette Sauce*
>   *à la mode*   *(see p. 350)*
> *6 boiled potatoes*   *Tarragon*
> *½ pound cooked green*   *Chopped parsley*
>   *beans*   *6 hard-cooked eggs*
> *1 cucumber*   *Cornichons (small sour*
> *4 to 5 tomatoes*   *pickles)*
> *1 head celery*   *1 onion, sliced*
> *1 green pepper*

Cut the beef into slices and then into smaller pieces. Combine with sliced potatoes, green beans, sliced cucumber, tomatoes (peeled and cut into sixths), finely sliced celery, and sliced green pepper. Dress with a good vinaigrette, heavily flavored with tarragon and chopped parsley. Garnish with sliced hard-cooked eggs, cornichons, and onion rings.

Tarte aux Apricots

> *Rich Pastry* (see *p. 359–360*)
> *Pastry cream*
> *Apricot halves*
> *Apricot Glaze* (see *below*)
> *Whipped cream* (*optional*)

Make Rich Pastry, chill, and place in a flan ring. Line pastry with foil, and fill ring with beans (to prevent pastry from puffing up). Bake at 425° for 10 minutes.

When cool, spread with a thin layer of pastry cream. Then fill with fresh apricots poached in a simple syrup and cooled. Top with an Apricot Glaze. Serve with whipped cream, if desired.

For the Apricot Glaze: Melt a 1-pound jar apricot jam in a heavy saucepan over high heat. When it is melted and bubbling, remove from fire and force through a fine sieve. Keep warm till ready to use. Also use as a glaze for tarts or cookies.

VARIATION: Add 2 tablespoons cognac, bourbon or rum to the jam when it comes to a boil, and let it cook down for 2 minutes before straining.

A MODEST BUT DELICIOUS LUNCHEON FOR 6

RISOTTO AL FRUTTI DI MARE

BEET AND EGG SALAD WITH

ONION DRESSING

CHOCOLATE GÉNOISE ROLL

Risotto Al Frutti di Mare

4 tablespoons butter
1 small onion, finely chopped
2 cups rice
1 cup white wine
Broth (chicken, beef or fish)
1 pound shrimp

1 pound crabmeat, scallops, lobster or mussels
12 to 14 small clams
Dash of sherry or port
Grated Parmesan cheese
Chopped parsley
Salt and pepper

Melt the butter in a heavy skillet, and sauté the onion till just golden. Add the rice, and toss with a fork for 3 or 4 minutes; do not let the rice brown. Add the wine, and cook until it has almost evaporated. Then add broth to cover, and cook until the liquid is absorbed. If rice is not yet tender (to your taste), add more broth, and continue cooking.

For the *frutti di mare:* You may combine any type of seafood for this dish. If you are using the combinaton suggested above, prepare each variety of shellfish separately—boil the shrimp and crab (or buy ready-cooked), and steam the clams. Combine all three and heat over a low flame with a little butter and a dash of sherry or port. Fold into the risotto. Add grated Parmesan to taste and chopped parsley. Taste for seasoning.

Beet and Egg Salad with Onion Dressing

> *6 to 8 cooked beets, peeled and coarsely chopped*
> *1 large onion, finely chopped*
> *8 hard-boiled eggs, finely chopped*
> *Mayonnaise*
> *Tarragon*
> *Greens*
> *Chopped parsley*

Combine the beets, onion and ⅔ of the egg. Bind with a tarragon-flavored Mayonnaise (preferably homemade, *see* p. 348), and arrange in a bowl bordered with greens. Decorate with chopped parsley and the remaining chopped egg.

Chocolate Génoise Roll

> *Basic Génoise recipe* (see *p. 361*)
> *1½ cups heavy cream, whipped*
> *2 tablespoons sugar*
> *2 tablespoons cocoa*
> *2 tablespoons Grand Marnier*
> *6 ounces semisweet chocolate bits*
> *1 cup sour cream*

Bake génoise in an 11- by 14-inch pan that has been buttered and lined with baking paper. When done, turn out on waxed paper. Allow to cool, and then spread with the whipped cream, flavored with sugar, cocoa, and Grand Marnier. Roll carefully by lifting the waxed paper at one end and allowing the génoise to fall gently inward. As you continue to lift the paper, the cake will roll forward. Finally, roll onto a board or plate.

Ice with Helen Evans Brown's Chocolate Frosting: Melt the chocolate over hot water, and combine with sour cream. Blend well, and spread over roll.

AN EASY LUNCHEON OR SUNDAY-NIGHT SUPPER FOR 4

A light Swiss Neuchâtel would be pleasant with this meal.

SWISS TARTE À L'OIGNON

GREEN SALAD

COMPOTE OF PRUNES

Swiss Tarte à l'Oignon

Cream Cheese Pastry or Rich Pastry (see p. *359–360*)
3 tablespoons butter
3 onions, thinly sliced
Salt and pepper
Nutmeg
1 cup Gruyère, or Emmenthal, grated
5 egg yolks
1 cup cream

Line a 9-inch tin with pastry. Place foil over the pastry, and fill with dried beans. Bake at 425° for 10 to 12 minutes. Remove beans (reserve for future use) and the foil.

Melt butter in a heavy saucepan over medium heat. Add onions and seasoning. Cover, and steam until onions are just tender. Remove to pastry shell, and mix gently with the grated cheese. Blend eggs and cream, and pour over the onion-cheese mixture. Bake at 375° for 25 to 35 minutes or till custard is just set.

NOTE: The pastry shell may be made in advance and frozen, either baked or unbaked.

Compote of Prunes

I keep a jar of good prunes in my kitchen the year round, preserved in Marsala, port or sherry. Select about 2 to 3 pounds of
dried prunes of good quality, place in a crock, and cover them
with any of the three wines mentioned. They will be ready for
eating in three weeks.

Serve in a compote with whipped cream, flavored with the
same wine in which the prunes were steeped.

These prunes have many other uses—in soufflés, in hot com-
potes with other fruits, and as a flavoring for certain meats.

A HEARTY WINTER OR SPRING LUNCH
FOR 4

Beer is certainly the correct tipple for this luncheon.

IRISH STEW

HOMEMADE ROLLS

ONION AND ROMAINE SALAD

APPLES AND RIPE CHEDDAR CHEESE

Irish Stew

> *2 pounds lamb shoulder, cut in 1½-inch cubes*
> *4 medium onions, thinly sliced*
> *3 carrots, thinly sliced*
> *6 medium potatoes, sliced*

Salt and pepper
3 cups stock or water
Parsley

In a heavy casserole place alternate layers of meat, onions, carrots and half the sliced potatoes. Season with salt and pepper and add enough stock or water to cover the mixture. Secure the lid and simmer over low heat 1½ hours. Add the rest of the potatoes and simmer another 45 minutes. Arrange stew on a hot serving platter; garnish with chopped parsley.

Homemade Rolls

See p. 354.

Onion and Romaine Salad

1 head romaine
1 large Spanish, or sweet Italian, onion
Basic Vinaigrette Sauce (see p. 350)
Chopped parsley

Wash and dry the romaine and place in refrigerator till ready to use. Slice the onion very thin, blend with vinaigrette sauce in salad bowl, and allow to stand for 1 hour. When ready to serve, add romaine and toss. Sprinkle with chopped parsley.

Apples and Ripe Cheddar Cheese

A good Canadian, Vermont or Oregon cheddar is a delicious cheese in winter or spring. Be sure to get a nicely aged and flavorful one.

 A HEARTY, UNHURRIED LUNCHEON FOR 6

Begin with Madeira or sherry, served with cheese biscuits and olives. With the cassoulet drink a Châteauneuf-du-Pape or Beaujolais.

QUICK CASSOULET

GREEN SALAD

FRENCH BREAD

BROILED PEACHES FLAMBÉ

Quick Cassoulet

*3 cans cannelini, white
Great Northern
beans or kidney
beans
1 large onion, chopped
3 cloves garlic, chopped
4 tablespoons oil
1 tablespoon chili sauce
½ teaspoon thyme*

*3 lamb steaks
3 loin pork chops
Salt and pepper, if necessary
1 cup of broth or 1 bouillon cube dissolved in
1 cup water
4 or 5 slices of bacon
Bread crumbs*

Drain the beans. Sauté the onion and garlic in oil, and add to the beans, along with the chili sauce and thyme. Broil the lamb and pork until nicely browned. Cut meat into cubes, and add to the beans. Toss well. Place in an oiled casserole or baking dish, and add the broth. Taste for seasoning. Top with the bacon slices cut into small pieces. Bake at 350° for 20 to 30 minutes, sprinkle with crumbs, and return to the oven for 3 to 4 minutes.

Serve with a crisp green salad and French bread.

Broiled Peaches Flambé

*12 peach halves
12 tablespoons dark brown sugar
Butter
⅓ to ½ cup bourbon*

Arrange peach halves, cut side up, in a handsome skillet or broiling pan. Place 1 tablespoon sugar and a dab of butter in the center of each. Broil 3 inches from heat until sugar melts and peaches are heated through. Heat bourbon, pour over peaches, and ignite. Serve at once.

NOTE : These may be served on peach ice cream.

FORMAL LUNCHEONS

Formal luncheons are not as common in this country as they are abroad. However, some day it will occur to hosts and hostesses that this is an ideal way to entertain certain visiting personalities. Naturally, it is not a black-tie affair. Nor are the menu and table as elaborate as they would be for a formal dinner. Usually guests are bid for 12:30, with lunch served at 1 and the final course and coffee over by 2. The offering consists of apéritifs, three courses and one or two wines. You might start with cold or hot hors d'oeuvres and follow with a meat or fish dish and a vegetable or salad. Finish off with dessert and coffee—and brandies, if you wish. Although it is not customary to serve butter at a formal meal, you may want to serve it with the hors d'oeuvres and then throughout the meal.

Unless it is a very formal and important affair, choose lighter wines than you would offer for a dinner party. Beaujolais, Fleurie or Juliénas, and Muscadet or Pouilly-Fumé are a few perfect luncheon wines. And one should not forget the good wines of California, especially if the guest of honor is a foreigner.

Keep flower arrangements and table settings simple. Place cards are optional, although I still like to present a written menu. Formal luncheons should be lively and amusing and without an air of duty or protocol.

A FORMAL LUNCHEON FOR 6

Serve a brut champagne with this if you wish.

LOBSTER AND ZUCCHINI APPETIZER

TOURNEDOS AU POIVRE FLAMBÉ

GRILLED TOMATOES WITH DUXELLES

FRENCH BREAD   GORGONZOLA CHEESE

FRESH PEARS

Lobster and Zucchini Appetizer

> *6 medium zucchini*
> *Sauce à la Grecque (see p. 350)*
> *Greens*
> *3 or 4 lobsters—about 1½ pounds each*
> *Thousand Island Dressing (see p. 349)*

Poach the zucchini à la grecque. Remove from sauce and chill. They should be tender with just a touch of crispness in them. Arrange on 6 beds of greens, and decorate with slices of poached lobster tail and one lovely piece of lobster claw. Serve with Thousand Island Dressing.

Tournedos au Poivre Flambé

> *White peppercorns*
> *6 tournedos, about 6 ounces each*
> *Coarse salt*
> *6 tablespoons butter*

3 tablespoons oil
½ cup cognac
6 rounds fried toast
1 cup Basic Brown Sauce (see p. *344*)

Roll or pound peppercorns till they are coarse. You may also whirl them in a blender. Press into the tournedos along with some coarse salt. Heat butter and oil in pan and sear the tournedos on both sides. Reduce heat and let them cook gently till they have achieved your desired state of rareness. They should never be served medium or well done.

Remove to a hot platter and pour off excess fat. Return the tournedos to the pan and flame with cognac. Place toast rounds on platter, and top with tournedos. Add brown sauce to pan and heat through quickly. Pour around the tournedos. Place a broiled tomato on each plate, and garnish with watercress. If it is to be a very impressive party you may top each tournedo with a slice of truffle! Serve very hot.

Grilled Tomatoes with Duxelles

6 tomatoes, red and ripe
Salt and pepper
6 tablespoons Duxelles (see p. *353*)
Toasted buttered bread crumbs
Chopped parsley

Cut off ⅓ of each tomato and discard. Sprinkle tomatoes with salt and a touch of pepper, and broil 5 inches from heat for about 6 minutes. Spread with duxelles, and return to broiler for 3 minutes. Keep hot till serving time. Dust with crumbs mixed with parsley just before serving.

Fresh Pears with Gorgonzola

Choose the ripest and best pears available. Serve with fruit knives and forks, and pass the cheese. It should be a fine ripe one.

Serve good French bread throughout the meal and again with the cheese, in case there are those who prefer it to the pears. And if you wish to serve a red wine with the cheese and fruit, it might be a fine old port. This would complement both.

A FORMAL LUNCHEON FOR 6

CRUDITÉS

CRÊPES DE VOLAILLE

QUICK STRAWBERRY SHERBET

Crudités

Arrange a selection of cleaned and crisped raw vegetables on a platter—perhaps radishes, scallions and strips of cucumber. Pass the salt. Anchovies and good bread and butter go well here.

Crêpes de Volaille

2 fowl or roasting chickens *Parsley*
1 onion, stuck with cloves *Salt and pepper*
1 bay leaf *12 unsweetened crêpes*
  (see p. 362)

For the sauce:
  5 tablespoons butter *Dash Tabasco*
  5 tablespoons flour *1 cup heavy cream*
  1½ cups broth *3 egg yolks, lightly beaten*
  1 teaspoon salt *¼ cup sherry or Madeira*
  Pinch nutmeg

Poach the chickens in seasoned water till just tender. Do not overcook. Cool. Remove chickens, and reduce broth by one half over a brisk heat. Strain through a linen towel or napkin.

Prepare the crêpes. They may be done a day or several days in advance. Simply wrap in foil, and store in the refrigerator. They may even be frozen.

Cut the chicken into 1-inch pieces. Taste for seasoning. Prepare the sauce: Melt the butter in a saucepan, add the flour, and let cook for a·minute. Then add heated broth slowly, and stir till sauce thickens. Add seasonings and the heavy cream and then the egg yolks. (Do not allow the sauce to boil after this point.) Add sherry or Madeira.

Mix chicken with ⅔ of the sauce, and heat through. Wrap chicken in the crêpes. Arrange in a baking dish or ovenproof serving dish. Pour remaining sauce over top, and glaze in a 450° oven for a few minutes.

Quick Strawberry Sherbet

2 packages frozen strawberries
Kirsch or Grand Marnier

Dice berries, and place in a blender with about ¼ to ⅓ cup kirsch or Grand Marnier. Blend, and then pour into ice trays, a serving dish, or individual serving dishes or sherbet glasses. Return to freezer to stiffen. Decorate with fresh strawberries, if you wish.

A FORMAL LUNCHEON FOR 4 TO 6

MADRILENE WITH CHIVES AND SOUR CREAM

POACHED SALMON, BEURRE BLANC

NEW PEAS

NEW POTATOES WITH MINT

PRINCESS CHARLOTTE PUDDING

Madrilene with Chives and Sour Cream

Use canned madrilene. Pass a bowl of chopped chives and a bowl of sour cream, and let each guest help himself. Toasted crackers go well with this.

Poached Salmon, Beurre Blanc

*3-pound piece filleted
    salmon*
Court bouillon :
    *2 pounds fish bones and
        heads*
    2 bay leaves
    *1 onion, stuck with 2
        cloves*
    1 or 2 stalks celery
    *1½ tablespoons salt
        (approximately)*
    1 teaspoon peppercorns
    ½ teaspoon thyme

½ teaspoon tarragon
½ cup vinegar
*1 pint white wine or dry
    vermouth*
Sauce :
    ¼ cup white wine
    ¼ cup wine vinegar
    *1 tablespoon chopped
        shallots or onions*
    ¼ teaspoon salt
    1 grind black pepper
    *3 sticks chilled butter, cut
        into 24 pieces*

Combine the ingredients for the court bouillon, except for the wine, and add enough water to cover fish bones and heads—about 4 quarts. Bring to a boil, and cook for 15 minutes. Taste for salt, and correct the seasoning. Add the wine, and continue cooking for 5 minutes.

Wrap the salmon in cheesecloth, leaving long ends to use as handles, and lower into the court bouillon. Poach at a feeble bubble, allowing about 6 minutes per pound. Test fish often with a fork or toothpick until it flakes easily. Be careful not to overcook. Remove salmon to a hot serving dish or gratin dish, and keep warm.

For the sauce : Boil the wine, vinegar and onions together in a Pyrex or enamel saucepan until they are reduced to 2 tablespoons. Add salt and pepper. Remove the pan from the heat, and, with a wire whisk, beat in two pieces of butter. When this begins to cream, beat in another piece. Continue in this manner, holding pan over low heat or warm water, until all the butter is added. The resulting sauce will be creamy and light amber in color. Do not let it get too hot, or it will separate.

Serve with the fish.

New Peas

3 pounds new peas
2 to 3 cups water

Salt and pepper
6 tablespoons melted butter

Select the freshest, youngest peas you can buy, and store in the refrigerator until ready for shelling. Do not soak them in water after shelling. Bring 2 to 3 cups water to a boil—do not worry if this does not entirely cover peas—and add peas. Cook uncovered till just tender, about 10 to 15 minutes. Drain, season to taste with salt and pepper, and toss with the melted butter.

New Potatoes with Mint

Follow directions on p. 365 for cooking new potatoes. Allow 3 or 4 potatoes per person, depending on size of potatoes—the smaller, the better. When cooked, toss with butter and chopped fresh mint.

Princess Charlotte Pudding

6 egg yolks
6 tablespoons sugar
2 tablespoons cornstarch
2 cups scalded milk
½ teaspoon vanilla
1 tablespoon unflavored gelatin
¼ cup cold water
¼ cup toasted filberts
2 cups heavy cream
Sugar
Cognac

Combine egg yolks, sugar and cornstarch in top of a double boiler. Heat milk and add vanilla (kirsch or cognac may be substituted if you wish). Soak gelatin in cold water. Pour milk into egg mixture, stirring constantly and continue to stir over hot water till mixture thickens. Add gelatin and stir until thoroughly dissolved. Add toasted filberts, chopped or whirled in the blender, and the cream, whipped and blended with the sugar. Pour into 12 individual molds. Chill.

Serve with raspberry sauce, sauce Melba or with crème de cassis. All these are available bottled.

SUMMER LUNCHEONS

When I think of an ideal summer luncheon, I think of a day like this: I am sitting in a cool house in Provence with the hot sun beating down outside. A few yards from the house there is a large tree with thick foliage and deep shade beneath. Beyond is a field of bright flowers, a range of hills and a brilliant sky. Soon guests will arrive for lunch. It will be a cold one, prepared yesterday. I shopped for some of the hors d'oeuvres at the local charcutier and robbed the garden of crisp vegetables. We shall have drinks in the shade of the tree and then move indoors. The table is set with gay placemats and Provencal pottery of that indefinable golden shade. There is a centerpiece of zinnias, and carafes of white and rosé wine, well chilled.

There is salade de museau—made from the muzzle of the beef long cooked. It is sliced paper-thin and tossed with a vinaigrette, with chopped pickle, onion and parsley added. I bought a cervelat—a cooked one that has a richly seasoned flavor and is utterly delicious. I made some peppers à la grecque, which are now cool and reposing in their *ravier* with oil and vinegar and spice; also some tiny onions, with the same beginning but to which I added a bit of tomato puree, some saffron and finally some white raisins, cooking the sauce till it made a glaze. There are fresh tomatoes and raw beets, just pulled from the garden this morning; and fresh basil has been chopped and mixed with the dressing for the tomatoes. There is a chicken—a poulet de grain bought from the *épicier* rather than the poultry dealer—because his are better. A sprig of fresh tarragon is in the chicken's tummy, and butter and salt and pepper were used to baste it first on one side and then on the other. The chicken is neither hot nor cold but that delicious in-between state where it has the quality of crisp warmth. The one hot dish of the meal will be haricots verts gathered just in time to cook. They will be buttered well.

Cheese and lovely fresh peaches will follow and some black, black coffee. This is summer lunching to me—color, good food, cooling wines.

 A SUMMER LUNCHEON FOR 6

This is an ideal luncheon for beer.

HOT RATATOUILLE WITH GRATED CHEESE

COLD ROAST BEEF WITH MUSTARD SAUCE

PICKLES   MELBA TOAST OR ROLLS

BLUEBERRIES WITH MAPLE CREAM

Hot Ratatouille with Grated Cheese

This great dish of Provence may be varied in so many ways. Here, we add mushrooms in quantity and cheese.

3 cloves garlic, finely chopped
2 onions, cut in thin slices
⅓ cup olive oil
1 green pepper, cut in thin rounds
2 medium eggplants, diced
6 to 8 very ripe tomatoes, peeled, seeded, and

diced, or 1 20-ounce can Italian plum tomatoes
1 teaspoon dry basil, or ¼ cup fresh chopped basil
1½ teaspoons salt
1 pound mushrooms, sliced
Grated Parmesan cheese

Sauté garlic and onions in oil till soft. Add pepper and eggplant, and cook for 5 minutes over medium heat, tossing well and shaking pan. Add tomato and seasonings, and simmer 30 minutes, covered for half that time. Add mushrooms, correct seasoning, and continue cooking till mushrooms are just cooked through. Serve sprinkled with grated cheese.

Cold Roast Beef with Mustard Sauce

This should be cooked to rare perfection. Merely slice and arrange on a platter. Garnish with watercress and pickles of your choice.

For the Mustard Sauce: Combine 2 to 3 teaspoons dry mustard with 1 tablespoon oil and enough white wine to make a paste. Add a touch of salt and finely chopped tarragon.

You may serve the ratatouille and roast beef together if you wish.

Melba Toast

See p. 329.

Blueberries with Maple Cream

Sweeten blueberries with maple sugar or maple syrup. Serve with sour cream, and sprinkle with a dash of cinnamon, if you wish.

A SUMMER LUNCHEON FOR 4

Serve a good, chilled Sancerre with this luncheon.

CRUDITÉS, SAUCE NIÇOISE

BROILED CHICKEN, ROSEMARY BUTTER

SNOW PEAS WITH MUSHROOMS

COEUR À LA CRÈME WITH STRAWBERRIES

CRISP ROLLS

Crudités, Sauce Niçoise

The crudités should include scallions or green onions, radishes, celery, tiny artichokes, asparagus, turnips, carrots—all raw. Arrange on a platter, and chill.

For the sauce niçoise:

> *2 cloves garlic*
> *12 anchovy fillets*
> *18 capers*
> *25 soft black olives*
> *2 cups mayonnaise*

Chop garlic, anchovy, capers, and olives very fine, and blend with the mayonnaise at least 3 hours before luncheon. Serve separately as a dip for the vegetables.

Broiled Chicken, Rosemary Butter

> *2 small broilers or 4 squab broilers*
> *½ cup butter*

Salt and pepper
1 teaspoon rosemary

Split the chickens if they are large; for squab chickens, merely remove the backbones, and flatten. Rub well with ½ the butter. Salt and pepper. Place skin side down on a broiler rack, and sprinkle bone side with a little rosemary. Combine remaining rosemary and butter.

For broilers: Broil for 13 minutes 3 inches from heat, turn, brush with rosemary butter, and broil skin side for another 12 to 13 minutes.

For squab broilers: Follow instructions given above, broiling bone side 8 minutes, then turning for another 6 minutes.

Snow Peas with Mushrooms

1 pound snow peas
1 pound mushrooms
Butter
Salt and pepper
Chopped parsley

Trim snow peas, and cook in a small amount of boiling salted water till just heated through. Drain at once. Sauté mushrooms quickly in butter. Toss with the snow peas. Season to taste with salt and pepper, and garnish with chopped parsley.

Coeur à la Crème with Strawberries

See p. 185.

A HOT-WEATHER LUNCHEON FOR 6

Serve a good Chassagne Montrachet.

VEAL SCALLOPINE WITH LEMON

ROESTI POTATOES

ONION AND ORANGE SALAD

APPLES BONNE FEMME

Veal Scallopine with Lemon

1½ pounds veal scallopine
Flour
6 tablespoons butter
2 tablespoons olive oil
Grated rind of lemon
3 or 4 lemon slices
2 tablespoons lemon juice
White wine
Chopped parsley or tarragon

Dust the scallopine with flour, and sauté quickly on each side in the butter and oil. Add the lemon rind, slices, and juice, and simmer for 3 to 4 minutes. Add a dash of white wine (you may use vermouth). Remove to a hot platter, and sprinkle with chopped parsley or chopped fresh tarragon.

Roesti Potatoes

Parboil 6 medium potatoes. Peel and grate. Melt ¼ pound butter in a skillet, add potatoes and cook well till they form a crust. Press into a cake with spatula, and turn and cook on other side.

Salt and pepper to taste and add more butter if needed. When crisp and beautifully brown, slide out onto a hot plate.

NOTE: These may be made in small cakes and served individually.

Onion and Orange Salad

> *5 oranges*
> *1 large Bermuda or Texas onion, or 2 red Italian*
> *   onions*
> *½ teaspoon crushed rosemary*
> *6 tablespoons olive oil*
> *2 tablespoons orange juice*
> *1½ tablespoons vinegar*
> *1 teaspoon salt*
> *½ teaspoon freshly ground black pepper*
> *1 large, or 2 small, heads romaine or curly chicory*

Peel the oranges with a sharp knife so that the white film is entirely removed. Slice the oranges by cutting between each section, to loosen the fruit from its thin membrane. Slice onions very thin, and break into rings. Combine the orange and onion slices with the rosemary, and dress with the oil, orange juice, vinegar, salt, and pepper. Just before serving, add the greens. Toss well.

Apples Bonne Femme

For 6 persons, 6 good-sized, firm apples. Core, then peel ⅓ of the way down the apple. Place each apple on a round of toasted white bread, well-buttered and sprinkled with granulated sugar. Place 1 tablespoon sugar and as much butter as the core will hold into each apple. Top with another tablespoon sugar and a chunk of butter. Place these in a well-buttered baking dish and bake at 350°, basting every 15 minutes with the juices in the pan and additional butter and sugar, if necessary, until the apples are tender but not mushy.

Serve warm with heavy cream, which you may wish to season with a little grated nutmeg.

AN UNUSUAL LIGHT SUMMER LUNCHEON
FOR 6

Depending on the filling, woven eggs, a specialty of Thailand, may be served as a first course, a luncheon dish or a dessert. Here, it is just right for a light midday meal.

WOVEN EGGS

TOSSED GREEN SALAD

RASPBERRIES IN RED WINE

Woven Eggs

> *9 eggs*
> *Peanut oil*

For the filling:

> *1 cup thinly sliced scallions (white portions)*
> *6 tablespoons peanut oil*
> *1½ pounds lean pork, finely ground*
> *1½ teaspoons anchovy paste*
> *1½ teaspoons grated lemon peel*
> *3 teaspoons lemon juice*
> *3 tablespoons tomato ketchup*
> *3 teaspoons finely chopped fresh coriander or ¾ teaspoon ground coriander seeds*
> *¾ cup finely ground peanuts*

Prepare the filling first. Sauté the scallions in the peanut oil till they are soft but not brown. Stir in the ground pork, and cook till brown, breaking up the meat with a fork. Blend in anchovy paste, lemon peel, lemon juice, ketchup, coriander, and peanuts. Continue cooking over low heat, stirring frequently, for 15 minutes longer. Correct the seasoning, adding salt if needed. Keep warm while you prepare the eggs.

Break eggs into a mixing bowl, and stir with a whisk until well blended. Do not beat. Strain through a fine sieve into another bowl. Then divide eggs equally between bowls, since the cooking will be done in two batches. In a shallow skillet heat peanut oil to a depth of about ¼ inch until it almost reaches the point of smoking. Remove pan from heat, and start immediately to "weave" in the eggs: Holding the first bowl about 6 inches above the edge of the skillet, dip into the egg with one hand and scoop up as much egg as can be held between the tips of the fingers. Dribble the egg into the hot oil in thin threads, weaving it into a lattice pattern. Continue the process until the egg is used up. Return the pan to moderate heat, and allow the eggs to cook until they are lightly browned on the underside. Carefully turn and brown on the other side. Remove to absorbent paper to drain, while you prepare the second batch of egg. Add more peanut oil if necessary.

Place the omelets on a warm serving platter and spread evenly with the filling. Fold the omelets in half to completely enclose the filling, and serve them at once with a garnish of raw bean sprouts and chopped chives.

Raspberries in Red Wine

For 6 persons, clean and pick over 1 quart raspberries and sugar them to taste. Arrange in a rather shallow bowl. Add 1 cup light red wine—a Beaujolais is ideal for this particular dish—and let them stand for 1 hour before serving.

A REFRESHING SUMMER LUNCHEON FOR 6

This meal calls for a young Chablis, well chilled.

> JAMBON PERSILLÉ
>
> CAESAR SALAD   MELBA TOAST
>
> STRAWBERRIES ROMANOFF

Jambon Persillé

> *2 pounds cold boiled or baked ham*
> *1 cup finely chopped parsley*
> *1½ to 2 cups clarified bouillon—beef or chicken, or*
>   *half and half*
> *1 envelope unflavored gelatin*
> *¼ cup cold water*

Remove all fat from ham, and cut in rather coarse julienne. It should be a ham with good flavor, not the run-of-the-mill boiled ham one buys in the supermarket. Canned Polish or Danish hams are excellent for this purpose. Mix some of the chopped parsley with the ham, and use the rest to line a mold. Fill the mold with the ham-parsley mixture.

Dissolve the gelatin and combine with ½ cup boiling bouillon. Stir until dissolved. Cool and combine with remaining bouillon. When it is just thick and syrupy pour over the ham and parsley. Chill in the refrigerator. Unmold on a platter, garnish with additional parsley, and serve with mustard or with Mustard Mayonnaise (*see* p. 349).

Caesar Salad

This famous salad is often served but seldom made correctly.

4 slices bread cut into
cubes
4 tablespoons butter
2 tablespoons olive oil
4 crushed garlic cloves
1 or 2 heads romaine,
washed, chilled and
dried
8 tablespoons olive oil
24 or more anchovy
fillets, diced

Juice of 1 lemon, or to
taste
Salt, if needed
Freshly ground black
pepper
1 egg, coddled 1 minute
Parmesan cheese, freshly
grated

Sauté the croutons in butter and 2 tablespoons olive oil, and add 3 garlic cloves to the pan.

Rub a glass or china salad bowl with the remaining garlic and add the greens. Pour over them the 8 tablespoons olive oil and toss well.

Add the croutons, the anchovies and lemon juice to taste. Toss lightly and taste for salt. Add freshly ground black pepper to taste, the coddled egg and a good handful of grated cheese. Toss well and add additional cheese if desired. Serve at once.

Melba Toast

See p. 329.

Strawberries Romanoff

Hull 3 pints of large, ripe strawberries and place them in a rather shallow bowl. Combine 1 can (6 ounces) frozen concentrated orange juice with an equal quantity of tawny port, and pour over the berries, allowing them to soak in this marinade for several hours. Add sugar if necessary.

When ready to serve, pile the berries in a serving dish. Serve the sauce in a pitcher, and pass a bowl of whipped cream, sweetened and flavored with a little port. Decorate with chopped pistachio nuts, if you wish.

LADIES ONLY

My mother had a great deal to say on the subject of ladies' luncheons, and not infrequently she found them a bore. Naturally, the company had something to do with the success of the occasion, but as often as not, Mother complained that the hostesses had fussed too much and offered every pickle, jelly and jam in the larder. Today's fashion of simplifying the table and slimming the figure has revolutionized the ladies' luncheon tradition. It is not unusual to serve only a main course and a dessert, with or without an alcoholic addition, although there are hostesses who prefer slightly more elaborate offerings.

Ladies' luncheons are the ideal time to be entirely feminine in the design of your table, to use the most delicate linens and most subtle flower arrangements, and to produce the most startling and delightful effects in your serving ware and its garniture. But, of course, the food—whether it is one dish or three—should be the chief conversation piece.

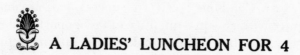 **A LADIES' LUNCHEON FOR 4**

This can be expanded easily to a luncheon for 6 or 8. Merely make two crab soufflés instead of one, and increase the number of oranges in the dessert. The mixture for the soufflé may be prepared ahead of time, the soufflé mold buttered, and the crabmeat placed in it. All that remains is for the egg whites to be beaten and the soufflé popped in the oven. By the time you have an apéritif it will be ready. For an apéritif there is nothing more refreshing than chilled white wine with a drop of cassis in it. Pass some good cocktail biscuits or salted Macadamia nuts with the drinks. If you wish to serve wine with lunch, continue with the same white wine used in the apéritifs; it might be a young Muscadet or a Pouilly-Fuissé.

CRAB SOUFFLÉ

MELBA TOAST

WATERCRESS AND RAW MUSHROOM SALAD

GRAPEFRUIT WITH SHERRY

Crab Soufflé

1 small onion, finely chopped	½ teaspoon freshly ground black pepper
5 tablespoons butter	Dash Tabasco
3 tablespoons flour	1 teaspoon tarragon
3 tablespoons tomato paste	2 tablespoons cognac
½ cup cream	4 egg yolks
1 teaspoon salt	6 egg whites
	1 pound crabmeat

Sauté onion in butter until soft. Add flour and stir, then add tomato paste and cream and stir again until smooth. Add seasonings, including cognac, and cool slightly. Add egg yolks and beat well.

Beat egg whites until firm but not dry. Fold into mixture. Butter a 1½-quart soufflé dish. Place a layer of crabmeat on the bottom. Add ⅓ soufflé mixture, then another layer of crab and the remaining soufflé mixture. Bake at 375° for approximately 30 minutes. You may serve with a hollandaise if you wish.

Melba Toast

See p. 329.

Watercress and Raw Mushroom Salad

> *½ pound freshest raw mushrooms*
> *1½ bunches watercress*
> *Vinaigrette Sauce* (see p. *350*)
> *1 tablespoon chopped parsley*
> *2 tablespoons finely cut chives*

Slice the mushroom caps very thin and combine with trimmed watercress. Toss with vinaigrette sauce, and sprinkle with chopped parsley and chives.

Grapefruit with Sherry

> *6 grapefruit*
> *Sugar to taste*
> *½ cup medium or cream sherry*

Peel grapefruit carefully, removing all white film. Slice neatly into segments with a sharp knife. Arrange in serving dish or individual serving dishes. Sprinkle with sugar, if necessary, and chill. Just before serving add sherry to taste. Or pass chilled sherry and permit guests to serve themselves.

 A LADIES' LUNCHEON FOR 8

A pleasant main dish with a most delicious soufflé for dessert makes entertaining as easy as you could want it. Tipple chilled dry sherry before lunch while you pass the olives and filberts. If you plan to serve a wine with lunch, make it a Pouilly-Fuissé or a California Traminer.

SHERRY   SPANISH OLIVES

TOASTED FILBERTS

VOL-AU-VENTS WITH CHICKEN AND

SWEETBREADS, SUPRÊME

PETITS POIS WITH MINT

ENDIVES WITH BEET DRESSING

APRICOT SOUFFLÉ

Vol-au-Vents with Chicken and Sweetbreads, Suprême

You may buy large vol-au-vents or small individual ones from a caterer or good pastry shop. If you use individual ones, bring them to the table hot and serve the chicken and sweetbreads from a separate bowl or tureen. The large vol-au-vents should be assembled beforehand. You may, of course, make your own vol-au-vents. Prepare a Pâte à Choux, as directed on p. 358, and then cut out the vol-au-vents to the size desired.

2 pounds chicken backs
1 pound chicken gizzards
1 onion, stuck with cloves
1 tablespoon salt
Water
4 whole chicken breasts
2 pairs sweetbreads
1 onion
1 carrot
1 stalk celery
1 cup white wine
1 pound mushrooms

For the sauce :
6 tablespoons butter
6 tablespoons flour
2 cups chicken broth
½ cup sherry or Madeira
1½ cups heavy cream
4 egg yolks
2 truffles
1 tablespoon lemon juice
2 tablespoons chopped
     parsley

Place the backs, gizzards, onion and salt in a deep pot, and cover with 2 quarts of water or more. Cook over low heat for 2½ to 3 hours, covered. Correct the seasoning and cool. Then chill, and remove excess fat.

Poach the breasts until just tender in 1 quart of the broth, adding salt if necessary. Do not overcook. Cool, and remove meat from bones. Return bones to broth, and reduce to 1 pint.

Allow the sweetbreads to stand in ice water for 1 hour, then trim. Dice the onion, and cut the carrot and celery in julienne strips. Place on the bottom of a large saucepan. Add the sweetbreads, the remaining quart of chicken broth and the white wine. Cover and poach for 20 to 25 minutes. Peel the sweetbreads, and return peelings to the broth. Reduce to 1 cup. Combine with the previously reduced broth. Strain and clarify.

Slice the mushrooms, and sauté quickly in 4 tablespoons butter. Remove the mushrooms and reserve the butter, adding 2 more tablespoons to the pan. Over low heat add the flour, and blend. Gradually stir in 2 cups of the reduced broth, and stir until thickened. Correct the seasoning, and add sherry. Then stir in the cream and egg yolks, and continue stirring till the sauce is perfectly smooth.

Cut the chicken and sweetbreads into bite-size pieces. Combine with the mushrooms and truffles. Heat with a little chicken broth, and combine with the sauce. Stir in the lemon juice. Keep hot over warm water. Correct the seasoning, and transfer to a warmed tureen; or ladle into vol-au-vent shells. Top with chopped parsley. If the vol-au-vents are 6 to 8 inches in diameter, serve cut in wedges.

Petits Pois with Mint

Use the frozen petits pois with butter sauce that come in a plastic bag. Follow directions on box. They are remarkably good. Add a little chopped fresh mint to the peas just before serving. You will need about 3 packages for 8 persons.

Endive with Beet Dressing

6 to 8 heads Belgian endive

1 large cooked beet
Basic Vinaigrette Sauce (see p. *350*)

Crisp the leaves of endive in cold water, and arrange them in a salad bowl. Grate the beet over them, and at the last minute add the dressing, and toss.

Apricot Soufflé

1½ pounds dried apricots
Sugar to taste
2 tablespoons cognac or ⅓ cup apricot liqueur
½ teaspoon salt
8 egg yolks
10 egg whites
1½ cups heavy cream, whipped
Sweet sherry or cognac

Soak the apricots in water overnight. Bring to a boil and cook for 5 minutes. Add sugar to taste and the cognac or apricot liqueur. Put through a food mill or a coarse sieve. You will need 2½ cups puree.

Combine the puree with the salt and egg yolks, and cook over low heat for 3 to 4 minutes to thicken. Cool slightly.

Fold in the whites, beaten stiff but not dry. Pour into 2 1½-quart soufflé dishes that have been buttered and sugared. Bake at 375° for 30 minutes or until brown and puffy. Serve with sweetened whipped cream flavored with a little sweet sherry or cognac.

 A LADIES' LUNCHEON FOR 6

This meal is composed of a rather pleasant first course, a cold main course, and a light dessert. It is simple to prepare, and the main course can be done a day in advance. Precede the lunch with a good dry sherry, and drink a light white wine with lunch if you wish.

CANAPÉ PROVENÇALE

COLD RED SNAPPER WITH SHRIMP AND

MUSTARD MAYONNAISE

CUCUMBER AND CHERRY TOMATO GARNISH

NESSELRODE PUDDING

Canapé Provençale

> *6 slices white bread*
> *Butter*
> *Garlic*
> *10 eggs*
> *½ teaspoon salt*
> *¼ teaspoon Tabasco*
> *3 tablespoons water*
> *18 anchovy fillets*
> *6 black olives*
> *Chopped parsley*

Cut the bread into rounds about 3 inches in diameter. Fry in garlic-flavored butter until crisp and brown. This may be kept warm in a napkin or foil for an hour or two. Just before serving, combine eggs with the salt, Tabasco and water, and scramble carefully. Do not overcook. Spoon the egg onto the fried toast, and garnish with anchovy fillets, black olives and chopped parsley.

Cold Red Snapper with Shrimp and Mustard Mayonnaise

> *1 or 2 red snappers—about 5 pounds in all*
> *2 pounds small shrimp*
> *1 onion*

1 sprig parsley
½ cup wine vinegar
1 tablespoon salt
Water to cover
1 lemon, thinly sliced
2 hard-boiled eggs, sliced
Mustard Mayonnaise (see *p. 349*)

Trim the fish, which is handsomer if it has its head. Clean and devein the shrimp. Combine the onion, parsley, vinegar, and salt with enough water to cover the fish, and pour into a long fish boiler. Wrap the fish in cheesecloth, leaving ends long enough to use as handles. Bring the liquid to a boil and cook for five minutes. Taste for salt. Lower fish into liquid and reduce heat to simmer. Allow 6 minutes per pound, or cook until fish flakes easily when tested with fork or toothpick. Remove from the bouillon and cool; then chill in refrigerator. Meanwhile cook shrimp in the same bouillon for 3 or 4 minutes. Remove, cool, and chill.

To serve: Remove skin from the snapper and arrange on a platter. Garnish with cooked shrimp, thinly sliced lemon and sliced hard-boiled eggs. Watercress is also a decorative touch with this. Serve with mustard mayonnaise.

Cucumber and Cherry Tomato Garnish

Thinly sliced cucumbers and cherry tomatoes may be used on the fish platter as an additional garnish or served separately as a salad. No dressing is needed.

Nesselrode Pudding

1 pint light cream
4 egg yolks
½ cup sugar
1 can (8¾ ounces) pureed chestnuts
¼ cup Malaga or sherry
½ cup currants
¼ cup seedless raisins
½ cup sugar

½ *cup water*
¾ *cup heavy cream*

Heat light cream in a saucepan until a film shines on top. Beat egg yolks until light and thick, then gradually beat in ½ cup sugar. Add heated cream gradually and pour back into the saucepan. Cook over a very low heat, stirring constantly, until custard thickens slightly and coats a spoon. Remove from heat, stir in chestnut puree and Malaga or sherry. Freeze, preferably in the traditional way, in an ice cream freezer, since the fruits are added later and should be all through the pudding when it is presented.

Cook currants, raisins, sugar and water together over a moderate heat until the fruit plumps up and the syrup thickens. Beat heavy cream until it holds a soft shape. Stir the fruit and the whipped cream into the frozen custard. Pack mixture into a melon or charlotte mold and freeze until firm, either in a freezer or in a container of ice and salt (4 to 6 parts ice to 1 part rock salt). Unmold on a handsome, chilled platter, and garnish with marrons glacé and whipped cream.

NOTE: To prepare fresh chestnuts, remove shell and inner brown skin of 20 plump chestnuts. Cook in a mixture of 1½ cups water, ½ cup sugar and about an inch of vanilla bean. When tender, drain off most of the syrup and either blend chestnuts in a blender or work through a sieve to make a smooth puree.

 A LOW-CALORIE LUNCHEON FOR LADIES

This luncheon follows the popular trend for luncheons that have simplicity yet a certain elegance. If you want to keep this truly low-calorie, you will eschew cocktails.

CONSOMMÉ WITH FRESH SORREL

TINY GRILLED LAMB CHOPS

CHERRY TOMATOES IN DILL

TOASTED PROTEIN BREAD

PINEAPPLE WITH KIRSCH

Consommé with Fresh Sorrel

2 quarts consommé (canned may be used)
½ pound fresh sorrel

Wash the sorrel well and cut it into thin strips. Heat the consommé to the boiling point. Serve in heated cups with a generous sprinkling of sorrel.

Tiny Grilled Lamb Chops

Ask your butcher well ahead of time to save you tiny rib chops and to French them. If they are 1-rib chops, serve 2 to a person; if they are double, have them cut full and serve 1 to a person. Provide some extras for those who have larger appetites.

Grill the chops quickly under a brisk heat, allowing about 5 to 8 minutes for 1-rib chops and 9 to 11 minutes for double. You can be the judge of how pink they should be. Salt and pepper the chops, and serve at once, with sprigs of watercress as a garnish.

Cherry Tomatoes in Dill

3 pints cherry tomatoes
1¼ teaspoons salt
2 tablespoons butter
1 tablespoon chopped fresh dill

Remove stems from tomatoes and place in top of a double boiler over hot water. Barely heat through, then add salt, butter, and dill, and heat for an additional 4 minutes. Serve with a little chopped parsley.

Pineapple with Kirsch

Arrange thin slices of ripe fresh pineapple on a platter or on individual dishes, and at the last minute sprinkle generously with chilled kirsch or framboise. Or you may add the brandy at table in case some guests prefer their pineapple plain.

DINNERS

INFORMAL DINNERS

If you enjoy your friends around you and enjoy cooking, then the idea of entertaining informally should appeal to you. The degree of informality will depend on how well you know your guests. You may cook and serve without the necessity of extra help.

It is my great joy to invite six or eight people for an informal, simple dinner, with one or two people to serve, or with one to supervise while I do much of the serving myself. On such an occasion I am apt to offer squab, for instance; one can nibble on the bones! Or I might produce a hearty dish of corned beef. I had a group in last summer for cold corned beef and tongue and a robust salad, followed by an old-fashioned bread-and-butter pudding. It was a sensation, and I knew that this homely menu would strike the right note.

Plan your food schedule carefully, and make your table as attractive as you can, then relax. No rush should show on these occasions.

As for wines—they can be as elegant or as simple as you wish. You might drink a carafe wine all evening, or you can bring out your choicest vintages, if you are certain your guests love wine. Don't waste your best on those who would rather have beer!

A DELICIOUSLY RICH DINNER FOR 8

Serve a Valpolicella with dinner. After dinner—espresso, and Galliano on the rocks.

PROSCIUTTO AND MELON

PASTA WITH WHITE TRUFFLES

CHICKEN WITH MADEIRA

ARTICHOKE SALAD   ITALIAN BREAD

FROZEN ZABAGLIONE

ESPRESSO

Prosciutto and Melon

Cantaloupe or Spanish or Persian melon is best for this. Serve melon in slices, with strips of prosciutto arranged over it. Have a pepper grinder handy, and let each person pepper his dish to taste. Westphalian ham may be substituted for the prosciutto.

Pasta with White Truffles

> *1 pound noodles, either white or green*
> *¼ pound butter*
> *8 ounces canned white truffles*

Boil noodles in plenty of salted water until just tender. (If you add a couple of spoonfuls of oil to the pot, the noodles will not stick together.) Drain and toss with the butter. Serve and top with freshly grated truffles, and spoon truffle liquid over pasta if you wish.

Chicken with Madeira (Venetian Style)

4 cloves garlic
2 sticks (8 ounces) butter
Freshly ground pepper
2 good-sized roasters
¾ cup Madeira

Chop garlic cloves very fine, and cream with 1 stick of the butter. Add 6 to 8 turns of the pepper mill. Divide garlic butter and add half to the cavity of each chicken. Butter the outside of chickens well with remaining butter, and salt them. Place them on their sides on a rack in a shallow roasting pan, and roast at 400° for 20 minutes. Baste and turn chickens over to opposite sides. Roast another 20 minutes. Turn breast sides up and baste (add additional butter if needed). Roast another 20 minutes or until chickens are tender.

Remove to a hot platter. Drain juices from the birds into pan, and add Madeira. Heat sauce thoroughly, and serve with the chicken, cut into quarters.

Artichoke Salad

Combine 2 packages thawed frozen artichoke hearts with 2 heads broken romaine leaves. Dress with a vinaigrette sauce.

Frozen Zabaglione

8 egg yolks (large eggs)
⅔ cup sugar
1 tablespoon grated lemon rind
1 cup Marsala, cognac or port
½ envelope gelatin, dissolved in 2 tablespoons water
3 tablespoons Grand Marnier
1 pint heavy cream, whipped

Beat egg yolks very well, and combine with sugar, lemon rind and Marsala. Continue beating over slightly boiling water until thick. Transfer pan to a bowl of ice, add dissolved gelatin and Grand Marnier and beat till cold. Fold in whipped cream, and spoon into individual dishes or a mold. Freeze several hours before serving.

AN UNUSUAL INFORMAL DINNER FOR 6

CLAM AND TOMATO BROTH

FILLETS OF LAMB WITH CEPES

GRATIN OF EGGPLANT

CRÊPES SOUFFLÉS

Clam and Tomato Broth

Combine tomato juice of good quality with clam juice, in equal proportions. Add a touch of basil and salt and pepper. Heat thoroughly. Serve with a dab of salted whipped cream.

Fillets of Lamb with Cepes

> *1 leg of lamb, boned*
> *6 tablespoons butter*
> *3 tablespoons oil*
> *2 cloves garlic*
> *1 teaspoon dried tarragon, or 1 tablespoon fresh*
> *   chopped tarragon*
> *Salt and pepper*

Cut the lamb into large cubes, about 3 inches square. Sauté in butter and oil until nicely browned. Add seasonings, and cook to the desired degree of rareness. Serve with cepes. These are Boletus mushrooms, available in tins. They also grow wild in parts of the country, but you must be a mycologist to identify the edible species.

Gratin of Eggplant

1 large onion, coarsely chopped
½ cup oil
4 tomatoes, peeled, seeded and chopped or ¾ can plum
tomatoes
1 large eggplant, sliced (unpeeled)
½ teaspoon thyme
½ tablespoon flour
Salt, pepper
Grated Swiss cheese

Sauté the onion in oil. Add the tomatoes and let them cook for 5 to 8 minutes. Add the eggplant and the thyme and cook very slowly. You may cover for part of the cooking time. When the eggplant is tender but not mushy, sprinkle in the flour and let it blend into the sauce. Salt and pepper to taste, add the grated cheese, and run under the broiler to melt.

Serve this hot or cold.

Crêpes Soufflés (for 12 crêpes)

12 dessert Crêpes (see p. 362)
1 recipe for Grand Marnier Soufflé (see below) or any
other sweet soufflé

Prepare the soufflé recipe. Butter a baking sheet. Arrange 2 to 3 tablespoons soufflé mixture on ⅔ of the crêpes and fold over ⅓ very lightly. Sprinkle lightly with sugar and bake at 425° for about 5 to 8 minutes or until the soufflé mixture is set. Serve very hot on hot plates. Pass a cognac vanilla sauce: Melt 1 pint vanilla ice cream and add cognac to taste.

For the Grand Marnier Soufflé:

3 tablespoons butter
3 tablespoons flour
½ cup milk, heated
¼ cup sugar
4 egg yolks
Grated rind of ½ orange

¼ cup Grand Marnier
5 egg whites, beaten stiff but not dry

Melt the butter over low heat, and add flour and stir for 2 to 3 minutes. Remove from heat, and stir until smooth. Add sugar and egg yolks, and blend well. Return to heat for a moment or two to thicken. Stir in orange rind and Grand Marnier. Cool slightly and fold in well half of the egg whites and then the second half more lightly. Either bake in a 1½–quart soufflé dish that has been buttered and well sugared, or use in crêpes as above.

AN EASY BUT IMPRESSIVE INFORMAL DINNER FOR 4

Some preparation may be done ahead. You might serve a Sancerre with the crab and a good Volnay with the meat course. Cognac would be pleasant after dinner.

CRABMEAT CHARENTAIS

ZRATYS NELSON WITH FRENCH FRIED ONIONS

BEAN SALAD

PEARS CONDÉ

Crabmeat Charentais

6 tablespoons butter
    (approximately)
4 thin slices French bread
3 or 4 scallions, finely sliced

1 green pepper, finely
    chopped
1 tablespoon grated carrot
⅓ cup white wine

Salt and freshly ground
black pepper
1 teaspoon chopped tarra-
gon leaves or ½ tea-
spoon dried tarragon

1 pound crabmeat
⅓ cup cognac
Lemon slices
Chopped parsley

In skillet or chafing dish, melt butter and brown the slices of bread very quickly. Remove them to a hot platter. Add more butter if desired, and cook scallions, pepper and carrot briskly for 2 minutes. Add white wine, crab and seasonings. Toss lightly to heat crabmeat thoroughly. Heat cognac and ignite and pour flaming over the crabmeat. Blend. Spoon over toast. Garnish with lemon wedges and chopped parsley.

Zratys Nelson

4 or 5 boiled potatoes
Butter
Salt and pepper
2 small cucumbers
8 mushrooms
2 tablespoons flour
1 cup cream
1 tablespoon tomato paste
8 medallions of beef, fillet or sirloin
French fried onions (see recipe below)

Peel and cut the potatoes in even rounds, and sauté in 3 to 4 tablespoons butter until nicely browned and crisp on the edges. Salt and pepper them. Arrange on a serving platter and keep hot.

Cut the cucumber and mushroom in thick slices and sauté in butter until the cucumbers are soft and the mushrooms slightly browned. Add the flour and mix well. Gradually add the cream, stirring constantly until thickened. Then add the tomato paste. Season to taste, and put aside to keep warm while preparing the beef.

Sauté the medallions quickly in butter on both sides. Salt lightly. Arrange over the potatoes, and cover with cucumber-mushroom sauce. Top with Cecily Brownstone's superb French Fried Onions.

For the French Fried Onions:

> *3 or 4 large Spanish onions*
> *Ice water*
> *1 egg, beaten*
> *1 cup buttermilk*
> *1 cup flour*
> *½ teaspoon salt*
> *½ teaspoon baking soda*
> *Fat for deep frying*

Slice the onions about ¼ inch thick, separate them into rings, and soak in ice water for a couple of hours. Drain, dry thoroughly, and dip in a batter made by mixing the egg with the buttermilk and adding the flour, sifted with salt and baking soda. Fry in deep fat at 375° until brown. Drain well on paper.

Bean Salad

> *1½ pounds young snap beans*
> *Salted water*
> *6 tablespoons olive oil*
> *2 tablespoons wine vinegar*
> *Salt and pepper*
> *3 tablespoons chopped onion*
> *2 tablespoons chopped parsley*

Cut ends from beans, but leave them whole. Boil in salted water until tender but still crisp. Drain. Remove to a flat dish. Add oil and vinegar, and season to taste. Cool. Serve with a garnish of the onion and parsley. Add more oil and vinegar if needed.

Pears Condé

> *6 to 8 medium pears, peeled and halved*
> *2 cups sugar*
> *1 cup water*
> *1 teaspoon vanilla*
> *Sweet Rice* (see *below*)
> *Candied fruit*

Chopped pistachio nuts
Whipped cream

Poach the pears until just tender in a syrup made by boiling together the water, sugar and vanilla. Serve warm on a border of sweet rice, and garnish with the candied fruit, nuts and whipped cream.

For the Sweet Rice:

> *¾ cup uncooked rice*
> *1½ cups boiling water*
> *2 cups scalded milk*
> *½ cup sugar*
> *Pinch salt*
> *3 tablespoons butter*
> *1½ teaspoons vanilla*
> *4 egg yolks, slightly beaten*

Cover rice with the boiling water, and let stand for 10 minutes. Drain. Combine scalded milk with the sugar, salt, butter and vanilla. Add to the rice, and then place in a shallow baking dish. Bake 30 minutes at 325°. Remove and stir in the beaten egg yolks.

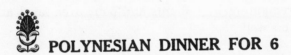 **POLYNESIAN DINNER FOR 6**

Here is a Polynesian dinner that can be done either indoors or outdoors, using a spit. It is a pleasantly different study in flavors and would probably be best accompanied by beer or champagne. I don't think any bread is necessary with this meal, save Melba Toast (*see* p. 329) with the salad. To finish off the dinner, serve good coffee and perhaps one of the coffee liqueurs, or Grand Marnier.

PACIFIC SHRIMP APPETIZER

DUCK GLAZED WITH CURRY AND HONEY

RICE PILAFF

SNOW PEAS AND MUSHROOMS

KUMQUAT PARFAIT

Pacific Shrimp Appetizer

4 to 6 heads Bibb or Limestone lettuce
1 pound tiny Pacific or Iceland shrimp
9 tablespoons oil, preferably olive
3 tablespoons wine vinegar
Dash or 2 Tabasco
2 to 3 tablespoons chutney
1 teaspoon salt
1 teaspoon freshly ground black pepper

Wash Bibb well to remove sand and grit. Dry thoroughly and chill. Combine with shrimp in a salad bowl—not a wooden one! Mix the remaining ingredients and pour over salad at the last minute. Toss well.

Duck Glazed with Curry and Honey

2 4 to 5-pound ducks, cleaned
2½ tablespoons curry powder
2 garlic cloves, finely chopped
1 teaspoon tumeric
½ teaspoon Tabasco
½ cup honey
¼ cup orange juice
¼ cup lemon juice

Rub the ducks inside and out with 1 tablespoon of the curry powder mixed with the garlic, tumeric, and Tabasco. If you are using a spit, truss, spit and balance the ducks. Roast over medium coals for about 1½ hours. During the last half hour of roasting, baste with a mixture of the honey, orange juice, lemon juice, and the remaining curry powder. Prick the skin from time to time to release the fat.

If you are using the oven, roast on a rack at 350° for 1½ hours. Baste frequently with the honey-curry mixture. Be sure to prick the skin, and raise the temperature to 475° for the last 15 to 20 minutes of cooking to crisp the skin. Serve the ducks quartered.

NOTE: These timings and temperatures should give you ducks medium done—that is, still a bit pink at the joints. If you like your duck well done, cook longer.

Rice Pilaff

> *2 cups uncooked rice*
> *2 large onions, sliced*
> *8 tablespoons butter*
> *4 cups or so stock, broth or bouillon*
> *Almonds and raisins (optional)*

Wash the rice and drain. Brown the sliced onions lightly in the butter and add the rice (and sliced almonds and raisins, if you wish). Cook over low heat for about 4 to 5 minutes, stirring it often to let it brown evenly. It should be just lightly colored. Heat the liquid to the boiling point and pour it over the rice until it is a good 1½ inches above. Cover the pan tightly and bake in a 350° oven for 25 to 30 minutes, or until all the liquid is absorbed. Serve with plenty of butter.

NOTE: This can also be cooked on top of the stove over very low heat.

Snow Peas and Mushrooms

> *1 pound mushrooms*
> *4 tablespoons butter*
> *½ pound snow peas*
> *Salt and pepper*

Slice the mushrooms, and sauté very lightly in butter. Cook snow peas in salted water till just tender. Do not overcook! Combine with the mushrooms, and season to taste. Add more butter if needed.

Kumquat Parfait

> *1 cup preserved kumquats (approximately)*
> *1 pint orange ice*
> *1 pint vanilla ice cream*
> *½ pint heavy cream, whipped*
> *6 whole preserved kumquats*

Chop the 1 cup kumquats rather coarsely. Cover the bottoms of 6 parfait glasses with orange ice, half of the chopped kumquats, and then small dips of ice cream. Add another layer of chopped kumquats, top with whipped cream, and garnish each parfait with a whole kumquat. Chill before serving.

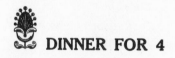 **DINNER FOR 4**

Drink a Prieuré Lichine or a Beychevelle. Serve favorite drinks before dinner with tiny green olives.

CURRIED PEA SOUP

PERDREAUX AUX CHOUX

BOILED NEW POTATOES

LEMON GRANITA

Curried Pea Soup

>1 package frozen peas
>1 medium onion, sliced
>1 small carrot, sliced
>1 clove garlic
>1 stalk celery with leaves, sliced
>1 medium potato, sliced
>1 teaspoon salt
>1 teaspoon curry
>2 cups chicken broth
>1 cup cream

Into small saucepan put peas, onion, carrot, garlic, celery, potato, salt, curry, and 1 cup of the chicken broth. Bring to a boil, cover, and simmer for 15 minutes.

Empty vegetables and liquid into container of electric blender. Cover and blend on high speed for 6 seconds. Remove cover and, with motor on, add remaining cup of chicken broth and the cream. Heat over simmering water, or chill and serve cold.

Perdreaux aux Choux

This dish should prove to anyone who doesn't already know it that cabbage is definitely a gourmet food.

>2 partridges
>1 old partridge (probably a hen), or a pheasant
>2 good-sized cabbages
>Bacon fat
>½ pound salt pork
>1 teaspoon thyme
>1 tablespoon parsley
>Salt and pepper
>2 to 3 cloves garlic
>¼ pound butter
>5 to 6 carrots, sliced
>2 onions
>1½ cup rich meat stock
>1 cup white wine
>1 large French or Italian sausage
>½ pound garlic sausages (or Italian sausages)

Clean and truss the two partridges. Remove the cabbage cores as you would for cole slaw; cover with boiling salted water, and blanch for 15 minutes. Drain. Separate the leaves.

Sear the old partridge in a little bacon fat in a deep pan. Add the salt pork, the flavorings, including salt and pepper to taste. Add the butter, carrots, onions, wine and broth. Cover with the cabbage leaves and simmer for two hours on a low flame. Thirty minutes before removing from the heat, add the large sausage, and fifteen minutes later, the smaller sausages. Meanwhile, have your oven preheated to 400°, and put in the two tender partridges to roast for 25 to 30 minutes. They should be basted two or three times with a mixture of melted butter, white wine, and salt and pepper.

At the end of two hours remove the old partridge from the pan. Cut all the meat from the carcass, and chop it finely. If you happen to have a duck press, put the bones through, and add the juice to the cabbage. Remove the onions. Cut the salt pork into slices and the large sausage into rounds. Chop the cabbage.

On a hot serving dish, arrange a layer of cabbage. Add the chopped meat from the old partridge and the two young partridges carved into serving pieces. Surround with the salt pork and both kinds of sausage. Serve with Boiled New Potatoes (*see* p. 365), well tossed with butter and chopped parsley.

Lemon Granita

> *½ cup sugar*
> *1 pint water*
> *½ pint lemon juice*

Make a syrup of the sugar and water by bringing them to the boil and boiling for 5 minutes. When the syrup is cold, mix it with the lemon juice, and freeze in the ice tray of the refrigerator at the normal temperature for making ice. Because of the sugar the freezing will take about an hour more than the usual time for making ice.

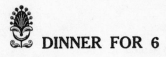 **DINNER FOR 6**

Drink Scotch or martinis before dinner and a pleasant Beaujolais or Fleurie during the meal.

TERRINE AUX AROMATES

GRILLED DEVILED BABY CHICKENS

WITH SAUCE BÉARNAISE

BARLEY WITH MUSHROOMS

MOCHA PARFAIT

Terrine aux Aromates

An unusual and delicious terrine that may be eaten hot or cold.

1 pound bacon
3 pounds spinach or 2 packages frozen chopped spinach
½ teaspoon thyme
½ teaspoon rosemary
3 tablespoons chopped parsley
Dash of nutmeg
1 medium onion, finely chopped
2 large or 3 small cloves garlic, finely chopped

1 tablespoon finely chopped fresh basil or 1 teaspoon dried basil
Dash of Tabasco
1 cup small black and green olives— Italian or French ones (pit before measuring)
1½ pounds coarsely ground pork, 75% lean, 25% fat
Salt and freshly ground black pepper

2 eggs	*2 large bay leaves*
⅓ cup cognac	*Flour and water*
½ pound sliced uncooked	
ham	

Use a terrine that may be covered tightly. Line bottom and sides with strips of bacon. Cook the spinach just enough to wilt and chop very fine. Drain well. If frozen spinach is used, merely thaw and press water through a sieve. Do not cook. Combine with half the seasonings and half the pitted olives.

Combine chopped pork with salt, freshly ground pepper and the remaining herbs and seasonings, the eggs and the cognac. Place half the pork mixture on the bottom of the terrine, and add in layers thin slices of ham, half the spinach mixture, pork —about half the remaining amount—then ham, spinach, and finally the rest of the chopped pork. Press it down well and place the two bay leaves on top.

Cover with foil, place the cover on top and seal with flour-and-water paste. Place the terrine in a pan and bake in a 350° oven for 1½ hours.

Grilled Deviled Baby Chickens with Sauce Béarnaise

6 squab chickens, about 1 to 1½ pounds each
½ cup soy sauce
½ cup sherry
2 tablespoons Dijon mustard
1 tablespoon Tabasco
½ cup olive oil
Melted butter
3 cups toasted bread crumbs
1½ teaspoons freshly ground pepper

Clean chickens, split each down the back, and marinate for 2 hours, turning often, in a mixture of soy sauce, sherry, mustard, Tabasco, and oil. Broil 6 to 8 minutes skin side down, then turn and broil another 6 minutes. Remove from oven, dip in melted butter, and roll in bread crumbs mixed with the pepper. Return to broiler for 2 minutes; watch carefully. Brush with butter, and broil another 2 minutes.

Serve with Sauce Béarnaise (*see* p. 347). Garnish with fresh watercress.

Barley with Mushrooms

> *½ pound mushrooms*
> *4 to 5 tablespoons butter*
> *1 large onion, peeled and chopped*
> *1 cup pearl barley*
> *2 cups broth (meat or chicken)*

Wipe the mushrooms with a damp cloth and slice them. Melt the butter and sauté the onions and mushrooms until soft. Add the barley and brown it lightly. Pour into a buttered casserole. Before you pour the broth over the barley, taste it for seasoning. If it has enough, the casserole will need no additional salt or pepper. Pour 1 cup of the broth over the barley in the casserole and cover. Bake in a 350° oven for 25 to 30 minutes and then uncover and add the second cup of broth, sprinkle the top of the casserole with toasted almonds, and continue cooking until the liquid is absorbed and the barley is done.

Mocha Parfait

> *½ cup sugar*
> *½ cup water*
> *1½ teaspoons instant-coffee powder*
> *1 cup (6-ounce package) semisweet chocolate chips*
> *2 eggs*
> *1½ cups heavy cream, whipped*

Combine sugar, water and instant coffee in a saucepan and bring to a boil. Boil for 3 minutes. Place chocolate chips in the blender and add sugar syrup. Blend for 6 seconds. Add eggs and blend for 1 minute. Remove and fold mixture into whipped cream. Pour into ice trays and freeze until firm in freezer section of refrigerator.

**AN INFORMAL DINNER FOR 6, WITH A
VIENNESE TOUCH**

STUFFED TROUT, PYRAMIDE

VIENNESE GOULASH

SPAETZLE

BEETS VINAIGRETTE

REHRUECKEN

Stuffed Trout, Pyramide

> *6 trout*
> *1 carrot*
> *6 mushrooms*
> *2 leeks*
> *1 stalk celery*
> *1 truffle*
> *4 tablespoons butter*
> *¼ cup cognac*
> *¼ cup port*
> *White wine*

For the sauce:

> *1 cup fish bouillon*
> *4 egg yolks*
> *½ cup heavy cream*
> *Salt and pepper*
> *Dash of paprika*

Cut carrot, mushrooms, leeks, celery and the truffle into narrow strips the size of match sticks. (Be sure to clean the leeks thoroughly.) Sauté in the butter for 2 minutes, then add the cognac and port. Sauté over high heat for another 2 minutes to reduce liquid to a glaze.

Split and remove backbone of the trout, and stuff each with the vegetable mixture. Poach fish in enough white wine to cover —about 5 minutes. Remove fish to hot platter while you prepare the sauce.

For the sauce: Combine fish bouillon with the egg yolks and heavy cream. Beat over hot water until thickened. Correct the seasoning. Add a dash of paprika.

Viennese Goulash

6 onions, peeled and
   thinly sliced
4 tablespoons butter
3 tablespoons oil
¼ cup vinegar
¼ cup paprika
3½ pounds beef, cut into
   cubes (cross rib,
   chuck, arm or rump)

Salt and pepper
1 teaspoon marjoram
½ cup tomato puree
Flour
2 cloves garlic, chopped
Chicken or beef broth
Beurre manié
Peel of 1 lemon
1 tablespoon caraway seed

Simmer onions in the butter and oil until golden. Add the vinegar and paprika. Then brown the meat in this mixture, tossing it well. Add salt, pepper to taste, marjoram, and tomato puree. Simmer for 1½ hours, or until liquid is practically reduced to a glaze. Sprinkle with flour, and add the garlic, and enough broth to cover. Simmer for 20 to 30 minutes. If the sauce is not thick enough, add tiny balls of beurre manié (butter and flour mixed). Whirl lemon peel and caraway in blender and add to sauce.

Spaetzle or Nockerli

2 eggs, lightly beaten
3 cups sifted flour
1 teaspoon salt
1 tablespoon melted butter
¾ cup water
Additional butter

Mix the eggs with the flour and salt until well blended. Add melted butter. Gradually add the water, and continue beating for about 4 minutes.

Make tiny balls of this dough, and drop into a pot of briskly boiling water. The spaetzle are cooked when they rise to the surface. Drain and allow to dry, then sauté quickly in hot butter.

Beets Vinaigrette

> *6 to 8 beets*
> *Water to cover*
> *Salt*
> *½ cup Vinaigrette Sauce* (see *p. 350*)

Cut off stems of beets, leaving about 2 inches—no less—and do not peel. Wash well, and plunge into boiling, salted water to cover. Cook covered for 20 to 30 minutes or until tender. When done, rinse in cold water and allow to cool. Slip off skins, and slice beets neatly. Cover with a vinaigrette sauce for 1 or 2 hours. Serve alone or on a bed of greens.

Rehruecken

> *Butter or margarine*
> *Dry bread crumbs*
> *5 medium eggs, separated*
> *2 whole medium eggs*
> *½ cup sugar*
> *½ teaspoon cinnamon*
> *2½ tablespoons finely*
> *   chopped citron*
>
> *¾ cup grated almonds*
> *   (reserve slivers to*
> *   decorate)*
> *⅓ cup grated unsweetened*
> *   chocolate*
> *½ cup semisweet chocolate*
> *1 tablespoon vegetable*
> *   shortening*

Butter two 10-inch Rehruecken pans or 1 large one, and dust with bread crumbs; or, use a melon-shaped mold.

Combine 6 egg yolks, the 2 whole eggs, and sugar. Beat till thick and lemon colored. Add cinnamon, citron, almonds, and grated chocolate. Mix. Beat egg whites till stiff but not dry, and blend well with the first mixture. Pour into prepared pans and bake for 30 minutes in a 350°–375° oven. Allow 45 minutes for a larger cake.

Press lightly to test doneness. If cake springs back, it is done.

Remove from pan, and let cool on a rack.

Melt semisweet chocolate and shortening over hot water, and spread over cake. Return cake to the oven, which has been cooling, and let it dry a bit. Decorate with almond slivers (to imitate lardoons in a saddle of venison).

 ## A LOW-CALORIE DINNER FOR 6

This is an elegant dinner with no particular richness or volume, but it will prove appetizing to those who are not dieting as well as to those who are. Furthermore, there is very little work for the cook. Serve cocktails to those who are not counting calories and Perrier or some other low-calorie drink to those who are; or serve champagne to everyone.

MELON WITH LIME WEDGES

LOBSTER À LA NAGE

BOILED NEW POTATOES

WATERCRESS   CUCUMBER FINGERS

CHERRY TOMATOES   CELERY

SHERRY JELLY

Lobster à la Nage

6 1 to 1½-pound lobsters
2 medium onions, sliced
4 carrots, sliced

2 cloves garlic
Several sprigs of parsley
4 cups clam broth
1 cup white wine
2 tablespoons salt
12 peppercorns
Water

Combine all ingredients in a deep pot, except the lobster, reserving a few sprigs of parsley for garnish. Pour in enough water to cover the lobsters when they are added. Bring to a boil and simmer for 10 minutes. Add the lobsters and return to a boil. Simmer for 18 to 20 minutes, then remove to a deep dish. Split the lobsters, crack the claws, and arrange on a platter. Garnish with parsley. Serve some of the broth separately, if you wish, and also serve an egg mustard sauce.

For the Egg Mustard Sauce:

3 whole hard-boiled eggs
3 hard-boiled egg yolks
1 clove garlic, minced
3 tablespoons Dijon mustard
2 tablespoons oil
1 teaspoon tarragon
½ teaspoon Tabasco
½ teaspoon freshly ground black pepper

Either blend the ingredients in an electric blender, or mash thoroughly with a fork, beating well to make a smooth sauce with the texture of a rather grainy mayonnaise. Correct the seasoning, if necessary, and garnish with chopped parsley.

NOTE: This sauce may be served with either hot or cold lobster.

Boiled New Potatoes

See p. 365.

Sherry Jelly

2 envelopes unflavored gelatin
1 cup cold water
Sweetener or artificial sugar
1½ cups boiling water
½ cup sweet sherry

Sprinkle gelatin on cold water to soften. Add sweetener or artificial sugar to taste and the boiling water. Stir till thoroughly dissolved. Add sherry and pour into a mold. Chill. Serve with heavy cream to those who want it.

This may also be made with port wine.

FORMAL DINNERS

Formal dinners a few decades ago were something appalling. The yard-square double damask dinner napkins, the cut glass, the crystal, the silver, and the menu itself all combined to make an event that would floor the average young host or hostess today. The courses—there were sometimes as many as seven—ran through soup, fish, entree, roast, perhaps game, dessert, and fruit. For each course there were wines. As soon as the dessert had been cleared away, there was coffee, port or brandy, and cigars for the gentlemen in the dining room, and coffee and port for the ladies in the sitting room or drawing room. The host took his cue to join the ladies, and then conversation or cards followed for an hour or two before the party broke up, usually by midnight.

Nowadays, with full-time servants at a minimum, formal dinners are far less of a production. The basic look remains the same—a perfectly set table with fine appointments. But one is apt to have the all-purpose wine glass instead of a variety of glasses. The menu usually consists of a first course, a main course with a complementary vegetable, often a cheese course for wine lovers, or a salad, dessert and sometimes fruit. Generally two wines, or two plus champagne, are sufficient. A Madeira or sherry might be served with the soup and another wine with the main course—probably a fine Burgundy or Bordeaux. If the host is an amateur of wines, he will choose a great wine of a fabulous year to accompany the cheese course. Often there is champagne with dessert or occasionally a fine sauterne or a Beerenauslese. I frown on dry champagne with dessert but enjoy a touch of sweet wine at times. Incidentally, if you are serving good wines, see that your flowers are not heavily perfumed!

Butter is seldom served at a formal dinner. A roll is placed on or beside the plate, and tiny hot turnovers or biscuits may be served with the opening course. If you are having a cheese course, pass French bread, preferably heated, as well as some good English or American biscuits.

In the event that the hostess or the host has prepared some of the food, instructions in serving should be given to the help before the guests arrive. At an informal gathering—even a black-tie occasion—either the host or hostess may go to the kitchen to check on matters or offer assistance. At a formal dinner only an unexpected crisis in the kitchen should take host or hostess away from their guests. The host should, however, help with opening the wines. Fine reds should be opened several hours ahead, and certain older wines should be decanted. The host should also see that white wines are not too chilled for serving, or they will lose their bouquet and flavor.

Provide legible and attractive place cards for your table, and it might be a nice touch to offer a card to each guest announcing his dinner partner. I also think it is important to do a handwritten menu; people like to know what they are eating. Two menus for one large table are ample. If you are fortunate enough to have a collection of porcelain menus (these can be written on with ink), so much the better.

As for pre-dinner drinks, I personally like to have a table set up in the living room to hold a large silver tray of bottles, decanters and ice. This is so much more elegant than a bar or a waiter who takes orders and makes drinks in the kitchen, and tricky portable bars are at the bottom of the list for a formal affair. There should also be brandies, whisky, soda and ice set up in the dining room and living room after dinner.

For detailed points of etiquette concerning a formal dinner, consult a good etiquette book. Be sure it is a sensible book, for some are inclined to be precious.

DINNER FOR 8 TO 12

ARTICHOKE BOTTOMS WITH FOIE GRAS

CHICKEN KIEVSKI

SEMOLINA GNOCCHI

BRAISED BRUSSELS SPROUTS

APRICOT ICE

Artichoke Bottoms with Foie Gras

Cook 12 large artichokes in acidulated, salted water till tender. Drain and cool. Remove leaves and chokes, and trim bottoms nicely. Fill hollows with foie gras or mousse. Top with a slice of truffle. These may be covered with an aspic.

Chicken Kievski (or Kiev)

12 flattened chicken breasts
Butter
Chopped chives
Chopped fresh tarragon
Salt and pepper
Flour
Beaten egg
Bread crumbs
Oil

Have the butcher bone the breasts, leaving the wing bone in; or do your own boning, which is simple enough. Pound the breasts between sheets of waxed paper. Be careful not to break the flesh. The resultant piece should be rather fan-shaped.

Make small, tapered "fingers" of butter—1 for each breast. Roll butter in chives and tarragon, and chill in freezer for 30 minutes.

Roll breasts around butter, tucking in the ends of meat to make a neat package. The chicken will adhere to itself nicely. Roll in flour, dip in beaten egg, and finally roll in freshly made bread crumbs. Cook in oil to cover, heated to 360°, till golden brown. Salt and pepper. Drain on absorbent paper.

VARIATIONS:

Niçoise: Blend the butter with chopped garlic, chopped black olives, and sweet basil before chilling. Serve the chicken with an anchovy sauce, if you wish.

Alsacienne: Spread the breasts with foie gras before rolling around the butter.

Semolina Gnocchi

> *2 cups milk*
> *1 teaspoon salt*
> *½ teaspoon pepper*
> *Dash nutmeg*
> *1 cup semolina*
> *½ cup grated Parmesan cheese*
> *2 eggs, beaten*

Bring the milk to a boil, and season it with salt, pepper, and nutmeg. Pour in the semolina, and stir until you have a thick mixture. Then stir in the cheese, remove from heat, and stir in the beaten eggs. Pour the mixture into a buttered dish or tin, making a layer about ¼ inch thick.

When cooled, cut into rounds with a cutter about 1½ inches in diameter, and arrange in an overlapping pattern in a fireproof dish. Pour a generous amount of melted butter over all, and brown under the grill or in the oven. A few minutes before removing, sprinkle with a handful of grated cheese. When this has melted, the gnocchi are ready.

Braised Brussels Sprouts

Choose 3 pints Brussels sprouts nicely matched for size. Melt 1 stick (¼ pound) butter in a heavy pan, and add sprouts. Salt and pepper to taste, cover, and cook over low heat for 20 minutes. Shake pan several times during cooking. When sprouts are tender to the fork—do not overcook—add a touch of lemon juice, and cook for a moment longer.

Apricot Ice

Prepare a syrup with 1 cup sugar and 2 cups water. Boil 6 minutes and cool.

Puree 3 cups canned apricots or poached fresh apricots. Add to the syrup with a dash of lemon juice and ¼ cup kirsch.

Pour into a mold, pack ice and salt around mold, and freeze. Or prepare in an old-fashioned freezer.

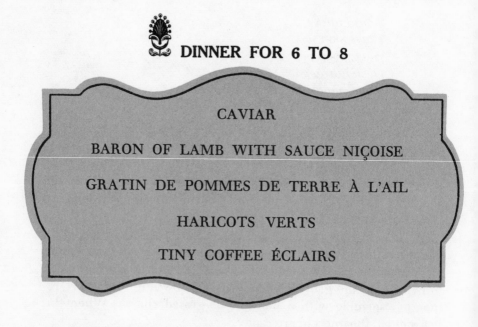

DINNER FOR 6 TO 8

CAVIAR

BARON OF LAMB WITH SAUCE NIÇOISE

GRATIN DE POMMES DE TERRE À L'AIL

HARICOTS VERTS

TINY COFFEE ÉCLAIRS

Caviar

It should be the best or none at all! Serve with lemon, and accompany with hot toast and sweet butter.

Iced vodka should also accompany this, or zubrowka, which is vodka flavored with sweet grass.

Baron of Baby Lamb with Sauce Niçoise

The baron consists of the two legs and part of the saddle. Rub well with salt and pepper and a bit of rosemary and garlic. Baby lamb is too delicate in flavor to stud with garlic. Roast at 325°, allowing about 12 minutes per pound, or until the meat thermometer thrust into the thickest part registers 155° to 160°. Serve at once with the pan juices and a Sauce Niçoise (*see* below).

Drink a fine Hermitage.

Sauce Niçoise

This is a version of béarnaise sauce and is delicious for its difference.

> *3 garlic cloves, sliced*
> *½ cup wine vinegar*
> *1 teaspoon salt*
> *½ teaspoon freshly ground black pepper*
> *3 egg yolks*
> *¼ pound (1 stick) butter*
> *Pinch of salt*
> *2 tablespoons chopped fresh mint leaves*

In a skillet or small saucepan place the garlic, wine vinegar, salt and pepper. Cook over a rather brisk flame until it is reduced to practically a glaze. Remove pieces of garlic, if you wish.

Prepare a basic hollandaise sauce in a double boiler: Combine the egg yolks, butter, and a pinch of salt. Let stand over warm water for ½ hour. Now heat the water, and, as you do, stir ingredients with a whisk or wooden spatula until the mixture is thickened and smooth. Add the vinegar glaze and the mint. Serve warm with the lamb.

To make in a blender: Place 4 egg yolks, rather than 3, in blender with the vinegar glaze and mint. Put top on blender, and turn on for a second, then off. Have the butter heated to the bubbling point (but do not let it brown), and pour gradually over the egg mixture while the blender is on at high speed until the mixture thickens and emulsifies. Keep warm over hot, but not boiling, water.

Gratin de Pommes de Terre à l'Ail

> *6 Idaho potatoes, thinly sliced*
> *4 cloves garlic, chopped*
> *2 tablespoons parsley*
> *1 tablespoon chives*
> *1 teaspoon thyme*
> *Salt and pepper*
> *½ cup or more oil*
> *⅓ cup water*
> *1 cup grated Switzerland Swiss cheese*

Arrange the sliced potatoes on a flat earthenware baking dish. Add garlic, parsley, chives, thyme, salt to taste and a little black pepper. Add the oil next and the water. Bake at 375° until tender. Sprinkle with grated Swiss, and return to the oven to melt the cheese.

Haricots Verts

Choose the smallest snap beans available in the markets. Leave them whole, merely cutting off the ends. For eight persons cook 2 pounds tiny beans in boiling salted water until just tender. Drain. Melt 6 tablespoons butter in a heavy skillet or sauté pan and sauté the beans very gently till well saturated with butter and tender to the bite. Add additional salt and freshly ground black pepper if needed.

VARIATION: Add buttered toasted almonds, crisp bacon bits or chopped parsley and chives to the beans.

They are also good cold with olive oil, vinegar and finely chopped raw onion added.

Tiny Coffee Éclairs

> *Pâte à Choux* (see p. *358*)
> *Crème Pâtissière* (see p. *213*)
> *5 teaspoons instant coffee*

1 package (6 ounces) semisweet chocolate bits
1 cup sour cream

Put pâte à choux in a pastry tube, and make small éclairs about 3 inches long. Bake and cool. Fill with coffee cream : Prepare a crème pâtissière, and flavor with 2 teaspoons of instant coffee. Glaze the éclairs with a mocha glaze : Melt chocolate over hot water, and combine with 3 teaspoons instant coffee. Stir into sour cream.

 AUTUMN DINNER FOR 8

Drink a Châteauneuf-du-Pape with the squab and finish off the dinner with a good Madeira.

MUSHROOMS IN MADEIRA CREAM

SQUAB WITH FORCEMEAT

PETITS POIS

SMALL FRENCH ROLLS

CHEESE

RASPBERRY SHERBET WITH PEACHES

Mushrooms in Madeira Cream

2 pounds mushrooms of fairly even size
¼ pound (1 stick) butter
3 tablespoons olive oil

1 teaspoon salt
1 teaspoon freshly ground black pepper
Tabasco
⅓ cup Madeira
3 egg yolks
1 cup heavy cream
8 or more slices fried toast
Chopped parsley

Trim stems from mushrooms, and sauté caps in butter and oil, tossing occasionally. Mushrooms should be still crisp when done; about 6 to 8 minutes cooking is ample. Season with salt, pepper, and Tabasco. Remove to a hot plate. Rinse pan with Madeira. Beat eggs lightly and mix with the cream. Add to the Madeira, and cook till the mixture begins to thicken. Remove from heat, and add mushrooms. Spoon over fried toast. Sprinkle with chopped parsley.

Squab with Forcemeat Stuffing

8 squab
12 shallots, finely chopped
Giblets
4 tablespoons butter
½ cup cognac, plus ⅓ cup
2 cloves garlic
1 pound pork, ground
½ pound veal, ground
1 cup crumbs
2 truffles, finely chopped
½ cup finely chopped
*   parsley*

1½ teaspoons salt
1 teaspoon thyme or rose-
*   mary*
½ teaspoon Quatre Épices
*   or Spice Parisienne*
2 eggs
8 strips bacon
Salt and pepper
Watercress
1½ cups Brown Sauce
*   (see p. 344)*

Sauté shallots and giblets in the butter for 3 to 4 minutes. Whirl in blender with ½ cup cognac and garlic. Combine with the pork, veal, crumbs, truffles, seasonings, and eggs. Blend well. Stuff the squab, and truss them. Arrange on a rack in a shallow baking dish. Lay a strip of bacon over each breast.

Roast at 450° for 15 minutes. Reduce heat to 350°, and roast for 30 to 40 minutes more. Baste with pan juices.

When squab are done, remove bacon; salt and pepper to taste, and blaze with ⅓ cup warmed cognac. Arrange squab on a platter. Garnish with a large bunch of watercress.

Chill pan juices over ice very quickly, and remove excess fat. Combine juices with brown sauce, and heat thoroughly. Correct the seasonings. Add a drop more cognac if needed.

Petits Pois

The frozen ones that come in a plastic bag are as good as any you'll ever eat. You will need about 4 packages. Serve with an extra dollop of butter and perhaps chopped fresh tarragon, if available, or parsley.

If you cannot find the frozen variety specified, look for a good brand of canned petits pois.

Raspberry Sherbet with Peaches

Arrange balls of good raspberry sherbet in a chilled glass bowl; top with fresh peach halves that have been lightly poached in vanilla syrup. Sprinkle with eau de vie de Framboise, or kirsch. Garnish with chopped pistaschio nuts.

 A FRENCH DINNER FOR 6 to 8

Start with sherry or Madeira, nuts and tiny cucumber sandwiches. Provide spirits for those who want them. Drink a Nuits-St.-Georges with the lamb.

CONSOMMÉ AUX PROFITEROLES

SADDLE OF LAMB PRINCE ORLOFF

POMMES PARISIENNE

ENDIVES BRAISÉES

FRAISES KATE

Consommé aux Profiteroles

Make a batch of Pâte à Choux (*see* p. 358) the day of the party. Place half of it in a pastry bag fitted with a small, plain tube. Squeeze pâte à choux into balls the size of a pea on a buttered baking sheet. Bake at 375° till they puff and brown. (Reserve the remaining pâte à choux, and bake a few large puffs for your next day's luncheon or dinner.)

The consommé may be canned, reconstituted.

> *5 cans beef broth*
> *1 bay leaf*
> *½ teaspoon Quatre Épices or Spice Parisienne*
> *1 pound ground beef without fat*
> *1 egg white (with shell)*
> *½ cup Madeira*
> *Chopped parsley*

Pour the cans of beef broth into a pot, and measure out and add three cans of water. Add the bay leaf, spices and meat. Bring to a boil, and simmer for 1½ hours. Beat egg white lightly and add to broth along with shell. Bring to boil again, and continue boiling 5 minutes. Remove from heat, and let stand for 5 minutes. Strain through a linen cloth. Add Madeira.

Serve very hot with the tiny profiteroles and chopped parsley added.

Saddle of Lamb Prince Orloff

Saddle of young lamb
1 pint or more Sauce Soubise (see below)
Truffles
Grated Parmesan cheese
Butter

Trim the saddle well and tie it. Roast it quickly in a 450° oven for 45 minutes, and reduce to 350° for additional 25 to 30 minutes. It must be firm but rare. In some places the saddle is called a "double loin."

Carve the fillets off the saddle in one piece. Spread the cavity with a film of sauce Soubise. Cut the fillets into scallops ½ inch thick. Brush each with sauce and reassemble, placing a thin slice of truffle between each scallop. Arrange a row of truffles on each side of the saddle, and top with additional Soubise. Sprinkle with grated Parmesan cheese, dot with butter, and run under the broiler to glaze and reheat.

For the Sauce Soubise :

Prepare a cream sauce with 4 tablespoons flour, 4 tablespoons butter, and 1 cup veal broth or chicken broth and ½ cup cream.

Stir in ½ cup onion puree :

Steam 1 cup finely chopped onion in 2 tablespoons butter in tightly covered saucepan until soft. Puree or put through the blender. Season the sauce Soubise with salt and pepper. You may add grated Gruyère cheese to this sauce for many dishes.

Pommes Parisienne

8 to 10 potatoes
1 pint oil heated to 370° in a large skillet
Salt and pepper

Peel potatoes, and cut with a small ball-cutter. Soak potato balls in ice water for 1 hour, then dry on absorbent towels. Cook in hot fat till golden brown on the outside and soft and mealy inside. Season with salt and pepper.

Endives Braisées

> *12 to 14 endives*
> *Beef broth or chicken broth*
> *6 tablespoons butter*
> *Salt and pepper*
> *Chopped parsley*
> *Marrow (optional)*

Split the endives. Poach in broth to barely cover till soft. Turn once during poaching. Remove endives, and reduce broth to a glaze. Add butter, and return the endives to the pan. Salt and pepper to taste, and add a touch of chopped parsley. (Marrow also may be added.) Cook briskly for several minutes.

Fraises Kate

> *1 quart strawberries*
> *Sugar*
> *1½ cups orange sections*
> *2 cans undiluted frozen orange juice*
> *2 quarts vanilla ice cream packed in a mold*
> *⅓ to ½ cup cognac*
> *Pistachio nuts, chopped*

Sugar the berries lightly. Thaw and heat the orange juice concentrate. Unmold the ice cream on a platter, and arrange the strawberries and orange sections around it. Also garnish the top with berries and orange sections. Add cognac to the orange juice, and bring to a boil. Serve the hot sauce with the ice cream and fruit. Sprinkle all with pistachio nuts.

**A SUPERB FORMAL DINNER FOR 8, NOT
TOO DIFFICULT TO PREPARE**

Drink a Château Cheval Blanc or a Château Ausone.

CLEAR GREEN TURTLE SOUP WITH MADEIRA

POPPY SEED ROUNDS

PERFECT ROAST CHICKEN WITH TARRAGON

POTATOES SAVOYARDE

GREEN SALAD, VINTNER'S STYLE

COFFEE MOUSSE

Clear Green Turtle Soup with Madeira

Naturally, you are not going to find a green turtle and make
soup. You will buy top-quality canned turtle soup and some
turtle meat; the latter is also available in cans.

> *2 large cans turtle soup*
> *1 can turtle meat*
>   *or*
> *3 cans turtle soup with meat*
> *Madeira to taste*

Dice the turtle meat. Heat the soup, and flavor to taste with
Madeira. Serve in cups. With the soup drink the same Madeira.

Perfect Roast Chicken with Tarragon

One of the simplest of dishes and one of the best, but it requires proper cooking.

> *3 or 4 large chickens or capons*
> *2 lemons*
> *A few sprigs fresh tarragon, or 1 teaspoon dried, for*
>   *each chicken*
> *Salt and freshly ground pepper*
> *6 to 8 strips bacon*
> *1 stick or more melted butter*

One-quarter of a chicken is the average serving, but you must remember that more people may want dark than white meat; or white than dark. Leftover chicken is no problem. It is excellent eaten cold, and it can be used in any number of dishes.

Wipe the outside of the chickens with a damp cloth, and dry. Clean the cavities by rubbing each with half a lemon. Remove the neck and the giblets. Pluck out any remaining pin feathers. If you can get fresh tarragon, crush a few sprigs and place into the cavity of each chicken; otherwise do the same with dried tarragon. Rub the chickens well with salt and freshly ground pepper. Then place them on a rack, turned on their sides, in a shallow roasting pan. Bard with strips of bacon. Place the giblets in the pan.

Roast at 400° for 25 minutes. Remove bacon, and turn chickens over to rest on other side. Brush well with melted butter and any fat in the pan. Roast 25 minutes more, basting once. Now place chickens on their backs. Baste well. Return to oven for 30 to 35 minutes, or until the skin is crisp and the meat is tender. Do not overcook! A little pink at the joints will never harm anyone.

Remove chickens from the oven, and let stand for 5 minutes. Cut into quarters, leaving one chicken whole to present on the platter. Serve the giblets and the pan juices, from which most of the grease has been removed. Garnish the platter with watercress.

Potatoes Savoyarde

> *8 to 10 potatoes*
> *Butter*
> *Salt and pepper*
> *Beef broth or consommé*
> *1 cup or more grated Gruyère*

Peel and slice potatoes very thin. Butter generously an oblong or round baking dish. Place a layer of potatoes in the dish, salt and pepper, then continue adding layers. Dot the top layer with butter. Pour in enough well-flavored beef broth or consommé to come almost to the top of the dish.

Bake at 350° for 45 minutes. Test for tenderness. If there is too much liquid left, pour off some of it. Sprinkle with the grated Gruyère, and return to oven till the cheese browns nicely and the potatoes are thoroughly cooked.

Green Salad, Vintner's Style

This should be made with walnut oil, if available. It is mainly a good, crisp green salad interestingly flavored with blanched fresh walnut halves and a dressing made partly with red wine. Sometimes shredded Gruyère is added to it.

> *6 heads Bibb lettuce*
> *1 head romaine*
> *1 bunch watercress*
> *1 cup walnut halves*
> *1 cup shredded Gruyère (optional)*

For the dressing:

> *1 cup oil, walnut or olive*
> *¼ cup red wine*
> *2 tablespoons vinegar*
> *1 teaspoon salt*
> *1 teaspoon freshly ground pepper*

Wash and dry the greens. Tear the larger lettuce leaves into smaller pieces. Arrange in a bowl, and add the watercress, walnut halves, and Gruyère (if you wish; remember, there is Gruyère in the potatoes savoyarde). Mix the dressing, pour over the salad at the last minute (watercress wilts easily), and toss.

Coffee Mousse

> *1 quart heavy cream, whipped*
> *1¼ teaspoons ground cinnamon*
> *½ cup sugar*
> *3 to 4 tablespoons instant coffee*
> *1 tablespoon gelatin, dissolved in ¼ cup water*

Whip the cream and add seasonings. Dissolve gelatin and melt over medium heat. Add to mixture. Freeze in a mold in freezer compartment or in an ice cream freezer.

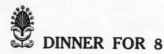 **DINNER FOR 8**

Drinks: With soup, Madeira or sherry. With main course, Château Lascombes or another good Médoc.

CRAB SOUP, MARGARET JENNINGS

STUFFED FILLET OF BEEF

FONDANT POTATOES

BROCCOLI, BEURRE NOIR

MINCEMEAT TART

Crab Soup, Margaret Jennings

> *1 pound crabmeat*
> *½ cup milk*
> *2 tablespoons butter*
> *2 cups Sauce Béchamel* (see p. 343)

1 cup cream, or more
Salt and pepper
⅓ cup Scotch whisky

Heat the crabmeat in the milk and butter. Prepare a light béchamel, and add the cream to it after it has come to the boiling
point. Add the crabmeat, and again bring to a boil. Season to
taste, and add more cream if the soup needs thinning. Just before
serving, stir in the Scotch. Serve in heated cups with a sprinkling
of finely chopped parsley.

Stuffed Fillet of Beef

8 chicken livers
Butter
Salt and freshly ground black pepper
6 tablespoons cognac
1 fillet of beef (5 to 6 pounds)
6 truffles
½ teaspoon rosemary
1½ cups Sauce Espagnole (see p. 344) *or canned beef*
    gravy
½ cup Madeira

Sauté chicken livers in 3 tablespoons butter for 3 minutes, tossing pan to cook livers evenly. Salt and pepper livers lightly, and
flame with half cognac. Remove livers, and reserve pan juices.

Make an opening in the fillet with a larding needle, or have
your butcher do it for you. Stuff the fillet alternately with
chicken livers and truffles (reserve liquid from can). Rub the
surface of the meat with butter, rosemary, salt and pepper.

Roast on a rack at 450° for 30 to 35 minutes, or until the
meat reaches an inner temperature of 125°. Baste with butter,
if needed, during roasting. Remove to a hot platter. Flambé
with remaining cognac. Combine pan juices with juices from the
sautéed livers, the truffle juice, the sauce espagnole, and the
Madeira. Simmer 2 or 3 minutes. Correct the seasoning.

Garnish platter with watercress. Serve sauce in a sauceboat.

Fondant Potatoes

3 pounds small new potatoes
¼ pound (1 stick) butter, softened
Salt and pepper

You must use a heavy pan for this. Scrape potatoes, and arrange in one layer in the pan. Add butter, cover the pan, and place over medium heat for 15 minutes or so. Turn the potatoes, re-cover, and continue cooking, shaking the pan occasionally, till the potatoes are just pierceable and tender. Add salt and freshly ground pepper to taste.

Broccoli, Beurre Noir

8 medium sections broccoli
Boiling salted water
6 tablespoons butter
Dash of lemon juice

Cook the broccoli till tender but still crisp. Drain, and keep hot. Melt butter in a pan, and shake over a fairly high flame till it colors. Add a dash of lemon juice. Serve over the broccoli.

Mincemeat Tart

1 Rich Pastry recipe (see p. 359–360)
2 cans mincemeat
3 apples, grated but not peeled
⅓ cup cognac
1 or 2 apples, thinly sliced
Sugar
Apricot Glaze (see p. 38)

Prepare the pastry, chill, and roll to fit an oblong flan ring, a 9-inch ring, or a 9-inch pie tin. Chill again, thoroughly.

Combine mincemeat, grated apple, and cognac. Fill the pie shell with this mixture, and press it down lightly. Cover with apple slices arranged in a pattern. Sprinkle lightly with sugar. Bake at 375° for 30 to 40 minutes or until apples are soft. Remove from oven and cool. Glaze with apricot glaze. Serve warm.

EASY TO PREPARE DINNERS

I have often said, when people complained about the time it takes to cook, that one can do a fine dinner for guests in an hour—an unforgettable dinner. And it *is* possible. One cannot, of course, produce a pot au feu or quenelles de brochet in that amount of time, but one can easily assemble an hors d'oeuvre and soup, a main course such as a chicken sauté, a veal scallopine or a sauced tournedos, and a vegetable, salad, cheese and simple but distinguished dessert—without sitting down to the table breathless. This doesn't take magic but merely good planning and deft execution. Such meals may prove far more memorable than those which take long preparation, and they are certain to be better enjoyed by the cook.

Here are nine dinners. Some are menus in which I take great delight. All are relatively easy to prepare—and without the aid of instant foods or packaged mixes. One or two menus require greater preparation than the others but not enough to tax the willing cook.

A VERY SPECIAL STEAK DINNER

A good Beaujolais should accompany this meal.

STEAK AU POIVRE FLAMBÉ

GALETTE POTATOES

FRESH ASPARAGUS, VINAIGRETTE

CHEESE

Steak au Poivre Flambé

Choose a good porterhouse or sirloin steak about 2 inches thick. Trim excess fat from steak, and score remaining fat. About 20 minutes before cooking the steak, press 1 tablespoon cracked pepper into the meat with the heel of your hand. The pepper must be freshly cracked or ground to provide the proper flavor. To crack, use a rolling pin or a meat pounder, or give it a brief whirl in the blender. The steak may be either pan-broiled in a heavy skillet or broiled in the oven, but I suggest pan-broiling as the better method for this, although it is a smoky process.

To pan-broil : Rub a heated skillet with a little beef fat. Allow the pan to become very hot, then place the steak in the pan and sear for 3 to 4 minutes on each side. Reduce the heat slightly, and continue cooking, turning once or twice, until the meat is done to your taste (10 to 12 minutes for rare). Test by cutting near the bone with a sharp knife.

Just before removing steak to a hot platter, pour ⅓ cup cognac over steak, and flame. Pour pan juices over meat, and serve, carved in slices.

Galette Potatoes

See p. 367.

Fresh Asparagus, Vinaigrette

Cook asparagus in boiling salted water. I use a large skillet, in which the asparagus fits very nicely, and cook it at a fast boil. The spears should be tender but still crisp. About 6 to 8 minutes does the job. Remove asparagus, drain, and cool.

Serve with a mustard-flavored vinaigrette, made by blending the following ingredients:

> *3 tablespoons wine vinegar*
> *1½ teaspoons Dijon mustard*
> *8 tablespoons oil*
> *Salt and freshly ground pepper*
> *Chopped parsley*

Blend the vinegar and mustard before adding oil. Then salt to taste, give it a few grinds of pepper, and add the parsley.

Cheese

A good Pont l'Évêque or a ripe Brie would be in order to finish off this meal, served with French bread and biscuits.

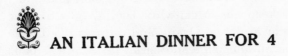 AN ITALIAN DINNER FOR 4

Drink a good Chianti. There are some excellent ones on the market. Consult the wine chart, p. 375–380.

ANTIPASTO

SPAGHETTI ALLA CARBONARA

GREEN SALAD

GORGONZOLA AND PEARS

Antipasto

Buy Italian salami and prosciutto at your local delicatessen or Italian market. (Prosciutto is now available in tins.) Arrange on a platter with hot peppers, if you like them, and radishes, which are especially good with this combination. Serve grissini or other bread sticks, and provide coarsely ground pepper for the prosciutto.

Spaghetti alla Carbonara

> *1 pound spaghetti*
> *½ pound thickly cut bacon*
> *⅓ cup white wine or dry vermouth*
> *2 eggs, well beaten*
> *½ cup or more freshly grated Romano or Parmesan cheese*
> *Freshly ground pepper*

Cut bacon into dice about ½ inch square. Sauté till cooked through but not crisp. Remove from pan, and add wine. Cook down and keep hot. Meanwhile cook spaghetti to your taste— well done or al dente. Drain, and return to kettle. Immediately add the bacon and wine and bacon fat from the pan. Mix, then add the eggs and cheese. Toss as you would a salad. Add a few grinds of pepper. Make sure the egg adheres to the spaghetti and cooks in the hot fat; if it still looks raw, toss some more over low heat. Serve with additional cheese.

NOTE: Not authentic, I know, but I have done this dish to great acclaim with Virginia ham instead of bacon. Also, macaroni may be used instead of spaghetti.

Gorgonzola and Pears

Select a good ripe Gorgonzola, and serve with ripe fresh pears. A simple and fitting end to this meal.

 A SEAFOOD DINNER FOR 6

Serve white wine cassis before dinner—use a California Mountain White or a Chablis—and serve the same wine with the lobster. With the salmon drink a light Burgundy—a Beaune or a red Chassagne-Montrachet.

COLD BABY LOBSTER, SAUCE VERTE

THIN RYE BREAD AND BUTTER

SALMON BRAISED IN RED WINE

BOILED NEW POTATOES

OMELET SOUFFLÉ

Cold Lobster, Sauce Verte

> 6 lobsters (1 pound each, or more if you wish to be generous)
> Pickled walnuts
> Hard-cooked eggs

Olives
2 cups mayonnaise
½ cup spinach
3 tablespoons chopped chives
3 tablespoons chopped parsley
1 teaspoon tarragon
1 tablespoon chopped mint
1 garlic clove

Cook the lobsters in boiling salted water—put them in head first —for 5 to 6 minutes after the water returns to the boiling point. Remove and cool. Split, and remove the stomach and intestinal tract; reserve the greenish-colored tomalley. Cut the meat into bite-size pieces, and crack the claws.

Arrange on serving plates. Garnish with pickled walnuts, hard-cooked eggs and olives. Two hours before serving, combine mayonnaise with the spinach, herbs and garlic, all finely chopped. Mix in the tomalley. Serve with the lobster.

Braised Salmon in Red Wine

6 to 8 pounds salmon
2 medium onions, thinly sliced
2 stalks celery, cut in strips
1 carrot, cut in thin strips
3 sprigs parsley
1 leek, cleaned and cut in strips
8 tablespoons butter

Salt
1 quart (or more) red wine
1 teaspoon thyme
1 bay leaf
18 small white onions
1 pound mushrooms

Place the sliced onions, celery, carrot, parsley and leek in the bottom of a large fish cooker or braising pan with 5 tablespoons of the butter. Cover and let cook over a medium flame until the vegetables are soft. Salt the salmon inside and out, and place it on this bed of vegetables. Add red wine to half the depth of the fish in the pan, and put in the thyme and bay leaf. Bring just to a boil. Cover the fish with a piece of cooking parchment, and place it in the oven for about 40 minutes or until the salmon is cooked through. Meanwhile, brown the small onions in 3 table-

spoons of butter, and let them cook through in a covered pan. Sauté the mushrooms lightly in the remaining butter, and season to taste.

Baste the fish in the oven from time to time. When it is cooked, arrange it on a hot platter and surround it with the onions and mushrooms. Strain the sauce, and if you wish it thickened, add beurre manié (butter and flour mixed). Taste for seasoning, and serve it separately.

Boiled New Potatoes

See p. 365.

Omelet Soufflé

> *8 eggs*
> *½ cup sugar*
> *⅓ cup cognac or rum, plus ½ cup*
> *Granulated sugar*

Separate the eggs, and beat the yolks until light and lemon-colored. Gradually beat in the sugar. Add ⅓ cup of cognac or rum. Beat the egg whites until firm, and fold ⅓ of them into the yolk mixture. Then cut in the rest of the whites. This soufflé is cooked in a skillet. Select a heavy metal one with a metal handle, for it must be ovenproof. I generally use a 10-inch cast-aluminum skillet for this recipe. Heat the skillet on top of the stove, and butter it well. Sprinkle with granulated sugar. Pour the soufflé mixture into the skillet, and bake at 375° about 15 minutes. Remove it from the oven, and serve from the skillet. Sprinkle with granulated sugar, pour ½ cup of cognac over it and ignite. Serve at once. Makes 8 servings.

VARIATION: Omit the cognac from the basic mixture, and substitute ¼ cup lemon juice and the grated rind of the lemon. This has a sharper flavor.

A SPRING DINNER FOR 6

A good Chambertin is a wise choice for a wine to be served throughout this dinner. Preceding dinner, with drinks, you might serve smoked salmon on pumpernickel.

HINDQUARTER OF BABY LAMB, PROVENÇALE

FLAGEOLETS   SAUTÉED TOMATOES

GRUYÈRE SOUFFLÉ

FRUIT

Hindquarter of Baby Lamb, Provençale

1 hindquarter of baby lamb
3 cloves garlic, finely chopped
Salt
1 teaspoon freshly ground black pepper
½ cup olive oil
1 cup white wine
1 cup pitted black olives (Italian or Greek)

Mash the chopped garlic cloves into the salt, and rub lamb well with this mixture. Then rub with the pepper and with enough of the olive oil to coat thinly. Combine the remaining oil with the white wine for basting.

Place on a rack in a shallow pan. Roast at 325°, allowing 15 minutes per pound. Baste several times during roasting with the oil and wine mixture. When the roast is done, remove to a hot platter. Skim excess fat from pan. Add olives, and cook 5 minutes. Pour this sauce over the heated Flageolets (*see* recipe below, or serve in a sauceboat.

Carve the lamb in thin slices.

Flageolets

Since flageolets are not to be found in this country except in cans, we must rely, for the most part, on those imported from France. They are very good and save you the work of starting from scratch.

For each can of beans, sauté 1 garlic clove in a tablespoon of olive oil for a few minutes, then remove the clove. Toss the beans in the hot oil, and cook just long enough to allow the beans to heat through. Correct the seasoning.

Serve with the pan juices from the roasted lamb, prepared as described above.

Sautéed Tomatoes

Halve 6 good ripe tomatoes. Place 2 tablespoons olive oil in a sautéing pan. Add tomatoes, cut side down. Sauté over very low heat for 30 to 40 minutes, or until the underside has more or less caramelized. Salt and pepper to taste.

Gruyère Soufflé

Oftentimes a cheese soufflé and fruit make a superb dessert course. My dear friend Simone Prunier, of Prunier's in London, has offered this combination many times at dinner parties, with great success. The basic mixture can be made ahead and the egg white added just before the soufflé goes into the oven—as you sit down to the lamb, probably; or after your oven has reached a higher temperature, if you choose to cook it that way.

> *3 tablespoons butter*
> *3 tablespoons flour*
> *¾ cup milk*
> *½ teaspoon salt*
> *½ teaspoon Tabasco*
> *5 egg yolks*
> *1 cup grated Gruyère cheese*
> *6 egg whites*

Make a cream sauce: Melt the butter, add flour, and cook several minutes before stirring in the milk, which has been warmed. Continue stirring till the mixture thickens. Add seasonings, and remove from heat. Cool slightly, and then stir in the egg yolks. (Warm them first by adding a few tablespoons of the mixture.) Add the cheese, and return to heat just long enough to melt the cheese; do not allow to boil. Cool. Beat egg whites till stiff but not dry. Fold ⅓ of the whites into the cheese sauce rather thoroughly, then gently fold in the remaining whites. Pour into a buttered 1½–quart mold, with a collar of brown paper tied around it to extend 2 or 3 inches above the top of the dish.

Bake at either 325° for 40 to 45 minutes or 400° for 25 to 30 minutes, depending on the timing of the rest of your dinner.

Serve at once. Follow with fresh fruit.

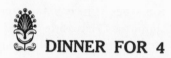

DINNER FOR 4

PAILLARD OF VEAL

SPINACH WITH CREAM AND NUTMEG

SLICED ORANGES WITH GRAND MARNIER

Paillard of Veal

This requires 4 thin slices from the leg, pounded; they should be about ⅛ inch thick. Brush the paillards with butter, and broil quickly in a very hot oven. Salt and pepper to taste, and remove to hot plates. Add a dollop of butter and a sprinkling of parsley.

Spinach with Cream and Nutmeg

> *2 packages frozen chopped spinach*
> *3 tablespoons butter*
> *1 tablespoon flour*

3 tablespoons heavy cream
⅛ teaspoon nutmeg
Salt

Thaw and drain spinach well. Chop again. Melt butter in a skillet, add flour, and stir in cream. Cook till thickened. Combine with spinach. Salt to taste and add nutmeg. Cover, and heat over very low flame, stirring once or twice; or heat in a double boiler over hot water.

Sliced Oranges with Grand Marnier

4 large or 6 medium oranges
¼ cup Grand Marnier or more
Sugar (optional)

Peel oranges, leaving no white skin on the outside. This can be done easily by using a sharp knife to peel the oranges, instead of peeling by hand. Slice oranges and arrange on plates. Sugar, if necessary. Add a little Grand Marnier to each portion.

DINNER FOR 4

GRILLED CHEESEBURGERS

MUSHROOM-ROMAINE SALAD

TOASTED ROLLS

QUICK RASPBERRY SHORTCAKE

Grilled Cheeseburgers

> *2 pounds chopped chuck or round*
> *1 teaspoon salt*
> *½ teaspoon freshly ground black pepper*
> *¼ teaspoon Tabasco*
> *½ teaspoon mustard*
> *1 cup loosely packed shredded cheddar or Gruyère cheese*

Mix seasonings and cheese with beef. Form into cakes about 1½ inches thick. Grill or pan-broil to your taste; or ask your guests how rare they would like their meat. Do not overcook. Serve on hot plates with mustard.

Mushroom-Romaine Salad

> *1 large head romaine*
> *½ pound raw mushrooms, sliced*
> *6 to 8 scallions, finely cut*
> *6 tablespoons oil*
> *2 tablespoons vinegar, or to taste*
> *¼ cup chopped parsley*
> *1 teaspoon salt*
> *Freshly ground black pepper*

Break romaine into salad bowl. Add sliced mushrooms and scallions. Blend oil, vinegar, parsley, salt and pepper. Add to salad, and toss just before serving.

Quick Raspberry Shortcake

> *1 or 2 packages frozen raspberries*
> *4 slices Pound Cake (see p. 360–361)*
> *Heavy cream or sour cream*

Thaw the raspberries. Toast the pound cake on both sides. Remove to warm plates. Spoon raspberries over cake, and serve with cream. (Naturally, if they are in season, fresh raspberries, sugared, are preferable.)

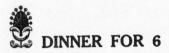 **DINNER FOR 6**

A pleasant white wine—a Muscadet or Chablis—would go well with the shad roe.

SHAD ROE POACHED IN BUTTER

BOILED NEW POTATOES

SAUTÉED ZUCCHINI WITH GARLIC

PINEAPPLE WITH KIRSCH

Shad Roe Poached in Butter

> *6 good-sized shad roe*
> *1½ sticks butter*
> *Salt and pepper*
> *Chopped parsley*
> *Lemon wedges*
> *Toast*

Use a heavy skillet with a cover. Melt butter over medium heat, and bathe each roe in the butter. Cover pan, and cook, turning once, for 12 to 15 minutes. Remove to a hot platter. Add salt, pepper, and chopped parsley to the butter. Spoon over shad roe. Serve with lemon wedges and toast.

Boiled New Potatoes

See p. 365.

Sautéed Zucchini with Garlic

> *6 small zucchini*
> *⅓ cup olive oil*

2 cloves garlic, finely chopped
Salt and freshly ground pepper
Lemon juice

Cut zucchini lengthwise in three strips each. Heat olive oil, and add zucchini and garlic. Sauté quickly until zucchini are tender but still somewhat crisp. Salt and pepper to taste, and sprinkle with lemon juice.

Pineapple with Kirsch

Choose a good ripe pineapple. Slice thin and cut off peel and prickly portions. Chill, and serve with sugar and kirsch. (A knife and fork are best for eating pineapple.)

 DINNER FOR 4

Serve a Cabernet Sauvignon.

KIDNEYS ON THE HALF-SHELL, FLAMBÉ

RICE WITH CHOPPED CHIVES AND PARSLEY

GREEN BEANS, VINAIGRETTE

GINGER SOUFFLÉ

Kidneys on the Half-Shell, Flambé

4 veal kidneys in part of their fat
Cognac
Salt and freshly ground pepper

Set the oven to 475°. Trim some of the fat from the kidneys and roast on a rack for 25 to 30 minutes. Turn once during the roasting. Remove to a grooved carving board or a flameproof platter. Cut the kidneys in half, and flambé with heated cognac. Salt and pepper to taste. Serve on hot plates. Spoon juices (from the board or dish) over the kidneys.

Rice with Chopped Chives and Parsley

Prepare 1½ cups rice in your favorite way, then blend with butter, chopped chives and chopped parsley.

Green Beans, Vinaigrette

These may be served either hot or cold.

> *1½ pounds green beans*
> *Salted water*
> *1 small onion, finely chopped*
> *Vinaigrette Sauce* (see p. 350)

Cook beans until tender but still firm. Drain. Combine with the onion and the vinaigrette sauce. If served cold, garnish with chopped parsley and onion rings.

Ginger Soufflé

> *3 tablespoons butter*
> *3 tablespoons flour*
> *¾ cup milk, heated*
> *Pinch salt*
> *5 egg yolks*
> *½ cup sugar*
> *½ cup finely cut preserved ginger*
> *6 egg whites*
> *Heavy cream, whipped*

Make a cream sauce: Melt butter in a saucepan, add the flour, cook for a minute, then add the milk slowly. Stir until thickened. Cool slightly. Beat in the egg yolks and the sugar. Return to low heat for a few minutes, stirring constantly. Add ginger, and cool slightly again. Beat egg whites till stiff but not dry.

Fold into cream sauce carefully, and pour into a 1½–quart soufflé dish that has been buttered and sugared. Bake at 400° for 25 to 30 minutes. Serve with whipped cream.

NOTE: Prepare the soufflé before dinner, except for beating and adding the egg whites. Butter and sugar the dish; have the oven heated to the proper temperature. Then take time to clear the table and prepare it for the dessert course while the soufflé cooks.

 ## A VERY INFORMAL BUT SATISFYING MEAL FOR 4 GOOD FRIENDS

MOULES MARINIÈRES

TOASTED FRENCH ROLLS

ROMAINE AND ONION SALAD

CHOCOLATE MOUSSE

Moules Marinières

4 quarts mussels
1 onion, finely chopped
3 ribs celery, finely chopped
3 garlic cloves, finely chopped
2 cups white wine
½ cup chopped parsley
1 tablespoon salt

Scrub the mussels well and "beard" them with a wire brush. Place mussels, vegetables, garlic, wine and salt in a large kettle.

Cover, and steam till the mussels open. Do not overcook, or they will be tough. Pour off the liquid, and strain through a linen napkin. Scoop mussels into soup plates or bowls. Add parsley to broth, heat for a minute or two, and ladle over mussels.

Toasted French rolls or French bread and butter should accompany this.

Romaine and Onion Salad

> *1 large or 2 small heads romaine*
> *1 large Italian or Spanish onion*
> *Vinaigrette Sauce* (see p. 350)

Wash and dry romaine leaves, wrap in towel, and refrigerate. Peel and slice onion thinly. Place in a salad bowl with the vinaigrette sauce. Just before serving, add the romaine, broken into pieces, and toss.

Chocolate Mousse

> *1 6-ounce package semisweet chocolate bits*
> *6 egg yolks, slightly beaten*
> *2 tablespoons cognac*
> *6 egg whites, beaten*
> *Dash salt*

Melt chocolate over hot water, add egg yolks and cognac, and blend well. Fold in egg whites, beaten till stiff but not dry, and the salt. Pour into individual pots or a glass dish, and chill. Make this the day before your dinner party.

DINNERS TO PREPARE IN ADVANCE

I have a predilection for rising early, and when I am preparing for a dinner party, I enjoy rising at 5:00 or 5:30 and going straight from the bath to the kitchen. I call this "cooking in the nude." It is so cool and quiet in the early hours and before midmorning one can have a whole dinner ready except for the final bits of cooking and the garnishings. You needn't get up before dawn, however, to give a dinner party. If you plan carefully, a fairly complicated menu can be assembled over a period of two or three days. Many frozen desserts may be made several days ahead; pastries and bread a week or two in advance, and frozen; crêpes, ready for filling, may be stored in the refrigerator for a week or in the freezer for a month or two. In fact, you might store away a whole buffet, providing you have enough refrigerator and freezer space, leaving only a few things to heat, dress, or garnish.

In the menus provided here, one or more courses can be prepared in advance. You will save more last-minute work if you lay out tablecloth, napkins and silver the night before, as well as serving dishes and other accessories. Ingredients for salads and garnishes can be prepared and refrigerated in plastic bags or foil. Stock your bar days in advance. If your schedule is really well thought out, you should be able to have a rest and a quick shower before the gala starts. There is nothing quite so satisfying as that lull before the first ring of the doorbell.

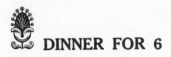 **DINNER FOR 6**

SEVICHE IN AVOCADO SHELLS

CHICKEN CHILI

WHOLE HOMINY

TORTILLAS

FRESH PINEAPPLE WITH RUM

Seviche in Avocado Shells

*1 pound firm-fleshed whitefish, boned, skinned and
   diced
1 cup lemon or lime juice
3 tablespoons olive oil
1 onion, chopped
1 small can green chilies, chopped
1 tomato, chopped
1 pinch oregano
Salt and pepper to taste
3 avocados, halved and seeded*

Marinate the fish in lemon or lime juice for at least 1 hour.
Drain, and add other ingredients (except avocado), mixing well.
Fill the avocado halves with mixture, and serve.

Chicken Chili

2 large fowl   *3 cloves garlic*
1 onion, stuck with cloves   *1 bay leaf*

2 hot peppers	*3 cloves garlic, finely*
Salt	*chopped*
Water	*1 tablespoon chili powder*
2 tablespoons chili powder	*1 teaspoon basil*
2 large onions, finely	*Fresh coriander*
chopped	*1 tin tomato paste*
6 tablespoons fat (3 each	*1 cup ripe olives*
chicken fat and but-	*Beurre manié*
ter)	*Sliced toasted almonds*
	Toasted filberts

Poach the chickens with the onion stuck with cloves, garlic, bay leaf and salt to taste.

When the chickens are tender, remove from the broth and cut meat from bones. Return carcasses to broth and cook for another 30 minutes. Add chili powder and hot peppers. Skim off excess fat. Strain broth through a linen towel. Reduce to 3 cups.

Sauté the chopped onions in fat and add garlic, seasonings and tomato paste. Add to reduced broth and add chicken. Correct seasoning and add about 1 cup ripe olives, and thicken with beurre manié (butter and flour mixed) if desired.

Serve with tortillas or with polenta. Garnish with toasted almonds and filberts.

Whole Hominy

Open and wash two No. 2½ cans whole hominy. Heat with 6 tablespoons butter in a covered pan over medium heat. Salt and pepper to taste and add ⅓ cup cream.

Tortillas

Tortillas may be bought in cans or from local Mexican shops in some cities. Cover with foil and heat.

Fresh Pineapple with Rum

Cut off the top, and peel the pineapple, removing the prickly portions. Slice, or cut in fingers, cubes or wedges. Remove the woody core. Sugar to taste, and add 1 ounce of dark rum per serving. Chill and let mellow for at least an hour.

AN ITALIAN DINNER FOR 8

Here is an interesting meal for 8 persons, with very little work to do at the last minute. The peppers may be prepared several hours ahead of time and held for the final baking. The crêpes for the cannelloni may be made the day before and refrigerated; or even days before and put in the freezer. Several hours before baking, assemble the cannelloni and make the tomato sauce. Pour the sauce over just before the dish goes into the oven. Clean the dandelions well in advance, crisp in water, drain, and refrigerate wrapped in a cloth until ready to use. Also prepare the peaches a couple of hours ahead of time, and chill.

Serve Americanos before dinner and Valpolicella with the meal.

STUFFED GREEN PEPPERS

CANNELLONI WITH TOMATO SAUCE

DANDELION SALAD

FRESH PEACHES WITH MARSALA

Stuffed Green Peppers

> 8 medium-sized green peppers
> 2½ cups croutons
> Oil
> 2 cloves garlic, finely chopped
> 16 anchovies, chopped
> ½ cup pine nuts
> ½ cup currants
> 2 tablespoons chopped parsley

> *2 tablespoons vermouth*
> *Salt and pepper*
> *Butter*

Blanch the peppers for 8 to 10 minutes, drain, remove the tops and the seeds.

Sauté the croutons in oil with the garlic till just golden, then mix with the anchovies, pine nuts, currants, parsley and vermouth. Salt and pepper to taste (remember, the anchovies contain a good deal of salt). Stuff peppers with this mixture and place in a buttered baking dish. Top each pepper with 1 tablespoon oil. Bake in a 350° oven for 30 minutes.

The peppers may be blanched, seeded and stuffed several hours before baking.

Cannelloni with Tomato Sauce

This is an Italian version of stuffed crêpes.

> *16 Italian sausages*
> *Tomato Sauce* (see *below*)
> *16 Unsweeteened Crêpes* (see *p. 362*)
> *1 pound ricotta cheese*
> *Grated Parmesan cheese*
> *Butter*

Place sausages in salted water. Bring to a boil and reduce to simmer. Poach for 12 minutes. Remove from water and when cool enough to handle, skin them and cut in long shreds.

Prepare a Tomato Sauce:

> *2 cloves garlic*
> *2 small onions*
> *2 tablespoons olive oil*
> *1 20-ounce can solid pack tomatoes*
> *1 teaspoon basil*
> *Salt and pepper*
> *1½ cans tomato paste*

Chop the garlic and onion very fine. Sauté in olive oil for 3 minutes. Add the tomatoes, basil, and salt and pepper, and bring to a boil. Reduce heat and simmer for 30 minutes. Add the tomato paste, correct the seasoning, and cook for another 15 minutes, then increase the heat and let the sauce reduce a bit. Stir frequently so that the sauce does not scorch.

To Assemble: Spread each crêpe with ricotta cheese, sprinkle with grated Parmesan, and give it a grind from the pepper mill. Add the sausage bits, roll the crêpes, and place them in a shallow baking dish so that they barely touch each other. Pour the tomato sauce over them, and sprinkle with additional grated cheese. Bake at 375° till bubbly.

NOTE: You may vary the filling by using poached brains cut in slices, or cooked chicken, veal, pork or ham, highly seasoned.

Dandelion Salad

Dandelion greens are in the market for a great part of the year, and they are cultivated in many sections of the country.

Crisp the greens in cold water, and toss at the last moment with a good vinaigrette sauce.

Fresh Peaches with Marsala

Peel and slice 8 to 10 ripe peaches. Add sugar to taste, and flavor with ⅔ cup Marsala. Frozen peaches may be substituted.

 DINNER FOR 4 TO 6

The shrimp and salad may be assembled well ahead of time, and the dessert may also be made ahead and kept warm. For the main course: Prepare the chicken, sauce and brioche dough or pastry crust. Just before sitting down to your first course, roll out the dough, cover the baking dish, and pop it into the oven. At the same time finish up the potatoes and keep warm over hot water. With the main course serve the same wine used in the coq au vin.

SHRIMP AILLADE

COQ AU VIN EN BRIOCHE

FLUFFY POTATOES

BEET AND ONION SALAD

PETS DE NONNE

Shrimp Aillade

1 pound cooked shrimp

For Aillade Sauce :

12 to 14 walnut meats, finely chopped
3 cloves garlic, finely chopped
¾ cup oil
1 tablespoon lemon juice
½ teaspoon salt
Chopped parsley

Blend ingredients for sauce. Mix with the shrimp and sprinkle with chopped parsley. Chill before serving.

Coq au Vin en Brioche

4 slices salt pork, cubed
Butter
6 chicken legs and thighs or 6 breasts
Flour
1 tablespoon oil
⅛ cup cognac
Bouquet garni (thyme, 1 bay leaf, sprig parsley, pep-
*   percorns)*
Red Burgundy to just cover

12 small white onions, peeled
18 mushrooms
Brioche or Plain Pastry dough (see *pp. 356 and 359*)

Try out the salt pork in a little butter. Roll chicken pieces in flour, and brown very quickly in 4 tablespoons of butter and the oil. Blaze with cognac. Add tried-out salt pork, bouquet garni and Burgundy. Cover, and let it cook for about 40 minutes or until tender.

Sauté the onions in a little butter until nicely glazed and just cooked through. Add the mushrooms, and allow them to mix and cook with the onions.

Transfer chicken to a shallow baking dish. Add onions, mushrooms and salt pork. Strain the sauce, and correct the seasoning. Pour over the chicken. Cool. When ready to serve, cover with a thinly rolled brioche or pastry crust. Bake in a 400° oven for about 25 minutes.

Fluffy Potatoes

4 to 8 potatoes
Boiling salted water
Salt and pepper
4 tablespoons butter
4 tablespoons heated cream (*or more*)

Peel potatoes, cut into halves or quarters, and cook in boiling salted water to cover. When tender, drain thoroughly and put through a ricer. Return to pan, season to taste with salt and freshly ground black pepper. Add butter, and beat thoroughly, preferably with a wire whisk. Then add cream, and beat it in well. If potatoes are not fluffy enough, beat in additional cream. Keep hot over a pan of hot water.

Beet and Onion Salad

1 can of beets or 5 cooked beets
1 Bermuda or red Italian onion
Greens
Vinaigrette Sauce (see *p. 350*)

Drain canned beets, or slice cooked beets. Peel and slice the onion very thin. Arrange on a bed of greens, and dress with a good vinaigrette sauce.

Pets de Nonne or Beignets Soufflé

> *1 cup hot water*
> *½ cup butter*
> *¼ teaspoon salt*
> *1 teaspoon sugar*
> *1 cup plus 2 tablespoons flour*
> *4 large or 5 small eggs*
> *Oil for deep fryer*
> *Granulated sugar*

Pour hot water over butter, and stir till melted. Add salt and sugar, and bring to a rolling boil. Add flour, and stir vigorously until the dough leaves edges of pan and forms a ball. Remove from heat, and beat in 1 egg. Beat in remaining eggs 1 at a time till the dough is waxy and well blended.

Heat oil in a deep fryer to 370°. Drop in dough by spoonfuls, or make small balls with lightly floured hands and fry until brown and puffy. Keep beignets in a warm oven. Roll in granulated sugar and serve hot.

NOTE: These may be served with a raspberry sauce or flamed with rum and sugared.

 A PROVENCAL DINNER FOR 4

The daube may be prepared a day or two ahead of time and reheated. It is one of those dishes which seem to improve with age. Vegetables for the first course and fruit for the dessert may be cleaned and sliced hours ahead and kept chilled in the refrigerator. All that remains for last-minute cooking are the peppers.

With the daube drink a good Châteauneuf-du-Pape; or if you wish to be truly Provencal, you might prefer a rosé.

CRUDITÉS

DAUBE PROVENCALE

POIVRONS SAUTÉ

FRUITS RAFRAÎCHIS WITH SABLES

Crudités

Prepare a Mayonnaise (*see* p. 348), and add to it 1 tablespoon Dijon mustard, a dash of Tabasco, and 3 tablespoons chopped parsley. Blend well. Serve as a sauce for the crudités. Arrange a selection of raw vegetables as attractively as possible on individual plates or on one large platter. You might combine cherry tomatoes, scallions, radishes, celery and asparagus. These may be eaten with the fingers. If you choose vegetables such as carrots, or celeriac, which can be cut in julienne strips or shredded, a fork is in order. One three-star restaurant in France serves a "bouquet of crudités" as a first course in which the vegetables are cut very fine and each is served in a different sauce. It is the most appetizing dish imaginable.

Daube Provençale

3 or 4 slices of salt pork	*1 teaspoon rosemary*
5 pound piece of beef,	*Several sprigs parsley*
shin or rump	*1 tablespoon salt*
2 pig's feet or 1 calf's foot	*2 teaspoons freshly*
2 bay leaves	*ground black pepper*
8 cloves garlic	*Red wine (about ⅘*
1 clove	*quart)*
1 strip orange peel	*1 pound macaroni*

Place the meats and seasonings in a crock, and cover with red wine. Let stand for 24 hours. Place in a heavy braising pan or casserole—*not an iron one*—and cook at the lowest possible temperature, about 200°, for 6 hours or more, until tender.

To serve hot: Remove from heat and let stand for 20 to 25 minutes. Skim off excess fat. Remove meat to a hot platter. Strain the sauce and serve part of it blended with 1 pound macaroni cooked in boiling salted water. This is called macaronade. The rest may be served with the meats.

To serve cold: Strain the sauce, let it cool, and remove the excess fat. Slice the meat, arrange in a serving dish, and cover with the sauce. Chill, then serve in its own jelly.

Poivrons Sauté

> *6 tablespoons olive oil*
> *3 cloves garlic*
> *5 to 6 green peppers, seeded and cut*
> *into strips 1 inch wide*
> *Salt and pepper*
> *Dash of vinegar*

Heat the olive oil in a skillet, and add the garlic and peppers. Sauté slowly, covering part of the time, until peppers are tender but not mushy. Salt and pepper to taste, and add vinegar.

Fruits Rafraîchis with Sables

Combine fresh fruits, according to your choice and the offerings on the market—perhaps grapes, melon balls and grapefruit sections; or sliced peaches and blueberries; or pineapple cubes, strawberries and bananas. Sugar if necessary, and flavor with kirsch or Grand Marnier. Chill well before serving.

Sables

> *1 cup flour*
> *½ cup sugar*
> *1 egg yolk*
> *7 tablespoons butter*
> *1 tablespoon cold water*
> *Salt*
> *1 teaspoon vanilla*

Sift flour and sugar together. Add egg yolk, butter cut in small pieces, water, and salt. Work the mixture quickly and blend into a ball. Add vanilla. Blend again. Chill for 30 minutes.

Roll ¼ inch thick on a floured board. Cut with serrated cookie cutter 3 inches in diameter. Place on lightly buttered cookie sheet. Bake at 350° till delicately brown. Cool on a rack.

 ## A MEXICAN DINNER FOR 6

You can have this dinner well in hand before any guests arrive. The flan should be made hours ahead so it will be thoroughly chilled. The mantequilla de pobre and salad should also be prepared in advance. Plan to put the carnitas in the oven an hour or so before your guests are due, which will allow an hour for drinking. Assemble the enchiladas last. Put them into the oven a half-hour before the Carnitas are ready to come out.

This meal calls for plenty of cold beer—Mexican, if you can find it.

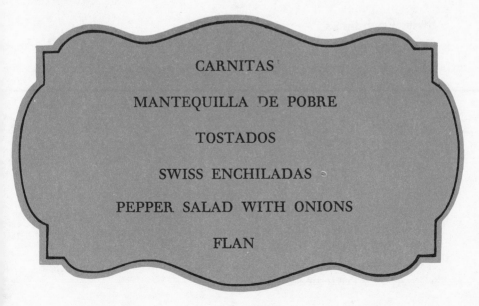

CARNITAS

MANTEQUILLA DE POBRE

TOSTADOS

SWISS ENCHILADAS

PEPPER SALAD WITH ONIONS

FLAN

Carnitas (Little Meats)

> *2 pounds lean pork (boneless butt)*
> *Salt and pepper to taste*

Cut the pork into 1-inch cubes, sprinkle with salt and pepper, and let stand on a rack for an hour or so. Place in a shallow baking pan in a 300° oven for about 2 hours, pouring off fat as it accumulates.

Spear with toothpicks, and serve with mantequilla de pobre and tostados.

Mantequilla de Pobre (Poor Man's Butter)

> *2 large tomatoes, peeled*
> *2 medium-sized avocados*
> *12 green onions, finely cut*
> *3 tablespoons red wine vinegar*
> *1 tablespoon salad oil*
> *Salt to taste*

Cut the tomatoes and avocados into small cubes; add onions, vinegar, oil, and salt. Toss gently until well mixed. Let stand at room temperature for about 30 minutes before serving.

Swiss Enchiladas

For the Stuffing:

1 onion, chopped	*1 dozen tortillas*
2 tablespoons oil	*Oil*
1 clove garlic, crushed	*3 cups hot cream*
2 cups tomato puree	*6 chicken bouillon cubes*
2 green chilies, chopped	*½ pound jack cheese*
2 cups chopped cooked chicken	*Garnish (avocado; hard-cooked eggs; or olives, green or ripe)*
Salt	

Prepare the stuffing first. Sauté the onion in the 2 tablespoons of oil until soft. Then add garlic, tomato puree, chilies, and chicken. Season to taste with salt, and simmer for about 10 minutes.

Fry the tortillas in about 1 inch of hot oil. Do not let them crisp, as they are to be rolled.

Heat the cream, and in it dissolve the bouillon cubes. Dip each tortilla into this cream mixture, cover it generously with the chicken filling, and roll it up. Arrange these rolls in a baking pan, and pour the remaining cream mixture over them. Top with jack cheese, sliced or grated, and bake in a moderate oven for about 30 minutes.

Garnish with the avocado or hard-cooked eggs, sliced, or with olives. This is not a hot Mexican dish. It is mild and delicious and a certain favorite with everyone. Anything with cream in it, by the way, is called "Swiss" in Mexico.

Pepper Salad with Onions

6 green or green and red peppers
1 or 2 red Italian onions
2 cloves garlic
Basic Vinaigrette Sauce (see p. 350)
1 tablespoon fresh basil, or 1 teaspoon dried basil

Seed the peppers and slice in rings as thin as possible. Peel onions and again slice as thin as possible. Combine and add finely chopped garlic and vinaigrette sauce seasoned with basil. Toss well, and allow to stand for an hour before serving.

Flan

This is a typical Spanish dessert, beautiful to look at and simple to make.

1¾ cup sugar
3 egg whites
8 egg yolks
2 tall cans evaporated milk
2 teaspoons vanilla flavoring
6 tablespoons cognac or rum

Put 1 cup of the sugar into a deep pan in which you can bake the custard. Place this over a low flame, and stir constantly until the sugar melts and turns a golden color. Tilt the pan, and allow the caramel to coat it entirely. Set this aside to cool while you make the custard.

Beat the egg whites and yolks together. Add the evaporated milk, the remaining ¾ cup of sugar, and vanilla flavoring. Mix well, strain into the caramel-coated pan, and place the pan in a larger pan containing hot water. Bake in a 350° oven for about an hour, or until a knife inserted in the center comes out clean. Cool slightly, and turn out on a platter while it is still warm (or else the caramel will stick to the sides).

When you are ready to serve, heat the cognac or rum slightly, pour over the flan, and ignite. Bring to the table blazing.

NOTE: Flans are best when made hours before serving and thoroughly chilled.

 A COMFORTABLE AND DELICIOUS DINNER FOR 6 OR 8

The estofat may be done one or two days ahead and merely reheated for the party. The potatoes may be partially cooked in advance and the second half of the preparation done at the last minute. The asparagus means last-minute work, but it's easy. The dessert is best made in the morning or several hours ahead.

You might begin this dinner by serving a good dry sherry and a bowl of olives, perhaps several varieties mixed. And if you wish to serve a first course, smoked salmon or smoked sturgeon, with thinly sliced cucumbers, would be perfect. Drink a good Châteauneuf-du-Pape.

ESTOFAT DE BOEUF

GLAZED POTATOES

GLAZED ONIONS

ASPARAGUS, VINAIGRETTE

LES OEUFS À LA NEIGE

Estofat de Boeuf

8 tablespoons pork drip-
  pings or goose fat
5 pounds rolled rump of
  beef
2 carrots
2 onions, stuck with cloves
4 cloves garlic
½ cup cognac

1 pint red wine
1 pound lean and fat salt
  pork
2 pig's feet
1 bay leaf
1 teaspoon thyme
¼ cup chopped parsley
Salt

Place drippings or fat in a deep kettle or braisière. Brown meat in fat on all sides over high heat. Add carrots, onion, and garlic. Place in a 450° oven uncovered for 15 minutes. Then add the cognac, wine, salt pork, pig's feet, herbs, and a small quantity of salt. Cover. Cook at 250° 4 to 5 hours, or until meat is very tender. Serve with glazed potatoes and glazed onions.

NOTE: This is also delicious when served cold, with the fat removed from the surface.

Glazed Potatoes

Boil 8 to 10 medium potatoes in their jackets until just half done. Peel, and cut in rather thick slices. Arrange in a baking dish with ¼ pound melted butter. Sprinkle with salt and pepper, and bake at 350° for 25 to 30 minutes, tossing gently with a fork several times during the cooking. When done, the potatoes should be nicely glazed, thoroughly tender, and crisp on the edges.

Glazed Onions

> *18 small white onions, peeled*
> *4 tablespoons butter*
> *½ teaspoon salt*
> *1 teaspoon or more sugar*

Heat the butter in a heavy skillet and add onions and sauté over brisk heat, rolling the pan so onions begin to brown on all sides. Sprinkle with salt and sugar and roll around well so that sugar will caramelize the onions and give them a pleasant glaze. Cover pan and steam the onions till just tender but not mushy.

Asparagus, Vinaigrette

For 8 persons, cook 5 pounds or more of asparagus, depending on size of stalks. Boil in salted water until just tender but still firm. (I find that an open skillet with enough water to cover the asparagus works as well as anything.) Drain, and serve with Vinaigrette Sauce (*see* p. 350).

Les Oeufs à la Neige

> *6 egg whites*
> *1¾ cups sugar*
> *3 cups milk*
> *1 teaspoon vanilla*
> *6 egg yolks*
> *1 teaspoon arrowroot*
> *Caramelized sugar*

Beat the egg whites very stiff, and add ¾ cup sugar, a little at a time, beating after each addition.

Heat the milk, 1 cup sugar, and vanilla to the boiling point. Keep at a feeble boil. Spoon up meringue about the size and shape of an egg and drop into the boiling milk. (You will need a second spoon to accomplish this.) Poach about 1½ minutes. Turn with a fork. Continue poaching about 2 minutes, then remove to a dry cloth to drain. When the egg white is cooked, strain the milk, and add the egg yolks, well beaten, and the arrowroot. Stir until it coats a wooden spoon. Cool in a serving bowl and float the meringue in the cream. Garnish with carmelized sugar, made by slowly heating about 1 cup sugar in a heavy-bottomed saucepan until it turns to a medium brown syrup.

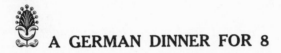

A GERMAN DINNER FOR 8

This rather rich dinner can be prepared ahead of time, except for the potato dumplings, which may be assembled ahead but must be cooked at the last minute. The champagne kraut must also be done at the last minute to insure crispness. Prepare the pea soup in advance up to the point of adding the cream. Then reheat in a double boiler and complete the recipe.

CREAM OF PEA SOUP

HASENPFEFFER

POTATO DUMPLINGS

CHAMPAGNE KRAUT

LINZER TORTE

Cream of Pea Soup

5 pounds fresh peas or 3 packages frozen peas
1 medium onion, sliced
4 tablespoons butter
Salt and pepper

1½ pints light cream
Chopped parsley
Chopped chives

Cook the peas and onion in boiling salted water till just tender. Drain, and puree, or whirl in a blender. Add butter and salt and pepper to taste, then add cream slowly. Serve very hot, garnished with the chopped parsley and chives.

Hasenpfeffer

2 hares, cut into pieces (legs and saddles)
Marinade:

Bottle red wine	*1 teaspoon thyme*
3 onions, thinly sliced	*Several sprigs parsley*
6 shallots, chopped	*Salt and pepper*
1 bay leaf	

Flour	*12 small onions, peeled*
4 tablespoons butter	*1½ cups bouillon*
3 slices salt pork, diced	*Arrowroot*
¼ cup cognac	*Chopped parsley*

Combine the ingredients for the marinade, and in it marinate the pieces of hare for 24 to 36 hours. Remove the pieces and dry; reserve the marinade. Flour the hare lightly, and brown in a skillet with the butter and salt pork. Remove to a casserole large enough to hold both hares, or to two smaller casseroles, if need be. Flame the hare with cognac. Add the onions, bouillon, and enough marinade to barely cover (or you may omit the bouillon and use only the marinade.)

Bake at 325° for 1½ hours.

Traditionally this sauce has currant jelly and sometimes kirsch added to it, and it is thickened with the blood and crushed liver of the hares. I think the flavors of the jelly and kirsch are unfortunate if you wish to enjoy a good wine with your meal; and the thickening process is obviously impossible unless you catch your own hare. I recommend that you thicken the sauce slightly with arrowroot and return the casserole to the oven for another 15 minutes. Taste for seasoning, and sprinkle with chopped parsley. Serve with potato dumplings.

Potato Dumplings

> *3 Idaho potatoes, peeled and boiled*
> *2 tablespoons butter, melted*
> *3 eggs*
> *1 teaspoon salt*
> *1 cup toasted bread cubes*
> *3 tablespoons oil*

Rice the potatoes, and combine with the butter, eggs and salt. Brown the bread cubes in oil, and add to the potatoes. Form mixture into smallish balls, the size of golf balls, with your hands, and cook in boiling salted water 12 to 15 minutes.

Champagne Kraut

> *1 head cabbage, fairly large*
> *4 tablespoons bacon drippings*
> *Salt and pepper*
> *1 bottle champagne (⅘ quart)*

Shred the cabbage, and braise it lightly in bacon fat, tossing well. Add salt and pepper to taste, then the champagne. Cover and cook for 10 minutes. Uncover, toss well, and continue cooking till cabbage is done to your taste. I prefer mine quite crisp.

Linzer Torte

> *1 cup unblanched almonds or hazelnuts*
> *1½ cups sifted flour*
> *1 cup soft butter*
> *2 hard-cooked egg yolks, mashed*
> *2 raw egg yolks*
> *½ cup sugar*
> *2 tablespoons dark, unsweetened cocoa*
> *½ teaspoon ground cloves*
> *¼ teaspoon cinnamon*
> *1 teaspoon vanilla*
> *1 teaspoon grated lemon rind*
> *1 egg beaten with*
> *   2 teaspoons light cream*
> *1½ cups thick raspberry jam*

Set oven at 350°. Lightly grease a cookie sheet. Grate almonds or hazelnuts fine. Mix flour and grated almonds together in a bowl. Make a well in the center. In well, place butter, mashed hard-cooked egg yolks, raw yolks, sugar, cocoa, spices, vanilla and lemon rind. Combine these ingredients into a paste, gradually incorporating the flour and almonds to make a dough. If dough is very soft, chill it slightly.

Roll half the chilled dough between sheets of wax paper to a thickness of ½ inch. Using a plate or pan as a pattern, cut out a round of dough 6 inches in diameter. Place on prepared cookie sheet. Brush lightly with egg mixed with cream.

Roll out remaining half of dough into a rectangle ¼ inch thick between sheets of wax paper. Cut into strips ¼ inch wide. Make a border on circle with some of the strips, pressing to make certain they are set on firmly. Brush with egg.

Fill shell with 1 cup raspberry jam. Using most of remaining strips, make a lattice across top of the torte. The ends of each strip should rest on the border. Brush ends of strips with egg. Make a second border on top of first, using last of strips. Press down firmly with the tines of a fork. Chill torte (or you can freeze it for baking later).

Brush lattice and border with egg. Bake 40 to 50 minutes or until torte is lightly browned. Jam will have darkened in baking. While torte is still hot, use remaining jam for color to fill in between lattice strips.

 AN EASY DINNER FOR 6

The entire meal may be prepared hours ahead of time. The only last-minute work is adding port to the melon, heating the macaroni dish, and tossing the salad. Drink a Beaujolais.

HONEYDEW MELON WITH PORT

MACARONI PARISIENNE

BEET AND CHICORY SALAD

BEL PAESE CHEESE

ITALIAN BREAD

Honeydew Melon with Port

Serve ¼ or ⅓ chilled melon to each person, depending on size
of both melon and appetites. Just before serving, add 1 or 2
tablespoons port to each portion.

Macaroni Parisienne

4 chicken breasts	Salt and pepper
¼ pound butter	1 cup cooked tongue
¼ cup Madeira or cognac	¾ cup cooked ham or
2 tablespoons flour	prosciutto
2 cups chicken broth	2 white truffles (canned)
1 cup cream	1 pound ziti (large maca-
Grated Parmesan cheese	roni)

Sauté the chicken breasts in 4 to 6 tablespoons butter, and toss
well so they brown lightly. Cook about 10 minutes. When they
are just cooked through, pour over them the Madeira or cognac.
Let cook down for a few seconds, and then remove the chicken.
Reserve pan juices.

Prepare a rich sauce with 2 tablespoons butter, the flour, and
the chicken broth. Add pan juices, the cream, and then the grated
Parmesan. Blend well. Season to taste with salt and pepper.

Cut the chicken, tongue, and ham into fine julienne; also julienne the truffles, saving half of a truffle to chop very fine.

Also chop one-third of the tongue very fine.

Partially cook the ziti in boiling salted water. Drain well. Combine with the cream sauce and the strips of meat and truffle. Spoon into an ovenproof baking dish, and sprinkle with the chopped tongue, chopped truffle, and additional grated cheese.

Bake at 350° for 15 minutes.

Beet and Chicory Salad

> *1 large onion, diced*
> *1 large cooked beet, diced*
> *Vinaigrette Sauce* (see *p. 350*)
> *1½ heads chicory* (*more or less, depending on size*)

Combine the onion and beet in a salad bowl. Add vinaigrette sauce and let stand 30 minutes. Add chicory just before serving, and toss.

Bel Paese Cheese

Be sure to allow the cheese to warm for several hours at room temperature. Serve with a good crusty Italian bread and butter.

 A HEARTY, DELICIOUS MEAL FOR 6 PEOPLE WHO LOVE PIG'S FEET!

The feet may be cooked several days in advance, leaving only the final grilling. With this meal drink beer or a fruity Alsatian Gewurztraminer.

TOMATO SALAD

FRENCH BREAD AND BUTTER

GRILLED PIG'S FEET, SAUCE DIABLE

CHIP OR FRENCH FRIED POTATOES

WATERCRESS

MUSTARDS

STEAMED APPLES

Tomato Salad

6 ripe tomatoes, or more, depending on size
6 tablespoons olive oil
2 tablespoons vinegar
2 tablespoons chopped fresh basil or
    1 teaspoon dry basil
2 tablespoons chopped parsley
Salt and pepper to taste

Scald tomatoes, or place over flame, to loosen skin. Peel. Slice very thin, and arrange on a serving dish. Spoon seasonings over the tomatoes a half-hour before serving. Crisp French bread and butter should accompany this.

Grilled Pig's Feet, Sauce Diable

6 pig's feet
6 pieces thin white cotton,
    1 yard long and 3
    inches wide

6 pieces white twine
6 tablespoons pork fat
Bread crumbs
Salt and pepper

Court Bouillon:
  1 pint white wine
  2 carrots
  2 cloves garlic
  1 teaspoon thyme

1 bay leaf
3 sprigs parsley
2 cloves
Salt and pepper
2 quarts water

Pig's feet may be bought ready for cooking. Ask your butcher to cut them long for you, or, if you go to Italian or Chinese markets, you will often find them already cut that way. Those usually found in the markets are cut below the hock and are very short.

First combine the ingredients for the court bouillon, and allow it to boil for 30 minutes to blend the flavors. Cool.

Wash the feet and brush them well. Wrap cotton cloth around each in tight overlapping bands and tie securely. This is to prevent the skin from breaking. Now place the pig's feet in the bouillon and let simmer, covered, until tender—about 3 to 4 hours. Remove the cooked feet from the bouillon, and unwrap the cotton. Place the feet on a platter and let them cool. Reshape, and trim off any loose ends. Prepare a Sauce Diable (*see* p. 345).

When ready to grill, rub pig's feet well with pork fat, and roll in dry bread crumbs. Grill under a broiler 5 inches from heat, turning often until nicely browned, or roast in a hot oven (475°) for 10 to 15 minutes.

Serve with the sauce diable, watercress, a variety of mustards, and crisply cooked potatoes.

Chip or French Fried Potatoes

See p. 368.

Steamed Apples

  1 stick butter
  6 apples, peeled, cored, and cut in sixths
  Vanilla
  Sugar
  ½ pint heavy cream, whipped
  ½ teaspoon vanilla

Melt butter in a heavy skillet, add apples and 1 teaspoon vanilla, and cover tightly. Steam over medium heat for about 6 to 8 minutes or until tender but not mushy. Shake pan several times during cooking. Add sugar to taste. Serve apples warm with whipped cream, sweetened, and flavored with vanilla.

 ## AN ELEGANT BUT RELATIVELY SIMPLE FRENCH MEAL FOR 6

The sole, its sauce, and the dessert may be made in advance. With this menu serve a Sancerre.

MELON

PAUPIETTES OF SOLE

POTATOES PERSILLÉS

PETITS POIS GRANDMÈRE

APRICOT AND PINEAPPLE FLAN

WITH ALMONDS

Melon

Choose a good ripe melon in season—you will need the cooperation of your greengrocer—and serve chilled, in slices, with lemon or lime wedges.

Paupiettes of Sole

½ pound salmon
2 eggs
½ cup chopped parsley
Salt and pepper

6 fillets of sole
White wine
1½ cups Sauce Velouté (see *p. 343*)
12 mushroom caps
6 artichoke hearts, previously cooked and trimmed
Butter

Grind the salmon, and mix with the eggs and parsley until it is smooth and pasty. Season to taste with salt and pepper, and spread on the fillets. Roll and secure with toothpicks. Poach the fillets in white wine to barely cover, basting well, until the fish is just cooked and flaky. Remove the fillets to a baking dish.

Prepare a sauce velouté, using 1 cup cooking liquid. Sauté the mushrooms and previously cooked and trimmed artichoke hearts in butter, and season to taste. Pour the sauce over the fish. Heat in 400° oven 20 minutes. Surround with artichoke hearts, top with the mushrooms, and garnish with the potatoes persillés.

Potatoes Persillés

2 pounds tiny new potatoes
6 tablespoons butter
Salt and pepper
Chopped parsley

Cut a band of skin off each potato (to allow the butter to be absorbed later), and boil in salted water till just tender. Drain, and toss with the butter, salt and pepper to taste, and about ⅓ cup (or to your taste) of chopped parsley.

Petits Pois Grandmère

2 packages tiny peas in butter (boil-in-plastic-bag
variety)
3 small onions, sliced
3 tablespoons butter
½ cup diced ham
Chopped parsley

Cook peas according to directions on package. Steam onions in butter till limp. Add ham, and heat for 3 minutes. Combine with the peas, and add 2 or 3 teaspoons chopped parsley.

Apricot and Pineapple Flan with Almonds

1 flan ring of Rich Pastry (see *p. 359–360*)
1 to 1½ cups pineapple preserves
⅔ cup toasted sliced almonds
2 cups cooked or canned apricot halves
1 cup apricot preserves for glaze

Prepare a flan ring as directed on p. 38. When cooled, spread the bottom with layer of pineapple preserves. Sprinkle the pineapple with sliced toasted almonds. Then top with either poached fresh apricots or with canned apricots that have been well drained. Finally brush with Apricot Glaze (*see* p. 38).

SUMMER DINNERS

Time was when housewives used to say on a summer's day they had to cook in the cool of the morning to have things cold for dinner. Indeed, many houses had summer kitchens, where the food was prepared to prevent the constant heat of the coal stove from raising the temperature of the living quarters. In this air-conditioned age it is possible for most people to prepare food at any hour of the day without fear of overheating the house, and it is possible to consume hot food on the hottest days. Cold food, however, continues to have a special appeal throughout the summer months, and it is a seasonal change to which I look forward with particular pleasure. I am of the opinion that most food tastes better cold anyway. A chicken roasted and allowed to cool slowly is a far more delicious dish to me than a chicken hot from the oven. Likewise, steak perfectly broiled, seasoned, cooled and sliced thin is even more succulent than steak rushed from the grill. Vegetables, too, seem to have more flavor when cold, and they lend themselves to a great variety of dressings and sauces.

It seems a good idea in any event to relieve a cold meal with at least one hot course—perhaps a hot first course or a hot dessert. If you must have a hot main course, go to the outdoor grill, and let the man of the house take over.

In summer, wines should be light and cooling. For the most part red wines are not so suitable as well-chilled whites and rosés. In fact, one could happily give up spirits for the summer and stay on a diet of wine.

Most cheeses are rather overpowering for summer fare. The Swiss cheeses and some of the goat cheeses are exceptions, but I believe that good red wine is so important to cheese that one should wait for a cooler season.

Summer dining can inspire all sorts of bright and amusing table settings and interesting backgrounds on the terrace or in the garden. This is the season to entertain in a relaxed and effortless fashion.

 A SUMMER DINNER FOR 4

Serve a chilled Beaujolais.

> DOUBLE CONSOMMÉ OF CHICKEN
>
> COLD BEEF EN DAUBE
>
> HORSERADISH CREAM
>
> RICE SALAD
>
> COFFEE GRANITA

Double Consommé of Chicken

1 fowl
3 pounds of chicken backs and necks
2 pounds of gizzards
1 onion, stuck with 2 cloves
1 rib celery
2 sprigs parsley
1 teaspoon thyme
Salt and pepper
Nutmeg
3 to 4 quarts water
2 egg whites (reserve shells)

Cook the backs, necks and gizzards with the vegetables and seasonings in water. Simmer for 2 to 2½ hours or until the broth is strong. Add the fowl, and continue cooking until fowl is tender—about 2½ hours. Remove fowl, and reserve; dice meat for other dishes.

Strain the broth, and discard the bones, etc. Beat the egg whites slightly, and add to the broth with the shells. Bring to a boil, and simmer 20 minutes. Strain through a linen napkin or towel.

Serve in demitasse or soup cups.

Cold Beef en Daube

See recipe (p. 145) for Daube Provençale. To serve cold, strain the sauce, and let it cool. Remove excess fat. Slice the meat and arrange in a serving dish. Cover with the sauce, and let it chill. Serve in its own jelly.

Horseradish Cream

> *1 cup freshly grated horseradish*
> *1 cup sour cream*

Combine and chill. Or take 1 cup sour cream and add bottled horseradish to taste.

Rice Salad

> *3 cups water*
> *1 bay leaf*
> *1 teaspoon salt*
> *1 pinch saffron*
> *½ cup converted rice*
> *½ cup oil*
> *2 to 3 tablespoons wine vinegar*
> *Freshly ground black pepper*

Bring the water to a boil. Add the bay leaf, salt, and saffron. Stir in the rice so that the water never stops boiling. Reduce the heat to low or warm. Cover and let it cook 11 to 13 minutes. Toss with a fork. Drain the rice and add oil, vinegar, and some freshly ground black pepper. Let it cook with this sauce. Then add :

⅔ *cup finely chopped onion*
⅓ *cup finely chopped seeded tomato*
½ *cup finely chopped celery*
½ *cup finely chopped green pepper*
¼ *cup raisins*
½ *cup pinenuts*
⅓ *cup chopped parsley*

Toss well and add more oil or vinegar and seasoning to the salad if needed. Spoon into a salad bowl. Decorate with sliced eggs and tomatoes, and serve very cold.

Coffee Granita

Make 1 quart of very strong coffee—espresso or regular coffee—and let it infuse over a "warm" pad for 30 minutes. Sugar to taste and stir till sugar is dissolved. Strain through a cloth into freezing tray. Freeze for 2 hours, stirring several times in order to break up the mixture. Serve with whipped cream if desired. A dash of cinnamon is delicious in it.

AN INTERNATIONAL DINNER FOR 8

You might serve tequila sours or Margaritas to begin, accompanied by tiny cocktail tamales or guacamole. Serve a white wine throughout dinner—perhaps a Muscadet or a Pinot Chardonnay.

SCALLOPS IN SEVICHE

VEAL CUTLETS SICILIENNE

HOT NOODLES WITH POPPYSEEDS

HOT TORTILLAS OR ROLLS

TOMATOES WITH BASIL DRESSING

SAVARIN WITH APRICOT GLAZE

Scallops in Seviche

2 pounds scallops
Juice of 12 limes or
   lemons (approxi-
   mately)
2 garlic cloves, chopped
   very fine
¼ cup chopped green
   onions
¼ cup chopped green
   chilies

½ cup olive oil

¼ cup chopped green
   peppers
¼ cup chopped parsley
¼ cup chopped cilantro,
   if available
¼ cup chopped shallots or
   chives
1 teaspoon mustard seed
1½ teaspoons salt
2 dashes Tabasco

Greens

Cover scallops with lime or lemon juice. Let stand in refrigerator 3 to 4 hours. Drain. Toss well with all of the seasonings and the olive oil. Let stand 1 hour. Line a glass dish with greens, and fill with the scallops. Serve with hot tortillas or rolls.

Veal Cutlets Sicilienne

*3 large, very thin cutlets,
    cut across leg*
¼ pound salami
*¼ pound mortadella or
    bologna*
*¼ pound prosciutto or
    cooked ham*
¼ cup fine bread crumbs
3 cloves garlic, minced

Chopped parsley
1 teaspoon basil
5 or 6 hard-cooked eggs
Olive oil
Salt and pepper
5 or 6 bacon slices
2 cups tomato sauce
2 whole cloves garlic

Leave veal slices in whole pieces, but remove bones. Pound veal very thin. Arrange slices side by side (the long sides adjoining) so they overlap slightly. Pound overlapping areas thoroughly to press them together. On veal arrange rows of overlapping slices of salami. Top with rows of sliced mortadella or bologna and finally with sliced prosciutto or cooked ham.

Sprinkle surface with fine bread crumbs, minced garlic, chopped parsley and basil. Down the center place a row of shelled, hard-cooked eggs. Sprinkle with olive oil, salt and freshly ground black pepper. Roll up very carefully as for jelly roll, making certain that eggs stay in place in center. Place roll in baking dish and top with bacon. Over all pour tomato sauce with whole garlic cloves added. Bake in moderate oven for 1 hour. Remove to a hot platter and slice or serve from baking dish.

NOTE : This is exceptionally good sliced cold.

Savarin with Apricot Glaze

½ cup warm water (105° to 115°)
*2 packages or cakes of yeast,
    active dry or compressed*
2½ cups unsifted flour
4 eggs, slightly beaten

1 tablespoon sugar
½ teaspoon salt
⅔ cup soft corn-oil margarine
Apricot Glaze (see p. *38*)
Fresh fruits and whipped cream or rum syrup

Measure warm water into small warm bowl. Sprinkle or crumble in yeast; stir until dissolved. Add to flour in large bowl; then add eggs. Beat with spoon for 2 minutes. Cover; let rise in warm place, free from drafts, about ½ hour, or until bubbly and doubled in bulk. Stir down; add sugar, salt and soft margarine. Beat again until dough is elastic when dropped from spoon (about 4 minutes).

Turn into well-greased 3-quart ring mold. Again let rise in warm place, until doubled in bulk, about 30 minutes. Bake in a very hot oven (450°) 10 minutes; reduce heat to 350°, and bake 20 minutes longer, or until done. Unmold. Brush with apricot glaze. When ready to serve, fill center with fresh fruits and whipped cream or pour rum syrup over the cake.

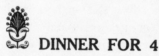

DINNER FOR 4

Serve a bottle of Sancerre or a California Riesling.

STRIPED BASS WITH CREAM SAUCE

BOILED NEW POTATOES

SPINACH WITH OIL AND GARLIC

FRENCH BREAD

CHEESE   APPLES

Striped Bass with Cream Sauce

> *3-egg omelet aux fines herbes (parsley, tarragon, or*
> *your choice)*
> *4 to 5 pound striped bass*
> *Chopped shallots or scallions*
> *Oil*
> *Salt and pepper*
> *1 cup white wine*
> *1 cup cream*
> *3 egg yolks*

Clean and split the striped bass.

Prepare the omelet aux fines herbes, and roll it into the fish as stuffing. Sew up the striped bass and place it on a bed of chopped shallots or onions in a well-oiled baking dish. Salt and pepper the fish, and add the wine. Bake at 400° for 25 to 30 minutes or until the fish flakes easily when tested with a fork. Remove the fish to a hot platter and take out the string or thread that you used to secure it. Strain the pan juices, and force the onion through a fine sieve. Reduce the juices slightly and add the cream mixed with egg yolks; stir until thick, but do not let it boil. Taste for seasoning and pour the sauce around the fish.

Serve with tiny Boiled New Potatoes and parsley (*see* p. 365).

Spinach with Oil and Garlic

> *2 pounds spinach*
> *4 tablespoons olive oil*
> *3 garlic cloves, finely chopped*
> *Salt*
> *Lemon juice*

Wash spinach well, and drain in a colander. Heat oil slightly in a heavy skillet, and add garlic. Add spinach, and toss, as you would a salad, over medium heat till spinach is just wilted and heated through. Add salt to taste and a dash of lemon. Serve hot.

Cheese

For dessert, serve a Roquefort and a sharp cheddar cheese, along with the best apples available and French bread and butter.

DINNER FOR 8

Chilled champagne is the proper choice for an apéritif. With it serve nuts or small cherry tomatoes.

A good white burgundy, such as a Puligny-Montrachet, well chilled, goes well with the sweetbreads. Serve a fine old Madeira with the dessert.

SHRIMP AILLADE

SWEETBREADS ALBERT

NUTTED ALA

SUMMER SALAD

STRAWBERRIES ROMANOFF IN

MERINGUE SHELLS

Shrimp Aillade

> *3 pounds tiny shrimp*
> *Tomato wedges, hard-cooked eggs, black olives*
> *4 cloves garlic, chopped*
> *1½ cups fresh basil leaves*
> *Salt and freshly ground black pepper*
> *6 ripe tomatoes, peeled, seeded and chopped*
> *1 cup olive oil*
> *Tabasco*
> *Lemon juice*
> *Chopped parsley*

The tiny Iceland shrimp are much better than larger shrimp for this dish. In many fine food stores in New York they come ready-cooked and frozen in blocks. The ready-cooked Pacific Coast tiny shrimp are equally good. In the South and Midwest, your best choice is the smallest fresh shrimp you can find. Poach shrimp until just done (about 2 or 3 minutes), shell and clean.

Arrange in an attractive serving dish. Garnish with tomato wedges, halved hard-cooked eggs and French or Italian black olives.

Serve with a sauceboat of aillade and toasted finger rolls. To make aillade, puree garlic and basil in a blender, or pound to a paste in a mortar. Season with salt and pepper, and mix with the chopped tomatoes. Gradually beat in oil, and add a dash of Tabasco and a little lemon juice. Let mixture stand 1 hour to mellow and blend flavors. Sprinkle with parsley. (This sauce may be made in advance.)

Sweetbreads Albert

1 leek, well washed	*Salt and pepper*
3 stalks celery	*2 cups white wine*
1 green pepper, seeded	*4 pairs sweetbreads*
2 small carrots, peeled	*1 tablespoon cornstarch*
6 shallots, chopped very fine	*3 egg yolks*
	Juice of 1 lemon
3 tablespoons oil	*Chopped parsley*

Cut the leek, celery, green pepper and carrots into fine julienne strips, and sauté with shallots in oil until lightly colored. Arrange the vegetables on the bottom of a deep saucepan, season with salt and pepper to taste, and add 1 cup white wine. Arrange sweetbreads (unblanched and unwashed) on the vegetables and cover. Simmer the sweetbreads and vegetables for ½ hour over medium heat.

Remove the sweetbreads and cool them between wet towels. Drain the vegetables, and save the liquid. Measure 1 cup of the liquid, add the remaining 1 cup white wine, and the cornstarch. Place in a saucepan, and simmer until slightly thickened.

Clean the sweetbreads, add the membranes and trimmings to the drained vegetables. Puree the vegetables in an electric blender and add to the thickened white-wine broth. Beat the egg yolks lightly and add. Cook slowly, stirring constantly, until the broth thickens, but do not let it boil. Add lemon juice, and taste for seasoning.

Slice the sweetbreads and place them on a hot platter in the oven for a few minutes to heat through. Pour the sauce over them, reserving some in a sauceboat to be passed separately. Garnish the platter with chopped parsley.

Nutted Ala

Ala is the name of a cracked-wheat product—a delightful change from other cereal dishes. It is particularly complementary to sweetbreads. Follow directions on the package of ala. (For 8 persons, you may have to double the recipe.) When the ala is done, add 1 cup toasted pecan halves and 4 tablespoons melted butter. Mix well.

Summer Salad

> *6 scallions*
> *1 heaping tablespoon fresh tarragon leaves*
> *Salt and freshly ground black pepper*
> *1 teaspoon dry mustard*
> *Olive oil*
> *Lemon juice*
> *Leaf lettuce or oak leaf lettuce*

Cut the scallions very fine, and chop the tarragon. Blend with salt and pepper to taste, and mustard. Add ½ cup olive oil and 1 teaspoon of lemon juice. Blend and let stand for one hour to mellow. Add more oil and lemon juice (to taste), and toss with the washed and dried greens at the last minute.

Strawberries Romanoff in Meringue Shells

> *8 individual meringue shells*
> *2 quarts ripe strawberries*
> *Sugar*
> *1 6-ounce can frozen orange juice concentrate*
> *1 cup port*

3 tablespoons Mandarine liqueur
2 cups heavy cream, whipped
Pistachio nuts

Buy meringue shells at a good bakery, or make your own according to your favorite recipe.

Hull the berries and sugar them if needed. (Remember, the wine and the orange concentrate have sugar, as does the liqueur.) Add the orange concentrate and port and let the berries mellow in this mixture for 2 hours. Toss them carefully several times. Add the Mandarine liqueur. Whip the cream just before serving. Fill meringue shells with berries, top with whipped cream, and garnish with chopped pistachio nuts.

BUFFETS

Grandmother, Mother and even you once had plenty of help in the home and probably a permanent servant. This is all but ancient history. Consequently the help-yourself fashion of entertaining grows more and more common. Many people who enjoy cooking have their kitchens designed to offer an attractive background for buffet service. Guests are invited to the kitchen to collect their food and carry it back to the dining room or terrace. This technique is casual and thoroughly functional. It has saved many a hostess a great deal of work.

Naturally there are formal buffets, too, where magnificent *pièces montées* and lusciously arranged platters are prepared by professional chefs to feast the eye as well as the palate. They should not be so slick and professional-looking, however, that they overpower your own style or violate good taste. A buffet of this type requires the attention of well-trained waiters or caterer's assistants. I have always felt that if one brings in caterers to reproduce food that one normally finds in a deluxe restaurant, why not invite your guests to the restaurant instead?

There is one rule of buffet service frequently overlooked: Offer one course at a time. It is a most distressing sight at a large buffet party to see plates heaped indiscrimately with cold duck, molded salads, tossed salads, ham, curried prawns and sundry other things. And there should be a fresh supply of plates available.

If you are serving a dinner for six or eight, or a luncheon for ten or twelve, you may wish to lay out tables for your guests. For a larger buffet, you will have to be more casual, but do not invite more guests than you can accommodate comfortably if they are expected to use knife and fork and balance a wine glass as well. A buffet may be anything from a breakfast of juice, toast and coffee to a ball supper with a hot table, a cold table and a drink table. The rules are the same. Looks count a great deal, and the service must be efficient.

LUNCHEON BUFFETS

 A SPECIAL PROVENÇAL BUFFET FOR 8

This menu you must serve to your most intimate friends. It is devastatingly good but very special—because of the high garlic content. Anyone who does not love the flavor of garlic has no place at your table on this occasion. Drink Pernod and a Provençal Rosé.

HERB BREAD

AÏOLI   CASSONADE

Herb Bread

> 1 large loaf French bread
> 1 small bunch parsley
> 8 to 10 scallions
> Small bunch chives
> 1 sprig fresh dill
> 1 stick (¼ pound) butter, or more
> ½ teaspoon salt

Split bread in half the long way. Chop the herbs and scallions, and combine with the butter and salt. Cream well. Spread mixture on each half of loaf. Press bread together again, firmly. Heat in 350° oven for 20 minutes. Cut in 1-inch slices.

Aïoli

This is a traditional Provençal sauce, delicious with hot or cold fish, cold vegetables, hot or cold meats, and cold fowl. One can make the sauce in either a mortar or a blender.

12 garlic cloves
3 egg yolks
Olive oil
Salt to taste
Lemon juice to taste

Mortar method : Pound the garlic in a mortar in a steady, revolving motion. Then add the egg yolks, and continue grinding. Finally, pound in olive oil, a tablespoon at a time (about 3 to 4 cups), till the mixture has the texture of a thick mayonnaise. Add salt and lemon juice to taste.

NOTE : Should the emulsion break down, remove it, clean the mortar, and start again, using 1 garlic clove, 1 egg yolk and a little oil. Then spoon in the first mixture, and continue stirring until the emulsion thickens.

Blender method : Make a heavy mayonnaise, using 3 egg yolks and 3 to 3½ cups of olive oil, or more, depending on the size of the yolks. This may be done in the blender, in the electric mixer, or by hand, as you wish. Then whirl 12 garlic cloves in the blender, with 1 egg yolk and a little oil. Combine this paste with the mayonnaise.

ACCOMPANIMENTS :

1) *Salt cod*
Two pounds filleted in one piece. Soak in water to cover overnight or for 8 to 10 hours. Change the water once during the soaking. Drain, and cover with cold water. Bring to a boil, and simmer for 10 minutes or until the fish is tender. Serve hot.

2) *Boiled potatoes*
Peel and boil 10 to 12 medium-sized potatoes in salted water until just pierceable. Drain, and dry over low flame. Serve hot.

3) *A cold or hot fresh fish*
Striped bass poached in court bouillon and cooled; or poached red snapper or halibut. Serve with a garnish of sliced cucumbers.

4) *Hard-cooked eggs*

Figure on at least 1 hard-cooked egg per person. Peel them, and arrange on a serving dish.

5) *Cooked vegetables*

Scrape 10 carrots, and cook in boiling salted water till just crisply done. Peel lightly 12 smallish zucchini, and cook them in salted water till just pierceable. Poach 12 medium white onions till tender. If asparagus is in season, cook 2 pounds until tender but still firm. Boil one artichoke for each person.

6) *Snails in their shells*—2 or 3 per person.

Arrange the assortment of foods on platters, and place around aïoli. Each person helps himself to the sauce and whatever he wishes to accompany it.

Cassonade

> *Brioche dough* (½ *recipe, p. 356*)
> *1 cup brown sugar*
> *4 egg yolks*
> *1 cup heavy cream*

Prepare brioche, roll out, and line a 9-inch pie tin that has been buttered. Let rise 5 to 10 minutes. Sprinkle brown sugar over bottom of the shell to cover evenly. Mix egg yolks and cream together, and pour over the sugar. Bake at 425° for 10 minutes. Reduce heat to 350°, and bake until the custard is set. Cool and serve.

A CRAWFISH FEAST FOR 6

Chilled aquavit and/or cold beer are traditional with spiced crawfish. A dramatic way to present the aquavit: Freeze the bottle into a square or cylinder of ice, leaving the neck free.

SPICED CRAWFISH

SLICED ONION AND TOMATO SALAD

WITH CUCUMBERS

HOMEMADE WHOLE-WHEAT BREAD   BUTTER

COEUR A LA CRÈME WITH STRAWBERRIES

Spiced Crawfish

These tasty shellfish are available in Louisiana, Oregon, Washington, Wisconsin, Minnesota and may sometimes be ordered from good fish merchants in other areas, who often ship by air direct to the customer. If crawfish are not available, substitute small lobsters or large shrimp.

> 2 quarts red wine (a good California
>   bulk wine is excellent)
> 1 quart water
> 3 bay leaves
> 4 cloves garlic
> ¼ cup Tabasco
> 2 tablespoons salt
> 3 sprigs parsley
> 6 to 8 whole allspice
> 1 teaspoon tarragon
> 6 to 8 dozen crawfish

Bring the wine, water, bay leaves, garlic, Tabasco, salt, parsley, allspice and tarragon to a boil in a deep pan. Lower the heat and simmer 10 minutes. Add the crawfish and cook 8 to 10 minutes or until just done but not mushy. Drain. (Save the bouillon; it will make the base for a fine bisque.)

Allow 12 to 16 crawfish per person and serve chilled. Provide small picks to extract the meat. They are best without sauce, but you may add a bowl of French dressing or mayonnaise for dunking if you wish.

Homemade whole-wheat bread with plenty of sweet butter is a good accompaniment.

If you use small lobsters, estimate 2 or 3 per person.

Sliced Onion and Tomato Salad with Cucumbers

> *5 or 6 red onions, peeled and thinly sliced*
> *5 or 6 ripe beefsteak tomatoes, peeled and thickly sliced*
> *4 cucumbers, peeled and thinly sliced*
> *1 tablespoon chopped fresh dill*
> *Vinaigrette Sauce* (see p. 350)

Marinate the cucumber in a good vinaigrette sauce with the dill (if available) for 1 hour. Heap in center of a chilled plate. Place alternate slices of onion and tomato around the cucumbers. Serve with cruets of oil and vinegar and with salt and pepper grinders.

Homemade Whole-Wheat Bread

> *2 cakes or packages of yeast*
> *1½ cups lukewarm water*
> *1 tablespoon salt*
> *1 teaspoon sugar*
> *2 cups coarse whole-wheat flour*
> *2 to 4 cups white flour*
> *Cornmeal*

Dissolve the yeast in the warm water and stir in the salt and sugar. Add the whole-wheat flour a cup at a time, beating it in with a wooden spoon; or use the dough hook on your electric mixer at low speed. Add enough white flour to make a smooth dough. Cover the dough with a towel and let stand in a warm spot to rise until double in bulk.

Turn the dough out onto a floured board and shape it into two long French-style loaves. Arrange on a baking sheet heavily sprinkled with cornmeal. Let rise for 5 minutes. Slash the tops with a knife, brush with water and start the loaves in a cold oven. Set at 400°. Place a pan of boiling water in the oven and bake bread until crusty, about 40 minutes.

Coeur à la Crème with Strawberries

2 8-ounce packages cream cheese
1 cup sour cream
Fresh strawberries, or fresh strawberry preserves
French bread or brioche loaf

Blend the cream cheese and sour cream together to a smooth paste with a fork. If the mixture is too firm, add a little heavy cream.

Line two small (or one good-sized) heart-shaped straw or reed baskets, or porcelain molds, with cheesecloth. Press the cheese mixture into the molds. Place them on a rack over a bowl in the refrigerator and let them stand for several hours.

Unmold into a chilled serving dish and surround with fresh strawberries. Serve with fresh berries or preserves and French bread or brioche.

 # AN HORS D'OEUVRE LUNCHEON FOR 12

This delightful meal may be served outdoors or in with equal flair. Drink the white wines—California Chenin Blanc, Sauvignon Blanc, and Grey Riesling—chilled, before and during the meal. Add a touch of cassis to the before-lunch version if you wish. Iced mocha is simply a blend of coffee and chocolate—serve coffee- and chocolate-flavored liqueurs if you want to accent.

RAW FAVA BEANS

RADISHES

CRUDITÉS WITH ANCHOVY MAYONNAISE

TIAN

CRABMEAT ORIENTALE

BEEF SALAD PARISIENNE

LEEKS À LA GRECQUE

VARIETY OF BREADS   CHEESE

COLD ORANGE SOUFFLÉ

ICED MOCHA

Raw Fava Beans

Fava beans (or broad beans) are in the market a good part of the summer. They come in long, broad green pods and are delicious eaten raw with salt. Simply break open the pods, slip out the beans, and dip them in a bowl of coarse salt.

Radishes

Arrange white and red radishes on crushed ice. Serve with sweet butter; or wrap each radish with an anchovy fillet fastened with a toothpick.

Crudités with Anchovy Mayonnaise

12 to 14 anchovy fillets, coarsely chopped
2 cloves garlic, finely chopped
¼ cup chopped parsley
¼ cup chopped fresh basil
1 tablespoon coarsely chopped capers
1 tablespoon Dijon mustard
2 cups homemade mayonnaise
Thinly sliced cucumbers, sliced tomatoes, sliced onion,
*   whole scallions, grated carrots, grated raw beets*
*   or other raw vegetables*

Combine anchovy fillets, garlic, parsley, basil, capers, mustard and mayonnaise, and taste for seasoning. Use little salt in the mayonnaise; anchovies and capers have plenty. Arrange vegetables on a platter; dunk in anchovy mayonnaise.

Tian

Olive oil
2 pounds raw spinach, coarsely chopped
2 pounds raw Swiss chard, coarsely chopped
6 to 8 finger-size zucchini, cut in small dice
2 medium onions, coarsely chopped
3 cloves garlic, finely chopped
½ cup finely chopped basil leaves
2 tablespoons dried basil
Salt to taste
1½ teaspoons freshly ground black pepper.
8 eggs, slightly beaten
1½ cups grated Parmesan cheese
Bread crumbs

Cover the bottom of a large skillet with olive oil and add the spinach and Swiss chard. Cook until just wilted. Remove and drain. Press out all liquid. Add the zucchini, onion and garlic to the skillet and repeat cooking procedure.

Combine the vegetables, the fresh and dried basil, salt and pepper, and place in a lightly oiled, heavy earthenware casserole. Pour the eggs over the vegetables and top with the cheese and bread crumbs. Bake in a 350° oven until the eggs are just set and the cheese is melted and bubbly. Chill and serve cold.

Crabmeat Orientale

3 cups cooked rice
½ pound raw mushrooms, sliced
1 cup thinly sliced water chestnuts
1 cup finely chopped green pepper
3 pimientos, finely cut
2 cups crabmeat (fresh, frozen or canned)

¼ cup chopped parsley
¼ cup chopped chives
1 cup olive oil
3 tablespoons soy sauce
3 tablespoons vinegar
½ teaspoon Tabasco
2 teaspoons Dijon mustard
Greens

Combine all ingredients but the greens. Toss well. Arrange on a bed of greens.

Beef Salad Parisienne

2 cups sliced, boiled, small new potatoes
1 cup finely cut scallions
2 cups coarsely chopped celery, with tops
3 cups lean boiled beef, cut in slices and then into 1½ inch squares
12 to 14 sliced sour pickles
1 cup cherry tomatoes
¼ cup capers
½ cup green pepper strips

Greens
6 hard-cooked eggs
3 tablespoons Dijon mustard
1 cup olive oil
1 clove garlic rubbed into 1½ teaspoons salt
1 teaspoon freshly ground black pepper
⅓ cup vinegar
Dash of Tabasco
Pickled walnuts, sliced

Combine the potatoes, scallions, celery, beef, pickles, tomatoes, capers and green pepper strips, and toss together in a large bowl. Arrange on a bed of greens.

Shell 3 hard-cooked eggs, reserve the whites, and mash the yolks with a fork. Work in the mustard. Stir in the olive oil, garlic-flavored salt, pepper and vinegar. Add a dash or two of Tabasco, and pour this dressing over the beef salad. Garnish with 3 quartered hard-cooked eggs, the sliced pickled walnuts and the 3 egg whites, chopped.

Leeks à la Grecque

⅓ cup olive oil
2 tablespoons wine
   vinegar
1 clove garlic, chopped
½ cup white wine
1 teaspoon salt
½ teaspoon freshly
   ground black pepper

1 sprig parsley
Good pinch of thyme
12 leeks
Water
1 tablespoon chopped
   parsley
Dash of Tabasco
White wine (optional)

Mix together the oil, vinegar, garlic, wine, salt, pepper, parsley and thyme, to make a sauce à la grecque. Wash the leeks and soak them well to be sure that all the grit is gone. Run them under cold water for a few minutes. Arrange the leeks in a flat pan and pour the sauce à la grecque over them. Add enough water, or white wine and water mixed, to cover. Simmer until just tender, and cool in the broth. Remove the leeks to a serving dish, and cook the broth down. Add chopped parsley and Tabasco, and pour over the leeks. Chill.

Cold Orange Soufflé

1 cup cold water
2 envelopes unflavored gelatin
8 eggs, separated
½ teaspoon salt
2   6-ounce cans frozen orange juice concentrate
1 cup sugar
1 cup heavy cream, whipped

Place water in the top of a double boiler and sprinkle the gelatin over the surface to soften. Beat the egg yolks lightly and add them with the salt. Mix well. Place over boiling water and cook, stirring constantly, until the gelatin dissolves and the mixture thickens a bit, about 4 minutes.

Remove from the double boiler and stir in the orange concentrate. Chill until the mixture drops from a spoon into soft mounds. Beat the egg whites until stiff but not dry. Gradually beat in the sugar and continue beating until the egg whites are stiff. Fold the whites into the orange mixture and then fold in the whipped cream.

Arrange a collar of doubled waxed paper around a 2½-quart soufflé dish. The collar should come 2 inches above the top of the dish. Fasten it with gummed tape. Pour the mixture into the dish and chill until firm. Remove the collar and decorate with orange sections, if you like, before serving.

 ## COUNTRY SUNDAY LUNCH FOR 6

Serve Summer Cocktails: Fill a large wineglass with ice. Add 2 tablespoons of raspberry syrup or Framberry liqueur, 2 ounces of Lillet, 1 ounce of eau de vie de framboise or kirsch. Stir and fill the glass with Perrier water.

During the meal, drink a good chilled Alsatian Riesling or Traminer. Served chilled kirsch or framboise with the coffee.

CERVELAT SALAD

COLD BARBECUED LOIN OF PORK

HORSERADISH APPLESAUCE

HOT FAVA BEANS WITH FRESH HERBS

MUENSTER CHEESE, FRESH CHERRIES

Cervelat Salad

6 knockwurst or Swiss-style cervelat
1 medium onion, finely minced
6 sour pickles or sweet gherkins, thinly sliced
1½ tablespoons Dijon mustard
1 cup mayonnaise
3 tablespoons sour cream
Romaine

Chopped parsley, chopped gherkins
Hard-cooked eggs, halved

Cook the knockwurst, and cool and skin them. Slice rather thinly, and combine with the onion, sliced pickles, mustard and mayonnaise. Toss well. Add the sour cream and toss again. Arrange on a bed of romaine, and garnish with chopped parsley and chopped gherkins. Surround with halved hard-cooked eggs.

Serve with thin buttered pumpernickel.

Cold Barbecued Loin of Pork

5- to 6-pound pork loin roast
Dry mustard
Thyme
Sherry
Japanese soy sauce
3 cloves garlic, finely chopped
2 tablespoons grated fresh ginger,
  or 6 pieces of candied
  ginger cut into slivers
1   8-ounce jar apple or currant jelly

Have the roast boned and tied. Rub with dry mustard and thyme. Make a marinade of ½ cup sherry, ½ cup soy sauce, garlic and ginger, and pour over roast. Let the pork marinate for about 2 hours, turning it several times as it soaks. You may let it stand all night in the refrigerator and roast it early in the morning, if you wish.

To cook, remove from the marinade and arrange a meat thermometer in the thickest part of the roast. Cook at 325°, allowing about 25 minutes per pound. Baste with the marinade. When the thermometer reads 175°, the pork is done.

Melt the jelly in a heavy pan over a medium flame and when it is bubbly, add 1 tablespoon soy and 2 tablespoons sherry. Let it cook down for a minute or two, stirring constantly. Spoon over the pork and cool in a chilly room. Do not refrigerate unless the day is exceptionally hot.

Garnish the platter with sliced tomatoes, thinly sliced onions and sliced cucumbers. Serve with horseradish applesauce.

Horseradish Applesauce

Combine 2 cups applesauce and 6 tablespoons fresh grated horseradish or 4 tablespoons bottled horseradish, drained. Blend well and chill. Vary the amount of horseradish to make the sauce hotter or milder.

Hot Fava Beans with Fresh Herbs

4 pounds fava beans (broad beans)
6 tablespoons olive oil
1 tablespoon butter
3 cloves garlic, finely minced
½ cup minced onion
Salt and pepper to taste
1 tablespoon chopped parsley
2 tablespoons chopped fresh basil

Shell the beans, and cook in boiling water until just tender. Drain. Heat the oil and butter, add the garlic, onion, salt and pepper, and cook 3 minutes. Add the beans and toss well. Then add the parsley and basil, toss again, and serve at once.

NOTE : These beans may be served cold. Simply add more olive oil and a little vinegar.

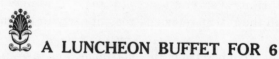

A LUNCHEON BUFFET FOR 6

SOUPE DE POISSON, MARSEILLAISE

TOASTED BUTTERED FRENCH BREAD

SLICED ORANGES, GRAND MARNIER

Soupe de Poisson, Marseillaise

¾ cup olive oil
3½ pounds fish—flounder, snapper, haddock
Salt and pepper
2 quarts water
2 large onions, chopped
1   29-ounce can Italian plum tomatoes
Pinch of basil
¼ pound spaghettini
Pinch of saffron
1 cup grated Gruyère cheese

Heat ½ cup of the olive oil in a deep, heavy pot, and sear the fish. Reduce the heat, and cook until fish is very soft. Salt and pepper to taste, and add the water. Simmer for 1 hour.

Sauté the onions in remaining olive oil, and when soft, add the tomatoes and basil. Cook for 15 minutes. Add to the fish pot, and simmer for 30 minutes. Press fish and vegetables through a food mill, and stir back into the broth. Add the spaghettini, broken into 1- or 2-inch pieces, and saffron. Cook 12 to 15 minutes, or until spaghettini is tender. Correct the seasoning.

Serve in bowls and sprinkle with Gruyère. Have plenty of hot buttered and toasted French bread ready to accompany this hearty soup.

Sliced Oranges, Grand Marnier

Peel 6 large oranges thoroughly to eliminate all traces of skin, then slice thin and arrange in a serving dish. Sprinkle lightly with 1 tablespoon sugar, and add Grand Marnier to taste. Decorate with candied violets or chopped pistachio nuts.

DINNER BUFFETS

 AN ALSATIAN BUFFET FOR 10

This is planned around one of the most delicious of all buffet dishes and one that guests always adore—choucroute garnie. It has become somewhat of a trademark for me over the years. Serve an Alsatian Riesling.

HERRING SALAD

CHOUCROUTE GARNIE

APPLE TART

Herring Salad

4 to 5 pickled herring
2 pounds new potatoes,
    cooked in their skins
2 apples, peeled and diced
6 cooked beets, peeled and
    diced
2 pounds cold veal, diced
2 to 3 medium-sized

onions, peeled and
    chopped
Sour cream
Mayonnaise
2 hard-boiled eggs, sliced
1 or 2 good dill pickles,
    cut in strips
Chopped parsley

Cut the herring in small dice. Peel and cut the potatoes in thin slices. Combine with the apples, beets, veal and onions. Add enough sour cream and mayonnaise to bind. Garnish with the sliced egg, pickle and chopped parsley.

Choucroute Garnie

My whole approach to this superb dish has changed in the last two years. I used to make it in the classic way, cooking the choucroute for hours with salt pork, sometimes pig's trotters and knuckles, and sausages. Finally, when it was done, it would be quite fatty with a flavor redolent of the various cuts of pork. Nowadays I prepare the choucroute and the garnie separately. For the choucroute: Place one or two slices of salt pork on the bottom of a deep kettle; or use fresh pork (sometimes the salt pork is strong and gives a disagreeable flavor). Add about 5 pounds of sauerkraut, washed and drained. Next add an onion, thinly sliced, and two or three finely chopped cloves of garlic. Give this a few grinds of the pepper mill. Cover the sauerkraut with white wine and water, and bring to a boil. Reduce heat, cover, and allow to simmer atop the stove for 4 hours or bake in a 325° oven for the same time.

For the garnie: Ham—Bake an 8- to 10-pound ham according to your favorite method.

Loin of pork—Roast a loin of pork well, basting it with apple juice from time to time. A 6-pound roast will take about 2½ hours at 325°.

Sausages—Poach 2 or 3 Polish, Italian or French sausages in red wine and chopped onion for 25 to 35 minutes.

Knockwurst—10 minutes before serving, place 12 to 18 knockwurst in a pan of water and poach them.

Potatoes—Boil 18 to 20 potatoes in their jackets.

To assemble: Arrange the sauerkraut on a great platter. Garnish with sliced ham, sliced pork and sliced sausages. Wreathe it with knockwurst. Serve with the boiled potatoes, mustards of all varieties, and either a good Alsatian Riesling or beer.

NOTE: To cook in the traditional way, place a large piece of salt pork into the pot with the sauerkraut. Add onions, garlic, pepper, white wine, and several pieces of pork hocks and a garlic sausage. Cook for one hour. Remove the salt pork and the sausage. Continue cooking for 2 more hours atop the stove or in the oven. Add knockwurst or other sausages, and remove when they are cooked. Roast a piece of smoked loin of pork separately. Serve with the sliced meats and boiled potatoes as above.

Apple Tart

> *Rich Pastry dough* (see *p. 359–360*)
> *6 to 8 cooking apples*
> *¼ pound butter*
> *1 teaspoon vanilla*
> *Sugar*
> *Apricot Glaze* (see *p. 38*)

Make a rich pastry and roll out to fit a 9-inch pan or flan ring. Peel and core the apples and cut them into sixths. Cut two of them again into paper-thin slices, and reserve. Melt the butter in a heavy skillet, and add the apples (in sixths) and vanilla. Cover and steam over medium heat until the apples are soft but not mushy—8 to 10 minutes. Taste for sweetness, adding sugar to taste.

Sprinkle the pastry with sugar and add the cooked apples, making them level at the top. Cover with the paper-thin apple slices arranged in a pattern. Sprinkle lightly with sugar. Bake 10 minutes at 425°. Reduce heat to 350°, and bake until the pastry is nicely browned and the apples on top are cooked through. Remove from the oven and cool. Cover with an apricot glaze.

 A SUMMER BUFFET FOR 8

Serve either champagne or a chilled rosé throughout; the champagne, of course, will add an extra festive touch.

COLD FILLET OF BEEF, JAPONAIS

RICE SALAD

LIZ LUCAS SHRIMPS

CHICKEN MAYONNAISE WITH WALNUTS

THINLY SLICED TOMATOES WITH BASIL DRESSING

ROLLS

PEACHES WITH BOURBON

ICED ESPRESSO

Cold Fillet of Beef, Japonais

1 large fillet of beef, 7 to 8 pounds, trimmed of all fat
1 cup Japanese soy sauce
1 cup olive or peanut oil
1 cup sherry
6 garlic cloves, chopped
1 teaspoon Tabasco
Dash freshly ground pepper

Marinate the fillet in the rest of the ingredients for 24 hours, turning several times. Remove and dry. Rub with oil, and roast on a broiling rack at 475° for 25 minutes, for very rare; 28 to 30 minutes for rare. Baste with the marinade 3 or 4 times during the roasting. Allow it to cool; if possible, do not refrigerate.

Arrange on a platter with watercress and tiny cherry tomatoes.

Rice Salad

4 cups cooked rice
½ cup chopped onion
½ cup finely diced celery
½ cup seeded, finely diced cucumber
¼ cup finely diced green pepper
Vinaigrette Sauce (see p. *350*)
Chopped fresh tarragon
Chopped parsley

Combine rice, vegetables, and vinaigrette sauce, and toss well. Arrange on a handsome plate or in a salad bowl. Sprinkle with tarragon and parsley.

Liz Lucas Shrimps

3 pounds or more cooked and shelled shrimp
3 medium onions, thinly sliced
4 slices lemon
Chopped parsley
Salt and pepper
¼ teaspoon Tabasco
Olive oil
3 bay leaves

Combine layers of shrimp, onion, lemon and parsley in a casserole or serving dish. Add seasonings and olive oil to cover. Top with bay leaves. Marinate for 6 to 8 hours. Serve in the casserole or dish.

Chicken Mayonnaise with Walnuts

4 cups chicken meat, cut in generous pieces (all white meat for elegance, white and dark for best flavor)
1 cup broken walnut meats (reserve about a dozen halves for garnish)
1½ to 2½ cups mayonnaise, preferably homemade, with a touch of sugar
Salt and pepper
Tabasco

Greens
Capers
Hard-cooked eggs

Combine chicken, walnuts, and mayonnaise. Taste for seasonings, adding salt and pepper, if necessary, and a dash of Tabasco. Spoon into a bowl lined with greens. Garnish with additional mayonnaise, capers, hard-cooked eggs and walnut halves.

Thinly Sliced Tomatoes

Peel tomatoes, slice thinly, and arrange on a platter. Sprinkle with salt, pepper, chopped fresh basil, and chopped parsley. Dribble oil over lightly, and add a touch of lemon juice.

Rolls

Provide a variety of hard rolls, perhaps some of rye. These will be pleasanter with the cold food if they are served warm.

Peaches with Bourbon

12 to 14 ripe peaches
Simple syrup (3 cups sugar, 3 cups water)
½ cup bourbon

Boil sugar and water together for 10 minutes. Peel peaches, and dip into syrup to poach till just tender. Add bourbon.
Serve cold with or without cream.

A PLEASANT BUFFET FOR 8, ESPECIALLY SUITABLE FOR SUMMER

Serve Vin Blanc Cassis or Champagne with the nuts and Muscadet or Riesling throughout the rest of the meal.

SALTED FILBERTS

SALADE NICOISE

CORN BREAD

COQ AU RIESLING

BOILED NEW POTATOES WITH PARSLEY

STRAWBERRY TART

Salade Niçoise

> *3 cans solid-pack white tuna*
> *Greens*
> *3 cans anchovy fillets*
> *4 ripe tomatoes*
> *8 hard-cooked eggs*
> *Pimientos*
> *Ripe olives*
> *Vinaigrette Sauce* (see *p. 350*)

Open the tins of tuna, and drain off the oil. Place in center of a large platter covered with greens. Arrange anchovy fillets around the tuna. Quarter the tomatoes and the eggs. Arrange around the edges of the platter. Garnish with strips of pimiento and ripe olives. Serve with a vinaigrette sauce heavily infused with garlic and basil.

VARIATION: Also prepare thinly sliced cooked new potatoes with oil and vinegar; and cooked, crisp string beans with oil and vinegar. Arrange with the rest of the ingredients on a platter, and top with onion rings, chopped parsley and chopped fresh basil.

Corn Bread

> *2 cups corn meal*
> *1 cup flour*
> *3 teaspoons baking powder*
> *¾ teaspoon salt*
> *2 eggs*
> *1½ cups milk*
> *½ cup melted butter*

Sift the dry ingredients and combine with the well beaten eggs and milk. Blend well and finally stir in the melted butter. Pour into a shallow, well-buttered baking pan, and bake at 425° for 15 to 20 minutes or until delicately brown.

This is delicious for cocktail hors d'oeuvres when split, buttered, and sandwiched with slivers of Virginia ham.

Coq au Riesling

> *2 2½- to 3-pound chick-*
> *ens, quartered*
> *Flour*
> *6 tablespoons peanut oil*
> *4 slices salt pork, soaked*
> *in water, drained,*
> *and diced*
> *8 shallots or scallions,*
> *finely chopped*
> *24 small white onions*
> *3 carrots, cut in rounds*
>
> *½ cup cognac*
> *1½ teaspoons salt*
> *1 teaspoon pepper*
> *Chopped parsley*
> *2 cloves garlic, chopped*
> *2 cups white wine*
> *1 pound mushroom caps*
> *Beurre manié (flour and*
> *butter kneaded to-*
> *gether)*

Cut and flour chicken, and brown lightly in oil. Remove chicken pieces to a hot platter. Add salt pork, shallots or scallions, onions, and carrots to peanut oil. Brown lightly. Return chicken pieces to pan, and blaze with warmed cognac. Toss well, season with salt, pepper, parsley, and garlic.

Add wine, and simmer for 20 minutes, covered. Add mushrooms, and turn chicken pieces. Continue cooking till mushrooms are done, and chicken is tender. The sauce may be thickened with beurre manié.

Serve with small Boiled New Potatoes (*see* p. 365) tossed in butter and chopped parsley.

Strawberry Tart

> *Rich Pastry dough for 2 crusts* (see p. *359–360*)
> *1 quart or more ripe strawberries*
> *2 cups (about 2 jars) currant or damson jelly*
> *1 pint heavy cream*
> *3 tablespoons sweet sherry*

Line 2   9-inch pastry tins or 2 flan rings (either round or oblong) with pastry. Fit a piece of foil inside each tin to permit you to fill it with dry beans or peas. (This will weight down the crust and prevent it from puffing up during the baking.) Bake at 400° for 10 to 12 minutes. Remove foil and beans. Reserve beans for future baking. Cool pastry.

Arrange hulled strawberries in baked shells. Empty jelly into saucepan, and boil for 3 minutes. Cool slightly. Spoon melted jelly over berries to glaze.

Serve with heavy cream, whipped and flavored with sherry.

A BUFFET FOR 8 OR 10

Serve cocktails and sherry with the first course. With the main course and the cheese, serve a good regional Bordeaux—a St. Émilion or a Médoc—and plenty of it!

ANGUILLES AU VERT

THINLY SLICED SALAMI

THINLY SLICED HEAD CHEESE

CRISP RAW VEGETABLES

RYE BREAD AND BUTTER SANDWICHES

BONED AND ROLLED TURKEY

BEER-GLAZED HAM

BOILED NEW POTATOES WITH HERBS

ROLLS AND SWEET BUTTER

DIJON MUSTARD   WATERMELON PICKLES

CHEESE BOARD

HEAVENLY CROWN

Have sets of plates ready for the cold dishes, the hot ones and for cheese and dessert. For your centerpiece arrange a beautiful bowl of fruit, which may be eaten with the cheese and dessert.

Anguilles au Vert

> *1 cup olive oil*
> *3 pounds eels, cut in 1¼ inch slices and skinned*
> *1 quart broth*
> *½ cup or more chopped herbs (parsley, tarragon, chives, basil and spinach)*
> *Juice of 3 lemons*
> *1 pint white wine*
> *Salt and pepper*

Heat the oil. Sauté the pieces of eel in the hot oil for 5 minutes, turning them to cook on all sides. Add the broth, bring to a boil and cook for 5 more minutes. Add the herbs, lemon juice, wine, salt, and pepper to taste and bring once more to a boil. Turn off the heat and let stand until cool. Serves 6 to 8.

Boned and Rolled Turkey

> *1   10- to 12-pound boned turkey*
> *⅔ cup butter*
> *1 cup finely chopped onion*
> *½ cup finely chopped celery*
> *1 tablespoon tarragon*
> *½ cup finely chopped parsley*
> *2 cups crumbs*
> *1 egg*
> *Salt and pepper*

Melt the butter in the skillet and sauté the onions and celery. Add the tarragon, parsley and crumbs. Remove from the fire and add the egg, and salt and pepper to taste. Spread this on the surface of the boned turkey, roll very tightly and tie. Brush with butter. Place on a rack in a baking pan or broiling pan and roast at 350° for 1½ to 2 hours, testing with a meat thermometer to achieve 165° internal temperature. Baste occasionally with butter.

NOTE: 1 cup of finely chopped mushrooms, chopped giblets, chopped truffles, small sausages or chopped nuts may be added to the stuffing.

Beer-Glazed Ham

1 smoked or ready-to-eat ham
1 cup brown sugar
3 tablespoons prepared mustard
½ cup beer or ale

Place ham, fat side up, in shallow baking pan. Bake in a slow oven (325°). If smoked, bake 25 minutes per pound, or until meat thermometer registers 160°. If ready-to-eat, bake 14 minutes per pound, or until meat thermometer registers 130°. Forty-five minutes before ham is done, take from oven and remove rind, if necessary. Score fat surface. Mix together brown sugar and mustard; stir to a paste. Gradually add beer, stirring until blended. Brush part of mixture over ham. Continue baking, brushing frequently with remaining mixture.

Boiled New Potatoes with Herbs

Prepare Boiled New Potatoes (*see* p. 365) and toss with plenty of butter, chopped parsley and chopped chives.

Cheese Board

A good selection for your cheese board might include Muenster, Camembert, Liederkranz and local cheddar.

Heavenly Crown

18 ladyfingers, split lengthwise
½ cup orange juice
1   6-ounce package semisweet chocolate
½ pound softened cream cheese
1 cup light brown sugar, firmly packed
⅛ teaspoon salt
3 egg yolks
3 egg whites
1½ teaspoons vanilla
1½ cups heavy cream

Place ladyfingers, cut side down, in a 375° oven for 5 minutes. Cool for about 10 minutes. Brush cut sides with orange juice.

Place approximately 22 pieces vertically around edge of a 9-inch spring form pan. Arrange remaining pieces on bottom of pan. Set aside.

Melt the semisweet chocolate over hot (not boiling) water. Remove from water and cool for about 10 minutes.

Meanwhile, blend together the cream cheese, ½ cup of the brown sugar, and the salt. Beat in the egg yolks one at a time, then stir in the cooled chocolate.

Beat the egg whites and vanilla together till stiff but not dry, then beat in gradually the remaining brown sugar, till stiff and satiny.

Fold the heavy cream into the chocolate mixture, and then fold in the beaten egg white mixture. Pour into the lined pan. Chill at least 5 hours or overnight. Yields approximately 12 servings.

 AN UNUSUAL, ELEGANT BUFFET PARTY
FOR 12

This calls for champagne; as a second choice, serve a good rosé.

TERRINE OF DUCKLING

HOT, VERY CRISP ROLLS

COUNTRY HAM WITH CHABLIS CREAM SAUCE

SPINACH GNOCCHI

FABULOUS SALAD

PRUNES, ALICE B. TOKLAS

Terrine of Duckling

1 Long Island duckling
1-inch strip pork skin
1 leek, well cleaned
1 sprig thyme
1 stalk celery
1 bay leaf
4 cups bouillon or stock
Water
1 pound chicken livers
1 pound lean pork
6 shallots
1 garlic clove

1 bunch chervil
5 eggs
1 tablespoon flour
1½ teaspoons salt
⅓ teaspoon pepper
¾ cup cognac
1 pound tongue
Truffles
¼ pound larding pork
1 envelope plain gelatin
¼ cup cold water

Skin duckling. To do this, cut duck skin from neck to vent along center of breast with very sharp knife. Pull back skin, using tip of knife to help cut connective tissue where necessary. Reserve skin. Cut meat from duck bones. Reserve pieces of breast. Place bones, neck and giblets in large kettle, reserving liver. Add pork skin, the leek, thyme, celery and bay leaf to bones. Add bouillon, or chicken bouillon cubes and water. Cover and bring to boil. Let simmer for 2 hours.

Meanwhile, put duck meat (except for breast), duck liver, chicken livers and pork through food chopper, together with the shallots, garlic and chervil. Add eggs to the chopped meat one at a time, pounding in well with mortar and pestle, or use a heavy bowl and wooden spoon. Then sprinkle in the flour, salt, and pepper, which have been mixed together. Add cognac, then mix well again.

If you have a blender, simply place 2 of the eggs in the glass container of the blender and add one-third of the chopped meat mixture. Blend well and pour into a mixing bowl. Repeat with 2 more eggs and half the remaining chopped meat. Blend the last egg with the rest of chopped meat and the flour, salt, pepper, cognac. Mix the three batches together thoroughly.

Line the bottom of a large oval terrine, or 2½-quart casserole, or smaller casseroles of total equivalent size, with the duck skin. Carefully pour in half of the meat and egg mixture. Arrange duck breast, strips of tongue and sliced truffles over this. Add remaining mixture. Top with thin strips of larding pork. Bake, uncovered, in slow oven, 300° for 2½ hours or about 1 hour for 16-ounce casseroles.

When broth has been boiling slowly for about 2 hours, remove cover and turn up heat to let broth reduce to about 1½ cups, including fat. Strain broth, then add the gelatin, which has been softened in cold water. Stir until gelatin is dissolved. When pâté is removed from oven, pour broth into casserole over pâté. Put a weight on pâté to keep it submerged in broth, and let stand for 2 hours. Remove weight, cover casserole, and refrigerate. Chill thoroughly before serving. Serve the terrine as a first course with rolls. It can be sliced or spread, as desired.

Country Ham

Real smoked country ham is available in many parts of the country. In and around New York there are at least six different varieties, and each requires different treatment. It is best to follow directions on the wrapping. However, most hams need final baking, even the ready-to-eat ones. Dust them well with brown sugar, crumbs, mixed spices (either Quatre Épices or Spice Parisienne, from Spice Islands), and a little dry mustard. The baking will give the ham a glaze. You may also glaze the ham if you are serving it cold—with an Apricot Glaze (*see* p. 38). When serving ham, slice very thin.

Chablis Cream Sauce

> *4 tablespoons butter*
> *12 shallots, finely chopped*
> *4 tablespoons flour*
> *1½ cups Chablis*
> *2 tablespoons tomato paste*
> *1 teaspoon salt*
> *½ teaspoon freshly ground black pepper*
> *1 cup heavy cream*
> *2 egg yolks*

Melt the butter in a heavy saucepan, and add the shallots. Cook until wilted and soft. Add flour, and cook briskly for 3 minutes. Stir in Chablis, and continue stirring till thickened. Add tomato paste and salt and pepper. Simmer 2 to 3 minutes, then stir in cream which has been mixed with the egg yolks. Stir till thickened, but do not allow to boil! Correct seasoning.

Pour into a sauceboat, and serve with the ham.

Spinach Gnocchi

1½ packages frozen spinach
2 tablespoons butter
½ pound ricotta cheese
Salt and pepper
Dash of mace
2 eggs, slightly beaten
3 tablespoons flour
⅓ cup grated Parmesan

Cook spinach in a heavy pan till just heated through. Drain well and chop fine. Press into a towel to drain off any remaining liquid. Combine with butter, ricotta, salt and pepper to taste, and mace. Cook 5 minutes or so over very low heat, stirring well. Remove from heat, and stir in beaten eggs, flour, and Parmesan. Cool and refrigerate for 2 hours.

Form into small balls or into cylinders about 1½ inches long, and roll in flour. Bring water to a boil in a large pot (gnocchi should not touch during cooking) and add the gnocchi. They are done when they rise to the surface. Remove at once and drain.

Serve with plenty of melted butter and grated Parmesan.

Fabulous Salad

It's decorative and delicious—and a conversation piece. Use a beautiful glass or china bowl to show it off.

12 heads Bibb lettuce
1 No. 2 can baby beets, drained
1 pound mushrooms
1 large bunch violets

Arrange the Bibb and the beets in the bowl. Slice the mushroom caps in rounds, and place over Bibb. Sprinkle with violets (sans stems).

Dress with:

¾ cup olive oil
¼ cup wine vinegar

1½ teaspoons salt rubbed with a garlic clove
1 teaspoon freshly ground black pepper
Toss at the last possible moment.

Prunes, Alice B. Toklas

48 large prunes, preferably pitted
2 fifths of port (approximately)
1 cup sugar
1 pint heavy cream, whipped
Macaroons

Soak the prunes in port to more than cover for 24 hours. Remove prunes, and add 1 cup more of port and the sugar to the wine. Place in a saucepan, add the prunes, and bring to a boil. Boil for 1 minute. Allow prunes to cool in the wine. Refrigerate for another 24 to 36 hours. Serve with whipped cream, and garnish with crumbled macaroons.

 AN ITALIAN BUFFET DINNER FOR 10

Serve a Soave or Verdicchio with the antipasto plate and Valpolicella, slightly cooled, with the main course. After dinner drink cognac with coffee.

ANTIPASTO PLATE

GREEN NOODLES BOLOGNESE

TENDERLOIN OF VEAL WITH BASIL AND

BLACK OLIVES

ZUPPA INGLESE

Antipasto Plate

Salami
Prosciutto
Capocollo

Shrimp Rémoulade
Mussels Rémoulade
Anchovies

Pickled Peppers
Artichokes Vinaigrette
Pickled Mushrooms
Pickled Beets

Celery
Carrot Sticks
Fennel
Scallions
Radishes

Eggs Mayonnaise
Cabbage Salad
Potato Salad
Coteghino with White Beans
Vinaigrette

Bread and Butter

You can make the Antipasto course as simple or as elaborate as you wish. Serve a selection from the dishes above, or the entire list. Some items, such as the pickled mushrooms or peppers, may be bought already prepared. The coteghino should be heated in water or red wine for about 30 minutes and served hot with a salad of white beans—either cannelini or Great Northern—dressed with a garlic-scented Vinaigrette Sauce (*see* p. 350). Arrange the antipasto in separate dishes on your buffet table with as much eye-appeal as possible, and serve casually with cocktails or one of the Italian wines suggested.

Green Noodles Bolognese

For the noodles :

> *5 or 6 cups flour*
> *6 eggs*
> *½ pound pureed spinach*

Make a ring of the flour, and place eggs and spinach inside. Blend, knead well, and pound. Use the electric mixer if you wish. Roll several times in noodle machine, or roll with rolling pin. Cut into strips, and dry slightly before cooking.

If you do not wish to take the trouble to make your own pasta, then buy it; excellent green noodles are put out by Buitoni.

For the sauce :

> ¾ *pound chopped beef*
> ¾ *pound chopped fat pork or 2 slices lean salt pork*
> *1 onion, finely chopped*
> *1 carrot, finely chopped*
> *1 stalk celery, chopped*
> *1 clove garlic, chopped*
> ¼ *cup chopped parsley*
> *Butter*
> *Salt and pepper*
> ½ *cup meat stock or bouillon*
> *1 tablespoon tomato puree*

Combine the meat and vegetables, and sauté in butter until nicely colored. Salt and pepper to taste, and add half the broth. Cook down, then add the remaining broth and the tomato puree. Cover, and cook 1 hour longer.

To assemble :

> *1 or 2 tablespoons cream*
> *Parmesan cheese, freshly grated*

Combine cooked noodles with the sauce, and then add the cream and Parmesan. Toss well.

Tenderloin of Veal with Basil and Black Olives

> *Veal tenderloin (boned loin), about 5 pounds, for*
>   *roasting*
> *Olive oil*
> *3 cloves garlic, finely chopped*
> *2 tablespoons fresh basil or 1½ teaspoons dried basil*
> *Salt and pepper*
> *2   6-ounce cans tomato sauce*
> *1 cup Italian or Greek olives*
> ½ *cup sherry or Marsala*

Rub veal well with 4 tablespoons olive oil, and a bit of the garlic and basil, and salt and pepper. Place in a baking dish. Combine tomato sauce, remaining garlic and basil, and olives, and pour around veal. Add 2 tablespoons olive oil.

Roast at 325° for approximately 1½ hours. Baste twice during this time. Add sherry or Marsala, and continue cooking till veal is tender.

Remove veal to a hot platter. Correct seasoning of tomato sauce. Slice veal and serve with the sauce.

Zuppa Inglese

1½ pounds pound cake or a large Génoise (see *below*)
Crème Patissière (see *below*) *or Bavarian cream*
Cognac, rum, sherry or Marsala
Chopped candied fruits—about ½ pound
Meringue

For the Génoise:

6 eggs
1 cup sugar
Pinch salt
1 teaspoon vanilla
1 cup sifted flour
½ cup clarified butter

Combine the eggs with the sugar in top of double boiler over hot, not boiling, water. Beat thoroughly for about 15 minutes with a whisk or electric beater. The mixture must be very thick, pale in color and ribbony. Flavor with salt and vanilla. Fold in the flour a little at a time, carefully. Finally fold in the clarified butter.

Pour into a long pan (11 inches by 14 inches) or into a large loaf tin, and bake at 350° for about 40 minutes, or until a cake tester comes out clean.

For the Crème Patissière:

2 cups milk
1 inch vanilla bean or ½ teaspoon vanilla
½ cup less 1 tablespoon flour
½ teaspoon cornstarch
½ cup sugar
4 egg yolks

Heat milk with vanilla bean or vanilla. Combine flour and corn-starch and add to sugar and egg yolks, in a saucepan. Beat thoroughly. Pour a little of the hot milk into the egg mixture, and stir well. Over low heat gradually combine the 2 mixtures, stirring constantly until they are thickened, but do not let the mixture boil.

For the Meringue:

> *4 egg whites*
> *4 tablespoons granulated sugar*

Beat egg whites until they form soft peaks. Gradually beat in sugar, and continue beating until glossy. To assemble: Cut the cake into 2 or 3 layers, and add cognac, rum, sherry or Marsala to each layer. Be certain that you use enough to flavor cake properly, but not enough to cause it to disintegrate. Let stand for ½ to 1 hour. Spread the layers with the crème patissière and sprinkle liberally with chopped candied fruits. Place the layers on top of each other, and cover with the meringue. Place in a 375° oven for 15 to 20 minutes to brown the meringue delicately. Cool the cake, and serve in slices.

BUFFET SUPPERS

 A BUFFET SUPPER FOR 12

This might be an after the theatre, opera or concert supper. The lamb stew can be prepared in advance and the garniture added at the last minute. The salad can be ready for tossing and the cheese board and bowl of fruit arranged. All that remains is to cook the rice.

A pleasant Beaujolais will do well throughout this supper. Beforehand offer highballs or drinks on the rocks, and perhaps pass a selection of crisp raw vegetables to munch while supper is warming.

RAW VEGETABLES, DIPPING SAUCE

LAMB MARRAKECH   RICE WITH PINENUTS

CHEESE BOARD   FRENCH BREAD

FRESH FRUIT

Dipping Sauce for Raw Vegetables

Blend together

    18 anchovy fillets
    1 peeled lemon
    3 cloves garlic
    1 teaspoon black pepper

1 cup olive oil
½ cup parsley sprigs

Combine in blender and whirl for 1 minute. Correct seasonings.

Lamb Marrakech

7 pounds lean lamb (leg or shoulder), cut in 1½-inch cubes
1 cup peanut or olive oil
4 large onions, finely chopped
8 garlic cloves, chopped
2 tablespoons salt
2 teaspoons crushed red chili pepper
1 teaspoon Spice Parisienne
2 teaspoons tumeric
9 or 10 tomatoes—ripe large ones, peeled, seeded and chopped
2 cups raisins soaked in sherry

For the garniture:

1½ cups each toasted almonds and filberts
Crisp fried onion rings
Chopped parsley

Brown the lamb in the oil, and add onion and garlic to brown lightly. Add seasonings and tomatoes, and bring to a boil. Cover —adding a small amount of liquid if necessary—and simmer for 1½ hours, or place in a 350° oven uncovered and baste well from time to time till lamb is tender. If you do the latter, you may have to add more liquid or cover the pan for half the time. Add tomatoes and raisins and heat through. Serve with rice, garnish with toasted nuts, onion rings and parsley.

Rice with Pinenuts

2 cups finely chopped onion
2 cups pinenuts
1½ teaspoons paprika
½ teaspoon Tabasco
1 cup olive oil
9 cups hot cooked rice

Salt and pepper
Chopped parsley
6 pimientos

Sauté onion, pinenuts, paprika and Tabasco in olive oil for 6 to 8 minutes. Toss with hot rice, using two forks. Season to taste with salt and pepper. Garnish with chopped parsley and chopped pimiento.

 A BUFFET SUPPER FOR 20

This late supper may be prepared ahead in your own kitchen, or you may have it catered and sent in before you return from the theatre or other entertainment.

If this is to be a celebration, serve champagne; otherwise, you might want to offer standard drinks, and chilled white wine. With the drinks serve a platter of cold poached shrimp, lobster slices, and whole raw scallops that have been marinated as in Seviche (*see* p. 137). Along with the seafood, pass bowls of cocktail sauce and tiny hot biscuits with butter.

COLD SEAFOOD PLATTER

SPLIT PEA SOUP WITH SAUSAGES

RYE TOAST AND BUTTER

CINNAMON STARS

ICE CREAM WITH MANGO MACADAMIA SAUCE

Split Pea Soup with Sausages

3 pounds split peas
1 ham butt with meat—
about 4 pounds
1 onion stuck with 2
cloves
4 garlic cloves
1 bay leaf
1½ teaspoons thyme

2 or 3 ribs celery
Water (about 6 quarts)
Salt and pepper
2 tablespoons tomato paste
¼ cup chopped parsley
2 or 3 Polish sausages
Croutons

Soak the peas overnight. Pick them over the next morning and combine with the ham butt, onion, garlic, bay leaf, thyme and celery. Cover with water. Bring to a boil, and boil rapidly for 30 minutes, stirring several times. Add salt to taste—about 2 tablespoons—and give several grinds of the pepper mill. Reduce the heat, cover and simmer for 3½ to 4 hours or until the soup is perfectly blended. Remove the ham, and put the soup through a sieve. Strip ham from the bones, and add small pieces to the soup. Correct seasoning, and add tomato paste. Cook down till soup has the texture of heavy cream. Just before serving add sausages heated and cut in thin slices. Garnish with chopped parsley and serve with garlic buttered croutons.

Cinnamon Stars

1 pound unblanched almonds
5 egg whites
Dash salt
2 cups sifted confectioners' sugar
2 teaspoons cinnamon
1 teaspoon grated lemon rind

Work almonds through a nut grinder or blend in an electric blender. Do not use a food grinder because it makes the nuts too oily. Beat egg whites with salt until they hold a soft shape, then gradually beat in the confectioners' sugar and continue beating until the mixture holds stiff peaks when you lift up the beater. Stir in cinnamon and grated lemon rind. Take about one-third of the egg white mixture and place in a separate bowl to use later on as a glaze. Fold ground almonds into remaining two-thirds of the batter and mix in thoroughly.

Take half the mixture at a time and pat it to a thickness of ⅜ inch on a board or pastry cloth, lightly sprinkled with confectioners' sugar. If mixture seems sticky, dust the palms of your hands frequently with confectioners' sugar. Cut with a small star cutter and place on a greased cookie sheet. Brush the tops of each cookie with a generous coating of the reserved egg white mixture and bake in a preheated 300° oven for 20 minutes or until edges begin to get firm. Baking does not change the color, you will notice. Take the other half of the batter and repeat the operation. Makes approximately 5 dozen small cookies.

Mango Macadamia Syrup for Ice Cream

2 or 3   12-ounce cans preserved mangoes
2 cups sugar
2 cups Macadamia nuts

Bring the mangoes to a boil in a heavy saucepan, and add the sugar. Let them cook down for 8 to 10 minutes till nicely thickened. Add the Macadamia nuts and cool. Serve over ice cream with additional nuts, if you wish, and perhaps sherry-flavored whipped cream.

 # AN HORS D'OEUVRE SUPPER FOR
6 TO 10

Vegetables

Tomato Salad: Scald or hold over a hot flame 4 large or 6 medium tomatoes. Peel and slice very thin. Arrange on a plate or in a ravier. Dribble 3 tablespoons oil and 1 or 2 teaspoons wine vinegar over slices, and sprinkle with chopped parsley and chopped fresh basil. Salt and pepper to taste.

Cucumber Salad: Peel 3 medium cucumbers. Split them lengthwise, and remove seeds with the aid of a spoon. Slice thinly into a soup plate. Sprinkle with 1½ tablespoons salt, and cover with another plate. Hold firmly, and shake plates well for several minutes. Let cucumbers stand for 1 hour. Rinse in cold water, and drain. Dress with oil, vinegar and freshly ground pepper— and if you wish, a little chopped fresh dill or chopped chervil.

Green Pepper Salad: Seed three good-sized peppers, and cut them into thin shreds. Toss well with 6 tablespoons oil, 2 tablespoons wine vinegar, 1 clove garlic finely chopped, 1 teaspoon salt, and a few grinds of pepper. Allow to stand for 2 to 3 hours before serving.

Celery Salad: Cut 1 bunch celery into thin, thin slices. Toss with the following dressing: 8 tablespoons olive oil, 3 tablespoons vinegar, 1 teaspoon tarragon, 1 teaspoon salt, ½ teaspoon freshly ground pepper, 2 tablespoons Dijon mustard, and 1 teaspoon dry mustard. Allow to stand for 2 to 3 hours.

Onions Monegasque:

36 to 40 small white onions, of one size if possible	*Sprig of fennel*
	1 teaspoon sugar
	½ teaspoon thyme
4 tablespoons olive oil	*1 bay leaf*
⅔ cup white wine	*Pinch of saffron*
½ cup water	*1 cup currants or sultana raisins*
1 teaspoon salt	

Peel onions and place in a skillet or sauteuse, and add oil, wine, water and seasonings. Simmer until onions are just crisply tender. Add saffron and currants or raisins, and cook down. Remove onions, reduce sauce, and then pour over the onions. Serve cool.

VARIATION : 1 or 2 tablespoons tomato paste may be added.

Mushroom Salad: Slice raw mushrooms very thin. To ½ pound sliced mushrooms add ½ cup Vinaigrette Sauce (*see* p. 350) and ¼ cup finely chopped parsley.

Asparagus Tips: Drain 2 cans white asparagus tips, and arrange in a ravier or serving dish. Garnish with chopped hard-boiled egg and chopped pimiento. Serve with a bowl of mayonnaise.

Corn Salad: Drain 2 cans of whole-kernel shoepeg corn, and dress with a good vinaigrette. Garnish with finely chopped green pepper and a little chopped sweet pickle.

Potato Salad: See p. 370.

Fish

Tuna: Buy tuna packed in olive oil, if possible. Serve plain in a ravier or dish.

Sardines: Buy extra good sardines in olive oil. Boneless and skinless ones are more elegant, and there are some delicious spiced varieties to be found in fancy food departments.

Herring Salad: See p. 194–195.

Smoked Fish: A ravier of smoked eel, salmon or whitefish; also, a layer of anchovies in a dish, garnished with chopped parsley and chopped green onion and dressed with a little olive oil and lemon juice. (Plenty of parsley is the secret of this combination.)

Shrimp: Cooked and shelled shrimp in an herbed mayonnaise.

Lobster: If you wish to be especially generous, offer a lobster salad.

Meats and Eggs

Rolls of Cold Baked Ham: Your favorite type.

Salami: Cornucopias with an herbed cream-cheese filling.

Headcheese: Homemade, if possible.

Beef Salad: See p. 98.

Summer Sausage: Thinly sliced.

Cold Beef Rolls: Rare roast beef rolled with kumquat mustard.

Cervelat Salad: Peel and slice 3 cooked knockwurst. Combine with 2 cups thinly sliced boiled potatoes, 1 medium onion, chopped, 1 tablespoon capers, ⅓ cup chopped parsley, and mayonnaise to bind.

Chicken: Cold roast chicken cut in quarters. Arrange on a platter with watercress.

Eggs Mayonnaise: Hard-boiled eggs mashed with a good home-made mayonnaise.

Eggs in Jelly: Boil 12 eggs for 5 minutes. Place under cold water, then shell. Prepare jelly by softening 1½ envelopes gelatin in ¼ cup cold water. Add to 2 pints boiling consommé, and stir till dissolved. Pour a little into the bottom of 12 small round or oval molds. Allow to nearly set, then place a sprig of tarragon (if available) on jelly. Top with a slice of ham and then an egg. Cover with jelly. Let stand 1 hour or until jelly is set. Unmold.

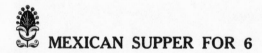

MEXICAN SUPPER FOR 6

Serve tequila sours made according to the recipe for regular sours, except that tequila should be used in place of whiskey, and lime juice in place of lemon.

There are a number of good imported Mexican beers on the market. Offer a selection, well chilled, to offset the high seasoning of the food.

Serve Kahlua in hot coffee or with coffee.

EMPANADAS

SOLE EN ESCABECHE

BEEF AND PORK CHILI WITH EGGS

BLACK BEANS AND RICE WITH CRACKLINGS

SALSA FRIA   RADISH SALAD

FRESH MANGOES

Empanadas

These delicious little turnovers may be filled with all sorts of savory tidbits. One of the best fillings is a mixture of chopped green chilies, olives and ham, bound with egg; other stuffings can be Jack cheese, chopped meats, or roast beef hash.

2¼ cups flour	2 cloves garlic, chopped
¾ cup lard	fine
1 teaspoon salt	⅓ cup olive oil
½ teaspoon freshly	1 pound roast beef hash
ground black pepper	1 tablespoon chili powder
Dash Tabasco	1 tablespoon chopped
Ice water	parsley, or fresh
1 medium onion, chopped	cilantro if available
	1 egg, beaten

Blend the flour, lard, salt, pepper and Tabasco; add as little ice water as possible (about 2 tablespoons) to make a firm dough. Chill for an hour in the refrigerator. Roll out on a floured board and cut into rounds as small or as large as you like, but large enough to hold stuffing when folded in half.

Sauté the onion and garlic in the oil. Add the hash and the

rest of the ingredients and blend well. Place a spoonful of filling on one half of each round of dough. Fold the other half of the dough over the filling to make a half circle or turnover. Seal the edges with a little water and make indentations with the tines of a fork. Brush with beaten egg and bake in a 375° oven until nicely browned. This will take about 12 minutes.

Sole en Escabeche

3 tablespoons butter
¾ cup olive oil
Flour
6 small fillets of sole
Salt, pepper
1 onion, thinly sliced and separated into rings
1 green pepper, cut in thin rings
1 clove garlic, finely chopped

½ cup orange juice
Juice of 2 limes
¼ teaspoon Tabasco
Orange slices
Lime slices
1 tablespoon orange zest (orange part of rind, grated or scraped)
Chopped fresh cilantro

Heat the butter and ¼ cup of the oil. Flour the fish fillets lightly and sauté them until delicately browned on both sides and just tender. Season to taste with salt and pepper.

Arrange the fillets in a flat serving dish and top with onion rings, pepper rings and garlic. Combine the remaining ½ cup oil, orange juice, lime juice, Tabasco and salt and pepper to taste. Blend well and pour over the fish while it is still warm. Let stand in the refrigerator 12 to 24 hours.

To serve, garnish with orange slices, lime slices and orange zest. You may top with additional green pepper rings and chopped cilantro.

Beef and Pork Chili with Eggs

6 onions, coarsely chopped
2 cloves garlic, chopped
⅓ cup peanut oil
2 pounds beef chuck, cut in 1-inch cubes

Flour
2 pounds pork loin, cut in 1-inch cubes
1 tablespoon salt
1½ teaspoons freshly ground black pepper

3 cups beef broth
  (approximately)
½ cup tomato paste
½ teaspoon Tabasco
4 tablespoons chili powder
  (or to taste)
1 cup ground nuts (al-
monds, peanuts,
  cashews)
8 hard-cooked eggs,
  quartered
Chopped parsley, or
  cilantro if available
Black olives

Sauté the onions and garlic in oil, adding more oil if necessary. Dredge the beef cubes with flour and brown in the pan with the onions. Add and brown the pork cubes. Season all with the salt and pepper. Pour over enough broth to barely cover the meat. Add tomato paste, and Tabasco. Simmer 1 hour.

Stir in chili powder and continue simmering until the meat is just tender. Add ground nuts and taste for seasoning. Cook and stir until the broth thickens. Just before serving, add quartered hard-cooked eggs. Garnish with parsley and olives.

Black Beans and Rice with Cracklings

1 pound black beans
Water
4 slices rather lean salt pork
1 onion, stuck with 2 cloves
1 bay leaf
2 hot chili peppers
Salt and freshly ground black pepper
Tabasco
Cooked rice
Bacon cracklings
Sour cream

Soak the beans overnight. Drain and add enough fresh water to come about 2 inches above the beans. Add the salt pork, the onion, the bay leaf, hot chili peppers, salt, pepper and a dash of Tabasco. Bring to a boil, lower the heat and simmer until the beans are tender but not mushy. Remove the onion, bay leaf and hot peppers and discard. Remove the salt pork and chop rather fine. Mix the pork with the beans and taste for seasoning.

Serve this dish with cooked rice; garnish the beans and rice with cracklings. (The packaged bacon cracklings used for hors d'oeuvres will do. Heat slightly and crumble a bit.) Provide a bowl of sour cream for those who like it with beans.

Salsa Fria

1 large can solid-pack tomatoes
1 can tomatillas (small green tomatoes)
1 can peeled green chilies, finely chopped
2 onions, finely chopped
10 scallions, finely chopped
Salt and freshly ground black pepper
1 teaspoon oregano
Chopped fresh cilantro if available

Chop the canned tomatoes coarsely. Peel the tomatillas. Blend the tomatoes, tomatillas, chilies, onions, scallions, salt and pepper to taste, oregano and a little cilantro. Chill.

Radish Salad

Slice red radishes very thin and marinate for several hours in oil, vinegar, salt and pepper. Serve on fresh crisp greens.

COCKTAIL
PARTIES

The ever popular cocktail party is an inferior form of entertaining at best, and there is a tendency to make it formal on occasion—something it was never meant to be. By all means have your house looking its best, use your best crystal and china, and have the food impeccably turned out, but don't be chi-chi. The results may be silly. Unless they are small gatherings around a tray with bottles and ice, cocktail parties should be planned so that the service is efficient and quick. Don't try to set up a professional bar in your house unless you have a barman to go with it, and you will need two if it is a largish party, and more if it is the "annual crush," which so many people use as a way to pay their social debts (and it is not really a very polite way). A large party will also need someone to tidy up from time to time. Some guests love to trail through a party leaving a wake of glasses, napkins and cigarette messes.

If you must do with a minimum of help or none at all, serve three varieties of drinks—and make good drinks—rather than attempt to offer a selection. The same holds true of cocktail food. Better to have two memorable snacks than hundreds of undistinguished canapés. In the menus provided here there is usually one item or two of substantial food. It goes without saying that the food should be attractive to look at and tasty as well.

While the cocktail party is the most popular way of entertaining it can also be the most difficult, since there is so much going on all at once. Don't make your drinks too weak, or your party won't be very lively. Neither make them too generous, or you will have a bunch of drunks on your hands. Plan four drinks per person, and have some supplies in reserve. Neither the host nor the hostess should drink unless it is something light. To give a good party you must be on the alert, though you appear to be entirely at ease. What a delight it can be to settle down later with your shoes off and have a few drinks in peace and quiet.

LARGE PARTIES

 A COCKTAIL PARTY À LA HELEN BROWN

Helen Evans Brown came one year to teach my classes the preparation of hors d'oeuvres. These were her suggestions for a party. Delicious they all are, and varied. Keep the drinks simple and offer the basic selection—Scotch, bourbon, martinis, sherry and perhaps Perrier for the nondrinkers.

SNITTERS

RILLETTES OR RILLONS

CHINESE GINGER AND PORK BALLS

STUFFED MUSHROOMS

PEANUT CRISPS

Snitters

Make tiny, open-faced sandwiches, using a variety of breads cut very thin and generously spread with sweet butter. Listed below are the delicacies you might use for fillings, together with a selection of garnishes. Be as deft and creative as you can in assembling fillings and garnishes. These can be lovely to look at, and delicious.

Fillings	*Garnishes*
Smoked Salmon	Sliced Lemon
Smoked Sturgeon	Olives
Rare Beef	Tomato
Ham	Chopped Onions
Tongue	Fried Onions
Veal	Pickles
Pâté	Prunes
Small Shrimp	Anchovies
Crab	Parsley
Lobster	Cucumber
Eggs	Chopped Aspic
Terrine	Scrambled Eggs
Cheese	Dill
Liver Paste	

Serve a bowl of crisp raw vegetables with the sandwiches and a mustard mayonnaise for dipping.

Rillettes or Rillons

1 pound lean pork, diced fine
2 teaspoons salt
Freshly ground pepper
¼ teaspoon nutmeg
1¼ pounds pork fat, diced fine
1 onion, chopped
¼ teaspoon ground cloves
¼ teaspoon thyme
1 bay leaf
Water to cover

(The difference between the two is that the rillettes are ground or pounded, the rillons left in small dice.) Mix ingredients, except bay leaf, cover with water, add bay leaf, and cook until the water has evaporated and the meat has browned. Remove bay leaf, drain off fat, and reserve. Return meat to heat and cook until crisp and brown. For rillettes, mash in a mortar or grind. Rillons are left as they are. Pack in pots, cover with reserved fat. Serve cold with toast or French bread.

Chinese Ginger and Pork Balls

> *1 pound ground pork*
> *2 tablespoons minced green onions*
> *1 egg·*
> *½ teaspoon salt*
> *¼ cup minced water chestnuts*
> *1 tablespoon grated fresh ginger*
> *1 tablespoon soy sauce*
> *Cracker crumbs, if needed, to make proper consistency*

Mix all ingredients, form into balls, then roll in cornstarch. Fry in deep fat (or pan fry). Serve on toothpicks.

Stuffed Mushrooms

Stuff large mushroom caps with the above mixture and sprinkle with sesame seeds. Bake in a 350° oven for 25 to 30 minutes.

Peanut Crisps

> *1 loaf bread, thinly sliced*
> *2 cups chopped salted peanuts*
> *1 cup peanut oil*
> *1¼ cups peanut butter*

Cut crusts from bread and cut each slice in half. Dry bread, including crusts, overnight in an unlighted oven, or in a warm place. Roll crusts to make crumbs, and mix with chopped salted peanuts. Combine peanut oil and peanut butter. Dip bread in the oil–peanut butter mixture, then roll in crumb mixture. Allow to dry. These will keep for weeks.

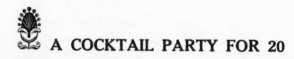

A COCKTAIL PARTY FOR 20

The drinks should be simple—Scotch, bourbon, martinis, gin and tonic, sherry. Blend some martinis ahead of time and chill them.

SALTED FILBERTS

POTTED SHRIMP PASTE

MELBA TOAST FINGERS

HOT ROAST LOIN OF SMOKED PORK

RYE BREAD ROUNDS

GERMAN AND FRENCH MUSTARD

SPICED ONIONS   CHERRY TOMATOES

SWEET AND SOUR PICKLES

THIN ONION SANDWICHES

Salted Filberts

Pour 1 to 2 pounds filberts onto flat baking sheets. Add ⅓ cup oil to each pan. Bake at 350° till nuts are delicately toasted. Sprinkle with salt—kosher salt is excellent for this—and shake well. Cool in baking pans.

Potted Shrimp Paste

> 2 pounds shrimp
> Salted water
> 1 clove garlic
> 1 bay leaf
> ⅓ cup wine vinegar
> ½ pound softened butter (approximately)
> ¾ teaspoon onion juice

½ teaspoon mace
Chopped parsley

Cook the shrimp in salted water to which you have added the garlic clove, bay leaf and wine vinegar. Three minutes after boiling should be ample. Remove shrimp, cool and clean. Chop coarsely and cream with softened butter, onion juice and mace. Add salt if necessary. Spoon into a serving bowl, and garnish with chopped parsley and a few whole shrimp. Serve with home-made Melba Toast (*see* p. 329), cut in strips about an inch wide.

Hot Roast Loin of Smoked Pork

Most good butchers carry smoked loin of pork. Buy a piece weighing 4 pounds or more. Roast in a 350° oven only long enough to heat through. Serve with thin slices of rye and pumpernickel and the mustards.

NOTE: You may baste the pork with Madeira or port during cooking, if you wish.

Spiced Onions

5 pounds small white onions, peeled
Salted water
1 large lump alum
1 quart cider vinegar
1 pint wine
1 pint wine vinegar
1½ pounds sugar
2 bay leaves
1 package pickling spices

Soak onions overnight in salted water. Drain, and pack onions in a large jar or crock with the alum. Combine the vinegar, wine, wine vinegar, sugar, bay leaves, and the spices. Heat to the boiling point, and boil for 4 minutes. Pour over the onions. Seal or cover the jar, and allow the onions to stand for 2 weeks before eating. These are thoroughly delicious.

Thin Onion Sandwiches

Cut good white bread into quite thin slices, and butter well. Salt and sprinkle with chopped parsley. Add thin onion slices, and top with another slice of buttered bread. Trim crusts, and cut into strips or "fingers." Pack in foil, and refrigerate till needed.

NOTE: Cucumber sandwiches may be made in the same manner. Simply substitute thinly sliced cucumbers for the onion.

 COCKTAILS FOR 25

You will need a barman and a waiter or two for this fairly elaborate party, and, if you can manage it, have help in the kitchen as well. Serve the usual drinks, but be sure you also offer such light things as sherry or Lillet, fruit juices, and Perrier.

SALTED ALMONDS

SALTED GARLIC PEANUTS

TERIYAKI STRIPS   FRENCH BREAD

BACON-WRAPPED PRUNES AND DATES

CHEESEBURGER BALLS

SHRIMP WITH GREEN MAYONNAISE

ANCHOVY RADISHES

FOIE GRAS SANDWICHES

SALMON-DILL PASTE WITH TOAST

Teriyaki Strips

> *1 quart Japanese soy sauce*
> *1 pint olive or peanut oil*
> *12 garlic cloves*
> *1½ cups slivered preserved or candied ginger*
> *1½ cups sherry*
> *1 tablespoon salt*
> *1 tablespoon Tabasco*
> *6 flank steaks (any you don't use can be frozen)*

Combine all the flavorings, and marinate steaks for several hours. Broil quickly—3 minutes to a side—and slice with a sharp knife in thin, diagonal slices. Serve on bread. Cook only one or two steaks at a time so they do not get cold.

Bacon-Wrapped Prunes

> *72 prunes*
> *72 strips Swiss cheese*
> *72 bacon strips*

Soak the prunes in water for 1 hour. Cover and bring to a boil. Cool in the water. Drain, and remove the pits. Fill each prune with a piece of cheese, wrap in bacon, and secure with a toothpick. Broil 4 to 5 inches from heat. Serve hot.

Bacon-Wrapped Dates

> *72 fresh dates*
> *Dry sherry to cover*
> *72 bacon strips*

Pit the dates, cover with dry sherry, and soak for several hours. Drain (reserve the sherry for a fruit cup later in the week), wrap with bacon, and broil till bacon is crisp. Serve hot.

Cheeseburger Balls

> *3 pounds lean ground chuck*
> *3 cloves of garlic, finely chopped*
> *3 teaspoons Dijon mustard*
> *¼ pound crumbled Roquefort cheese*

> 1½ teaspoons salt
> 1 teaspoon freshly ground black pepper
> Butter and oil

Combine all ingredients except butter and oil, form into tiny balls, and sauté in equal amounts of butter and oil. Shake the pan vigorously during sautéing so balls will roll and keep their shape. When done to your taste—do not overcook—remove to a platter, and impale each ball on a toothpick. Serve very hot—with a mustard-flavored Hollandaise, if you wish.

Shrimp with Green Mayonnaise

> 4 to 5 pounds (about 10 to 15 to a pound) large
>   shrimp
> 2 gallons water
> 1 cup vinegar
> 1 bottle white wine (⅘ quart)
> 3 garlic cloves
> 2 bay leaves
> 1 teaspoon thyme
> 1 onion, stuck with cloves
> 1 sprig parsley

Clean shrimp, leaving tail shell intact. Combine liquids and seasonings, and bring to a boil. Simmer for 10 minutes, then add shrimp and cook for 3 to 4 minutes. Drain and cool. Serve on a bed of parsley with green mayonnaise.

Green Mayonnaise

> 1 quart mayonnaise
> 1 cup finely chopped raw spinach
> 2 tablespoons chopped fresh tarragon
> ½ cup chopped parsley
> 2 tablespoons chopped chives
> 1 tablespoon Dijon mustard

Combine all ingredients, and blend well. Allow to stand for 2 hours before serving.

Anchovy Radishes

Clean several bunches of radishes, and crisp in cold water. Drain. Wrap an anchovy fillet around each radish and secure with a toothpick. Serve very cold.

Foie Gras Sandwiches

Butter thin slices good white bread, preferably homemade, with sweet butter. Spread with mousse of foie gras and top with another slice of bread. Cut in strips or fingers. Chill.

Salmon-Dill Paste

> *1 pound smoked salmon*
> *1 large onion, finely chopped*
> *2 tablespoons fresh dill*
> *Mayonnaise*
> *Sour cream*
> *Dill*
> *Parsley*

Dice salmon, and combine with onion and dill. Add enough mayonnaise and sour cream to bind ingredients and make a paste. Chill. Garnish with dill and parsley, and serve with pumpernickel or rye bread; or with tiny brioche, which can be purchased at some bake shops.

 A COCKTAIL PARTY FOR 30

Here is a party that embodies my approach to the cocktail hour. Instead of tray after tray of tiny morsels of food, we have a good, hearty offering. Serve the usual variety of drinks, but be sure to include some beer, champagne and chilled dry sherry.

The steak tartare should be served in a bowl surrounded with a selection of breads and crackers; or molded into a loaf and served on a chopping board. Pass the spareribs with plates and small paper napkins. Along with this, serve either a bowl of freshly shelled peas or fresh, raw asparagus tips—whichever is in season.

STEAK TARTARE

GLAZED SPARERIBS

RAW PEAS OR RAW ASPARAGUS TIPS WITH

COARSE SALT AND PEPPER

FRESHLY ROASTED SALTED PEANUTS

KNOCKWURST WITH SHALLOT MUSTARD

Steak Tartare

Use top round, sirloin or tenderloin. You will need about 5 pounds. Have it ground just before you use it. Using two knives, blend into the meat in the following order:

1) 18 to 20 anchovy fillets, well chopped. After blending, mold the meat into a mound, and do so after adding each of the ingredients.

2) 1½ cups or more finely chopped onion.

3) Make a crater in the center of the mound, and add 5 egg yolks, 1½ teaspoons salt, several grinds of black pepper, and several generous dashes of Tabasco.

4) 2 tablespoons Dijon mustard, about ½ cup capers, and about ⅓ cup finely cut chives.

5) About ¼ cup cognac.

Be sure all ingredients are thoroughly blended, then form into a loaf or loaves for serving. Sprinkle with chopped parsley if you wish. Keep chilled until ready to serve; and perhaps serve half the quantity at a time.

Glazed Spareribs

You will need about 20 pounds. Roast them, a few pounds at a time, with salt and pepper for 45 minutes in a 350° oven. This can be done well ahead of time. Cool the ribs, and cut them into individual portions.

Prepare a glazing sauce for each five pounds of spareribs:

> *1 cup Japanese soy sauce*
> *1½ cups tomato catsup*
> *1½ cups honey*
> *5 cloves garlic, finely chopped*
> *1 teaspoon Tabasco*

Mix all ingredients thoroughly. Place spareribs on racks over baking pans, brush well with the glaze, and roast for 10 minutes at 450° or until they are glossy and crisp. Baste several times during baking.

Knockwurst with Shallot Mustard

Buy 25 or 30 good, juicy knockwurst, and boil them in batches as you need them. Slice them in rounds, and serve with:

> *1 cup Dijon mustard*
> *1 cup Durkee dressing*
> *½ cup catsup*
> *½ cup chopped shallots or scallions*

Blend ingredients thoroughly. Add additional mustard to taste. This is even more delicious when a little chopped fresh tarragon is added.

 # A LARGE COCKTAIL CRUSH FOR 40

This is one of those parties which starts at about 6 or 7 o'clock and goes on till about 8:30 or 9:00 and provides enough food so that people do not need to go to dinner. I'd set up a full bar and also have some champagne and white wine with cassis. Thus you are apt to satisfy everyone. Coffee is a good idea at about 9 o'clock, with some sweet biscuits, perhaps.

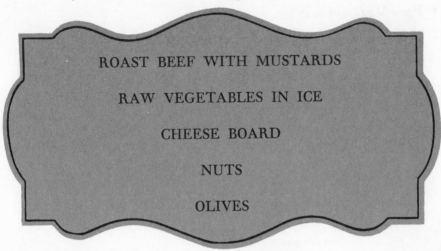

ROAST BEEF WITH MUSTARDS

RAW VEGETABLES IN ICE

CHEESE BOARD

NUTS

OLIVES

Roast Beef

I produce a full 7-rib roast and usually have it roasted by a restaurant where I dine often. It is delivered hot and served after a half hour. The chill is never in it, and it slices magnificently for sandwiches on thinly sliced dark bread and French bread. Serve a variety of mustards, as well as Burgundy mustard and mustard butter.

Burgundy Mustard

> *2 cups Dijon mustard*
> *12 small sour pickles*
> *1 small sweet pickle*
> *1 teaspoon dried tarragon or 1½ tablespoons fresh*
> *tarragon*

Chop the pickles and tarragon very fine and blend with the mustard. Garnish with finely chopped pickle.

Mustard Butter

Cream ½ pound sweet butter, and blend in 2 teaspoons dry mustard, 1 teaspoon freshly ground black pepper and a few drops lemon juice.

Raw Vegetables in Ice

Serve bowls of delicious raw vegetables in crushed ice The usual seasonals, such as celery, carrots, scallions and radishes, can be enhanced by cauliflower flowerets, broccoli flowerets, raw asparagus, thinly sliced turnips and raw mushrooms.

Serve with the following sauce, for dunking:

To ½ pint of homemade olive-oil Mayonnaise (*see* p. 349) flavored with capers, garlic, parsley, and ½ pint sour cream add:

> *3 garlic cloves, finely chopped*
> *2 tablespoons chopped capers*
> *½ cup chopped parsley*
> *1 teaspoon Tabasco*
> *½ cup chopped chives*

Cheese Board

I find that Switzerland Swiss is perfect for such a party as this. Put a large piece on a cheese board, and near it knives for cutting, crackers, water biscuits and breads.

Nuts and Olives

Salted almonds and filberts and both the Greek olives and the tiny Spanish ones are always welcome at a party. You can have bowls of these around in a number of places.

 ANOTHER LARGE COCKTAIL PARTY FOR 50

Here again you should set up a full bar, including some good wine and chilled beer. The food makes this fairly buffet-ish, although it is not a full supper. This could also be turned into a late after-theatre party, at which you would serve only beer and wines.

Tiny Danish pastries and coffee may be served at the end of cocktail time as a signal that the party is over.

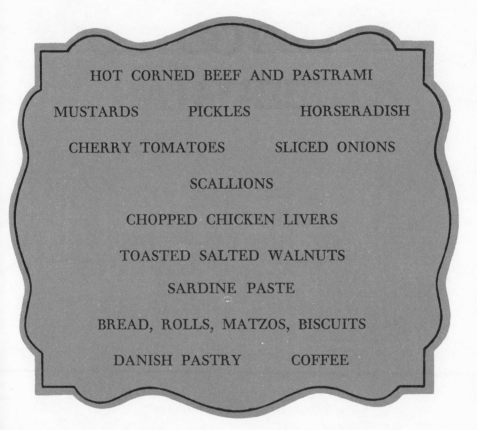

HOT CORNED BEEF AND PASTRAMI

MUSTARDS   PICKLES   HORSERADISH

CHERRY TOMATOES   SLICED ONIONS

SCALLIONS

CHOPPED CHICKEN LIVERS

TOASTED SALTED WALNUTS

SARDINE PASTE

BREAD, ROLLS, MATZOS, BISCUITS

DANISH PASTRY   COFFEE

Hot Corned Beef and Pastrami

I suggest that you order this from a good restaurant or Jewish delicatessen. Have someone on hand to carve it for you, and carve it to order as the guests indicate their preference. Provide a wonderful selection of bread and rolls, sweet butter, a variety of mustards, thinly sliced pickles, fresh horseradish, and sliced onions.

Chopped Chicken Livers

> *2 pounds chicken fat*
> *3 large or 4 medium onions, finely chopped*
> *1½ pounds chicken or duck livers*
> *Salt and pepper*

Chop the chicken fat in small pieces, and try out in a heavy skillet till the fat is thoroughly liquid and cracklings begin to form. Add ½ cup finely chopped onion, and cook till nicely browned. Strain through cheese cloth, and reserve both the fat and the cracklings. Place remaining raw onions in a heavy pot with a cover and cook in 4 tablespoons chicken fat. When the onions are soft and delicately colored, salt and pepper to taste.

Sauté the livers in the remaining chicken fat till they are just cooked through. Remove and chop rather finely. Toss in the pan with the fat, juices, onions and cracklings. Season to taste and cool. Serve in a chilled bowl with matzos and other good crackers and biscuits.

Sardine Paste

> *1 pound cream cheese*
> *1 large onion, grated*
> *½ cup chopped parsley*
> *½ cup chopped chives*
> *2 tablespoons or more lemon juice*
> *3 tins boneless and skinless sardines*
> *Salt and pepper*
> *Paprika*

Mash the cheese and cream it thoroughly. Beat in the onion, chopped parsley, chives, and lemon juice. Mash the sardines and beat into the cream cheese mixture. Correct the seasoning. Sprinkle top with paprika and additional chopped parsley, and serve with wedges of lemon. This is delicious spread on crackers, biscuits or thinly sliced bread.

You may double this recipe, if desired.

SMALL PARTIES

 A SIMPLE COCKTAIL PARTY
FOR 6 OR 8

Offer an assortment of cocktails and drinks without attempting
to produce everything in the bartender's handbook. You might
confine yourself to martinis, daiquiris and Scotch, for example.
The feature of the party will be the pâté de campagne.

PÂTÉ DE CAMPAGNE, PROVENÇALE

FRESH TOAST

ANCHOVIED RADISHES

GARLIC-FLAVORED OLIVES

Pâté de Campagne, Provençale

A delicious country pâté, easy to make and always welcome.

> *2 pounds lean pork, very coarsely chopped*
> *2 pounds veal, chopped rather finely*
> *1 pound ground pork liver*
> *1 pound fresh pork siding or fat bacon, diced*
> *6 garlic cloves, minced*
> *3 eggs*
> *½ teaspoon Spice Parisienne*

⅓ *cup cognac or whiskey*
1 tablespoon basil
1 tablespoon salt (*approximately*)
1 teaspoon freshly ground black pepper
Bacon or salt pork (*enough to line terrine*)

Combine all the meats and seasonings. If you wish to test for seasoning, sauté a small piece—about 1 tablespoon—in butter till cooked through.

Line a good-sized straight-sided terrine or baking dish with salt pork or bacon. A 2½-quart soufflé dish, heavy pottery dish or a large round Pyrex dish are ideal. Fill with the mixture and form a well-rounded top. Place a few strips of bacon or salt pork over the top, and bake at 325° for 2 to 2½ hours. I always cover it with a sheet or foil for the first hour or so of cooking. It will break away from the sides a bit when done.

Remove from the oven and cool. Weight it after the first half hour of cooling. Serve from the terrine or dish in generous slices with a sharp, heavy knife. Cover tightly with foil when replaced in the refrigerator.

Anchovied Radishes

Select tiny crisp radishes. Clean thoroughly and soak in ice water for an hour or so. Wrap each radish with an anchovy fillet, and secure with a toothpick.

Garlic-Flavored Olives

Buy the super-colossal California ripe olives. For 2 to 3 cups olives, add 3 tablespoons olive oil, 3 finely minced garlic cloves, and 1 tablespoon grated lemon rind. Let stand for 1 or 2 hours before serving.

COCKTAILS FOR 12 TO 15, WITH A MEXICAN FLAVOR

Serve your favorite potables, and in addition offer tequila sours.

CHILI CON QUESO   BREADSTICKS

FRITOS   CELERY

FRIED CHICKEN LEGS

CHEESE BOARD   BREAD AND CRACKERS

CAVIAR-STUFFED EGGS

Chili con Queso

2 cloves garlic, finely chopped
1   28-ounce can Italian plum tomatoes
Salt and freshly ground black pepper
2 cans peeled green chilies, finely chopped
1½ cups Velouté Sauce (see p. 344)
1 pound shredded Jack or cheddar cheese

Combine garlic, tomatoes, salt and pepper to taste. Cook down for 20 minutes over medium flame, stirring occasionally. Add chopped green chilies (be certain to remove the tiny seeds before chopping). Cook till thick and pasty. Add cream sauce and cheese, and place in chafing dish or electric skillet over warm heat.

Use for dipping breadsticks, fritos and celery.

Fried Chicken Legs

Buy 24 to 28 chicken legs. If you must buy thighs too, do so—use for another meal. Dredge with highly seasoned flour, using paprika, cayenne, dry mustard, salt and pepper. Fry the legs, a few at a time, according to your favorite method. Serve hot.

Cheese Board

Buy 4 or 5 varieties of cheese—perhaps Canadian cheddar, Roquefort, Switzerland Emmenthal or Gruyère, or Brie—and keep at room temperature for several hours before serving. Serve on a cheese board or a marble cheese dish with butter, and a selection of breads and English biscuits.

Caviar-Stuffed Eggs

> *18 to 20 eggs, hard-boiled and shelled*
> *¾ cup or more red caviar*
> *¼ cup grated onion*
> *Dash Tabasco*
> *Mayonnaise, if needed*
> *Chopped parsley*

Cut eggs carefully into halves lengthwise. Remove yolks, place in a bowl and mash with the caviar and seasonings until they form a paste. Stuff the whites either with a pastry bag and rosette tube or with spoon and fork. Decorate with a dab of caviar and a touch of parsley.

 AN APÉRITIF PARTY FOR 12

Apéritifs are ideal for a group you wish to entertain very informally, perhaps before you go off to the theatre or the horse show. Have a selection of such items as St. Raphael, Dubonnet, Byrrh, Campari, Cinzano, Cinzano Bianco, Punt y Mes, and sherry (preferably Amontillado, Manzanilla or Montilla). All of these delicious drinks should be served chilled or on the rocks, and, of course the Campari is excellent with soda or combined with sweet vermouth to make an Americano. The food should be casual, in the spirit of the party.

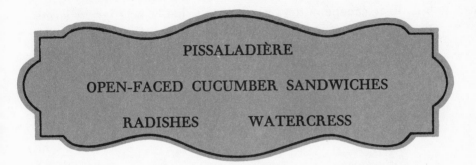

PISSALADIÈRE

OPEN-FACED CUCUMBER SANDWICHES

RADISHES   WATERCRESS

Pissaladière

This is the southern French version of pizza.

Brioche dough (see *p. 356*)
3 large onions, finely chopped
6 tablespoons butter or olive oil
Anchovy fillets
Black Italian-style olives

Mix one full recipe of brioche. After the first rising, punch down the dough and roll out ½ inch thick. Arrange in square or oblong baking tins. While the brioche is rising a second time, sauté the onions in butter or oil for 3 minutes. Cover and steam until they are soft and tender. Season to taste. Spread the onion over the brioche. Next arrange a lattice of anchovy fillets. Place black olives in the spaces between the fillets. Bake at 375° till the brioche is crisp and cooked through. Serve warm.

VARIATIONS: Add a spreading of tomato paste and sprinkle with finely chopped garlic and chopped fresh basil. Add thin slices of peperoni or salami.

Open-Faced Cucumber Sandwiches

24 very thin slices good white bread
Mayonnaise or Durkee dressing

24 slices hard-boiled egg
24 slices cucumber
24 capers or 24 rolled anchovies

Spread bread with mayonnaise or dressing. Cut in rounds with a biscuit or canapé cutter. Each round should be slightly larger than an egg or cucumber slice. Place a slice of cucumber and a slice of egg on the bread, and top with a caper or rolled anchovy. Serve as soon as possible, before bread becomes soggy.

 A CHAMPAGNE PARTY FOR 10 OR 12

Nothing is pleasanter, to my way of thinking, than a party with good champagne and plenty of time to relax and talk. This is possible with 10 or 12 guests. Be sure there is plenty of sitting space. The food should be simple but with a quality of elegance.

GOUGÈRE

TINY SAUSAGE ROLLS

VIRGINIA HAM SANDWICHES

WARM SALTED ALMONDS

Gougère

Pâte à Choux (see p. *358*)
½ cup grated Switzerland cheese
½ cup finely diced Switzerland cheese
½ teaspoon Tabasco

Make one full recipe of pâte à choux. Combine the grated and diced cheese with the choux paste and Tabasco, and fill a pastry bag, fitted with a large rosette tube. Force the paste into a ring or into individual rosettes on a buttered cookie sheet. Bake at 375° until well puffed and browned, or until the paste no longer tears. Serve warm.

Tiny Sausage Rolls

> *Cream Cheese Pastry or Plain Pastry* (see *pp. 360 and 359*)
> *24 to 36 well seasoned small pork sausages*
> *1 egg*
> *3 tablespoons cream*

Make one full recipe of pastry. Poach the sausages in boiling water for 5 minutes. Drain, and cool. Roll out the pastry, and cut into squares just large enough to encase the sausages completely. Arrange on a baking sheet. Brush with egg beaten with cream. Bake at 375° until the pastry is nicely browned and crisp. Serve warm.

Virginia Ham Sandwiches

You must use a real Smithfield ham for this. You may buy slices from most good delicatessens, or you may buy a whole ham ready-cooked and ready for the table.

Spread very thin slices of white and rye bread with sweet butter. Brush ever so lightly with a good mustard, and arrange paper-thin slices of ham on the bread. Top with another buttered slice of bread, and cut into fingers or triangles.

Warm Salted Almonds

Make your own salted almonds with fine Jordan almonds and butter and salt. Either cook them slowly atop the stove in a heavy skillet, or roast them in the oven at 350° with plenty of butter and coarse salt. Do not let them overcook, or they will have a scorched flavor. I find that if I use half butter and half peanut oil it gives the nuts a most pleasant texture.

For ten persons I would toast two pounds of nuts. Any left over may be frozen or kept in an airtight container.

A SMALL ELEGANT COCKTAIL PARTY
FOR 10

This is the type of cocktail party you give for a very close friend who loves the elegant things in life or for a visiting mogul who is tremendously important to you or to the community. In other words, it's a smash!

Fill a large silver punch bowl with ice, and in it chill champagne, vodka and zubrowka and perhaps aquavit. If guests demand other drinks, have the makings at hand, but the chilled selection in the punch bowl is appropriate for the food to be served.

Bring out small plates, knives and forks, and your best linen.

CAVIAR

SMOKED SALMON

FOIE GRAS

Caviar

Be certain it is the best, and serve it in a bowl of ice with a caviar spoon or fork. Put it in charge of someone who knows how to serve it without breaking the eggs and creating havoc with your best forty-dollar brand. With it serve lemon wedges, chopped onion and chopped egg, yolk as well as white. Keep fresh toast coming, and have dark bread, butter, and, if you wish, sour cream. You had better count on at least a kilo of caviar!

Smoked Salmon

If the Scotch salmon is available, by all means serve it; if not, then certainly the best Nova Scotia that you can find. If you have someone who can cut salmon beautifully in thin, longish slices, have him perform in the dining room. Otherwise, have it perfectly sliced beforehand. Serve capers, oil and lemon. Thinly sliced onion will appeal to many, as well. Pass the pepper grinder. Pumpernickel, hot toast and rye bread, sliced thin and buttered, are splendid with this.

Foie Gras

If you can get fresh foie gras, as is sometimes possible in New York and other cities, this will be superb. Otherwise, you will have to provide a large crock or two of the preserved goose liver. Here again it is important to have someone serve it properly. Toast and butter are necessary accompaniments.

ENTERTAINING
OUTDOORS

INDOOR – OUTDOOR
COOKING

Outdoor cooking has been a staple form of cookery for centuries, but it is only since the last war that it has gained general popularity in this country. There have always been garden parties and dinners on the terrace, but there has been nothing like the mass outdoor cooking that now takes place in suburban patios and on city terraces across the nation. The appeal lies in its simplicity, the unique flavor that can be achieved, and the chance to escape from the kitchen into the open air. Furthermore, its rugged approach to cooking gives the man of the house a chance to shine. Frequently it is a cooperative enterprise, with the host tending the grill or spit while the hostess makes preparation in the kitchen. Using both indoors and outdoors this way, all sorts of variations are possible—for example, an outdoor meal with embellishments from the kitchen; an indoor meal with one course prepared on the outdoor grill and brought to the dining room; or a first course prepared outdoors and served there with drinks, while the remainder of the meal is prepared and served indoors. In any case, cooking in the open air brings a novel and informal touch to any meal. There is no more delicious way to prepare meats if the grilling is done with care. Make certain you have proper equipment, and avoid overcooking.

AN OUTDOOR STEAK LUNCHEON
FOR 6 TO 8

SEAFOOD PLATE, PROVENÇALE

STEAK WITH ANCHOVY BUTTER

HASH BROWN POTATOES

PEA AND MUSHROOM SALAD

SOUFFLÉ GLACÉ GRAND MARNIER

Seafood Plate, Provençale

Greens
4 lobsters, poached, split, claws cracked
1½ pounds cooked lump crabmeat
3 pounds large shrimp (10 to 15 per pound),
poached and shelled
2 pounds bay scallops, marinated in lime juice for
1 hour
2 quarts mussels, scrubbed and steamed open

Place cracked ice on a large platter, decorated with greens, and arrange the seafood on the greens as attractively as possible—the lobster around the outside, a great pile of pink shrimp in the center, crabmeat on one side of the platter, and bay scallops on the other. First drain the lime juice from the scallops and mix the scallops with 1½ teaspoons salt and 2 tablespoons chopped parsley. Trim the platter with mussels on the half shell. Serve this sumptuous plate with sauce provençale.

For the Sauce Provençale :

> *2½ pints homemade Mayonnaise, made*
> *with olive oil* (see *p. 348*)
> *2 hard-boiled eggs, chopped*
> *2 garlic cloves, minced*
> *2 tablespoons chopped capers*
> *2 tablespoons chopped parsley*
> *2 tablespoons Dijon mustard*
> *Salt and pepper to taste*

Combine all ingredients, and allow to mellow for 2 hours before serving.

Steak with Anchovy Butter

> *2 large sirloin steaks, 2½ inches thick*
> *Salt and pepper*

Rub steak well with coarse salt and freshly ground pepper. Broil over coals at medium temperature, turning several times. Increase heat at the end of cooking time if a char is desired. Slice, and adds a spoon of anchovy butter to each serving.

For the Anchovy Butter :

> *¾ pound softened butter*
> *2 garlic cloves, minced*
> *12 anchovy fillets, finely chopped*
> *2 tablespoons chopped parsley*

Blend butter and seasonings thoroughly. Chill for several hours before serving.

Hash Brown Potatoes

See p. 367.

Pea and Mushroom Salad

> *3 pounds tender fresh peas or 2 packages frozen small*
> *peas*
> *Boiling salted water*
> *1 tablespoon sugar*

¼ *cup Vinaigrette Sauce* (see p. *350*)
½ *pound mushrooms, sliced*
2 *tablespoons fresh basil or 1 teaspoon dried basil*

Cook the peas in boiling salted water to which you have added the sugar. When just tender, drain, and add the vinaigrette sauce. Cool. Toss with the raw mushrooms, to which you have added the basil.

Soufflé Glacé Grand Marnier

5 eggs, separated
⅔ cup sugar
1 envelope unflavored gelatin
⅓ cup Grand Marnier
1 cup heavy cream, whipped
Macaroons
Candied cherries

Combine the egg yolks and sugar in the top of a double boiler and heat over hot water, beating constantly, until the mixture is thickened. Add gelatin that has been dissolved in ¼ cup cold water, and continue beating over ice until the mixture is cold. Gradually add the Grand Marnier. Fold in the whipped cream and stiffly beaten egg whites. Pour into a 1½-quart soufflé dish around which you have tied a collar of brown paper that extends 3 to 4 inches above the edge of the mold. Chill in the refrigerator for several hours. Remove the paper collar and decorate the top with crushed macaroons and candied cherries.

 AN OUTDOOR LUNCHEON OR DINNER FOR 10

This is a delicious summer meal and one that has an unusually good blending of flavors. The roast takes long, slow cooking over the coals; the vegetables can come from the kitchen at the last minute; and the dessert can be made early in the morning.

Chilled rosé is certainly the only wine to go with this food! You may want to precede it with long, cool drinks—perhaps gin and bitter lemon or tonic, garnished with a slice of lime or a sprig of mint.

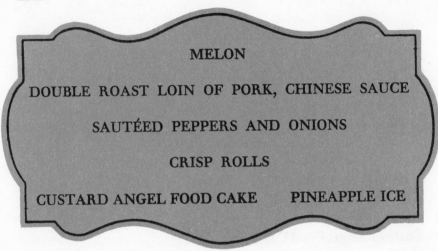

MELON

DOUBLE ROAST LOIN OF PORK, CHINESE SAUCE

SAUTÉED PEPPERS AND ONIONS

CRISP ROLLS

CUSTARD ANGEL FOOD CAKE   PINEAPPLE ICE

Melon

Serve wedges of peeled honeydew or Persian melon with coarsely ground black pepper and a little salt.

Double Roast Loin of Pork, Chinese Sauce

Have two loins of pork boned and tied together, with the fat outside. Rub the roast well with salt and a touch of rosemary. Balance on the spit and roast over good coals, allowing about 25 minutes per pound. Place a pan to catch the drippings as the roast turns. It should be basted at least six or eight times during cooking with Chinese Sauce: Combine ½ cup soy sauce, ½ cup tomato catsup, ¼ cup honey, and 3 cloves garlic finely chopped.

The pork should be roasted to 170° internal temperature and allowed to stand for 20 minutes before carving. Baste with the drippings and sauce while it is standing. Serve the basting sauce with the pork, first adding 1½ tablespoons dry mustard and toasted sesame seeds to taste.

This roast is also delicious when served cold with a mustard mayonnaise and a potato salad.

Sautéed Peppers and Onions

6 to 8 large green or sweet red peppers
2 Italian red onions
½ cup olive oil
1 clove garlic
Salt and pepper
1 to 2 teaspoons wine vinegar

Remove seeds from peppers and cut into strips about 1 inch wide. Peel and slice onions moderately thin. Heat olive oil in a skillet, and add the garlic clove. Then add the peppers and sauté slowly for 20 minutes. Add the onions, and cook covered for 10 to 12 minutes. Uncover, and continue cooking till peppers and onions are just tender. Salt and pepper to taste, and add a touch of wine vinegar just before serving.

Custard Angel Food Cake

1¼ cups sugar
½ cup water
8 eggs, separated
1 cup sifted cake flour
½ teaspoon salt
1 teaspoon cream of tartar
1 teaspoon vanilla

Combine sugar and water, and boil till it spins a thread (230° on a sugar thermometer). Beat egg yolks till very light and lemon-colored. While continuing to beat, pour hot syrup over yolks in a thin stream. The mixture should thicken noticeably. Sift the flour and salt seven or eight times, and measure. After the egg mixture has cooled to room temperature, fold in the flour.

Beat the whites till frothy, add the cream of tartar, and continue beating till the whites are stiff but not dry. Fold into the flour mixture, and add the vanilla. Pour into an ungreased tube pan, and bake at 300° for 1½ to 1¾ hours.

This is delicious served with a dusting of powdered sugar and accompanied by a good pineapple ice.

AN OUTDOOR DINNER FOR 4 OR 6

Here is a good, simple enough dinner enlivened by a few flourishes. Drink a young Beaujolais or a Juliénas with dinner. Have cognac with coffee after the blueberry tarts.

FIGS WITH BACON

DOUBLE ENTRECÔTE, MUSTARD HOLLANDAISE

FRENCH FRIED ONIONS

SLICED TOMATOES WITH BASIL

BLUEBERRY TARTS WITH WHIPPED CREAM

Figs with Bacon

2 or 3 figs per person
1 slice bacon for each fig
Freshly ground black pepper

Grill bacon over coals, wrap around figs, and serve with black pepper. Or place figs in the middle of a platter and surround with crisp bacon, allowing each person to help himself. This makes a delicious combination of flavors.

Double Entrecôte, Mustard Hollandaise

Double entrecôtes are from the first three or four ribs of beef. They should be cut one or two ribs thick, and the bone should be trimmed so that the steak resembles a gargantuan French lamb chop.

Grill the entrecôtes over medium coals to the state of doneness you prefer. If it is a 1-rib steak cut full, it will take about 20 minutes for quite rare. If it is a really thick cut, allow about 25 to 30 minutes, or test by cutting near the bone with a knife. A thick 2-rib steak will serve 3 to 4, according to appetite. Serve with a brisk mustard-flavored Hollandaise.

If you have any entrecôte left over, it is even more delicious cold the next day for breakfast or lunch.

French Fried Onions

See p. 84.

Sliced Tomatoes with Basil

Peel and slice beefsteak tomatoes. Salt and pepper them well. Prepare a dressing with:

> *½ cup finely chopped basil*
> *1 red onion, coarsely chopped*
> *1 tablespoon chopped parsley*
> *1 teaspoon salt*
> *1 teaspoon freshly ground black pepper*
> *6 tablespoons olive oil*
> *1 tablespoon lemon juice*

Arrange tomatoes on a platter, and spoon dressing over them.

Blueberry Tarts with Whipped Cream

> *1 quart blueberries*
> *½ cup water*
> *1 cup sugar*
> *1 teaspoon vanilla*
> *12 tart shells or 2 pie shells* (see *Plain Pastry,*
> *p. 359–360*)
> *1 pint heavy cream, whipped*

Wash and pick over the blueberries. Add sugar and water, and poach gently till just softened. Add vanilla, and cool. Spoon berries into the tarts, and serve topped with whipped cream.

*A formal dessert service for six. The dessert is
a Bavarian cream decorated with candied violets.
Fresh violets adorn the centerpiece, an antique
Italian candelabra. The table is distinctively laid
with vermeil, Wedgwood majolica and 19th-century
wine rinsers, used here as fingerbowls.*

A simple late supper
for two. Mr. Beard
is pouring himself a glass
of light red wine and
enjoying a dish of
cold chicken, along with
a salad of Bibb lettuce
and cherry tomatoes,
French bread
and Gruyère cheese.

An old butter churn has bee
converted into a handsome
rack for Mr. Beard's
impressive collection of
knives—primary tools
for any serious cook.

A curry buffet, with a large array of condiments and the Indian wafers known as "poppadums." The silver punch bowl holds a choice of chilled beer or champagne.

Mr. Beard in his New York kitchen with two versions of one of his favorite foods, oysters. Chilled oysters on the half shell are ready to eat. Meanwhile an oyster stew is in the making.

Mr. Beard decanting a rare old wine with a steady hand and an alert eye. Standard equipment for decanting includes a silver strainer and a candle to illuminate the sediment in the bottle.

AN UNUSUAL OUTDOOR DINNER FOR
12 TO 15

This dinner is possible for a very short season of the year, when kid is in the market. Italian butchers, especially, are apt to offer it in the spring; it is a specialty of the Easter season. Kid is deliciously tender meat, nicely flavored—and a surprise to guests. With it serve a pleasant California Zinfandel or a Pinot Noir. For cocktails, serve Negronis.

STUFFED EGGS

SCALLIONS   RADISHES

KID ON A SPIT   POTATOES ANNA

BIBB LETTUCE AND CHERRY TOMATO SALAD

FRENCH BREAD

FRESH STRAWBERRY ICE CREAM

Stuffed Eggs

12 to 15 eggs, hard-boiled and peeled
6 tablespoons softened butter
1 clove garlic, finely chopped
3 anchovies, finely cut
1 tablespoon capers
1 tablespoon chopped parsley
Mayonnaise

Cut eggs in half either lengthwise or crosswise. Remove the yolks and force them through a sieve into a bowl. Add the softened butter, garlic, anchovy and capers. Blend well, add the parsley, and correct the seasoning. Finally, add mayonnaise to bind, if necessary. Force through a pastry bag with a rosette tube into the egg halves. Chill before serving, and garnish the plates or platter with radishes and scallions.

Kid on a Spit

A whole kid will weigh 12 to 15 pounds. Reserve the liver, heart and kidneys. Rub the kid lightly with rosemary and garlic. Spit it well, and tie the front legs together, folding them under the body. Stretch the back legs out on the spit and tie together. Truss securely and balance. Roast over medium coals with a dripping pan in the firebox. Baste or brush with melted butter mixed with white wine and garlic.

While the kid is roasting, sauté the liver, heart and kidneys in butter. Slice very thin, and combine with 1½ cups Brown Sauce (*see* p. 344), ¼ cup Madeira, and about 2 tablespoons of chopped parsley.

When the kid is done, it should still be juicy, with the faintest blush of pink—about 150° when tested with a meat thermometer in the thickest part of the flesh. Serve with the brown sauce, which may be mixed with some of the drippings from the grill. Pass plenty of crisp rolls.

Potatoes Anna

See p. 369.

Bibb Lettuce and Cherry Tomato Salad

8 heads Bibb or Limestone lettuce
1½ pints cherry tomatoes
1 clove garlic
1 teaspoon salt
¾ cup olive oil
¼ cup wine vinegar
2 tablespoons fresh basil, finely chopped
Salt and pepper

Wash the lettuce thoroughly to rid it of sand, then drain and dry. Remove stems from cherry tomatoes, wash and drain. Combine with lettuce in a salad bowl, preferably not a wooden one. Crush the garlic clove, and rub it well into the salt. Add to the oil. Just before serving, pour oil on the salad and toss. Then add vinegar, basil and salt and pepper, and toss once again. Serve at once.

Fresh Strawberry Ice Cream

> *8 egg yolks*
> *2 cups hot milk*
> *1 cup sugar*
> *1 quart heavy cream, whipped*
> *3 cups ripe, sweet strawberries*
> *2 tablespoons Grand Marnier*
> *Port*

Beat the egg yolks lightly. Combine milk and sugar, and heat thoroughly. Pour over the egg yolks, while whisking constantly. Cook in a double boiler over hot water until slightly thickened. Chill, and fold in the whipped cream and 2 cups of the berries, crushed, and sweetened if necessary. Add Grand Marnier and freeze—either in your refrigerator or in an ice cream freezer. Sugar the remaining berries, flavor with a little port, and serve with the ice cream.

A MEXICAN-FLAVORED OUTDOOR DINNER
FOR 8

This is somewhat plain but good, hearty fare. It can be done almost at a moment's notice and can be expanded to accommodate extra guests. Beer makes a good accompaniment here.

GUACAMOLE WITH TOSTADOS

OR MELBA TOAST

GRILLED HAMBURGERS WITH GARLIC

ROLLS

PINTO BEANS WITH CHILI AND SAUSAGE

ORANGE AND ONION SALAD

FRESH MANGOES, CHERRIES AND APRICOTS

Guacamole

> *3 soft, ripe avocados*
> *1 cup thinly cut green onions*
> *2 tablespoons lime juice*
> *¼ teaspoon Tabasco*
> *1 teaspoon salt*

Crush avocados, and blend with the green onions. Add lime juice, Tabasco and salt. Correct the seasoning. Serve as a dip or spread with tostados or Melba toast (*see* p. 329).

NOTE: There are many versions of this. Some people add a little tomato paste; others, garlic. If you can get fresh coriander (cilantro), by all means add a good deal of it here. Use your imagination and your taste buds.

Grilled Hamburgers with Garlic

> *1 clove garlic for each pound*
> *1 teaspoon salt for each pound*
> *1 teaspoon freshly ground pepper for each pound*
> *½ teaspoon Tabasco for each pound*

*Chopped chuck or top sirloin—½ to ¾ pound per
  person*
Butter

Mince the garlic, and combine with other seasonings. Form
cakes of the meat, about 1 inch thick, and press seasoning into
the side of each cake. Grill over medium coals to suit the taste
of your guests. Remove from the grill, and top each hamburger
with a pat of butter.

Pinto Beans with Chili and Sausage

*1 pound pink pinto beans
Bay leaf
1 onion, stuck with 2 cloves
Salt to taste
¼ pound bacon, cut thick
4 cloves garlic, finely chopped
1 cup finely chopped shallots
1 teaspoon thyme
1 teaspoon ground cumin
4 tablespoons chili powder
1 cup tomato paste
2 tablespoons wine vinegar
2 pounds pork sausages, preferably chorizos*

Soak the beans overnight. Drain, and add fresh water to reach
1½ inches above the beans. Add the bay leaf, onion, and salt
to taste. Bring to a boil and cook till the beans are just tender.
Drain, and reserve liquid.

Meanwhile, sauté the bacon cut into small cubes. Remove and
add garlic and shallots to the fat. Cook till just soft. Add the
thyme, cumin, chili powder, tomato paste and vinegar, and
blend with the beans, adding about 1 cup of the bean liquid.
Place in a baking dish, and cover with a piece of foil. Bake at
350° for 1 hour. Add the sausages, which have been poached in
water for 10 minutes. Return the baking dish to oven till the
sausages are browned—about 35 to 40 minutes. Add bean
liquid during cooking if necessary.

Orange and Onion Salad

> *2 oranges*
> *2 sweet onions*
> *Curly chicory or romaine*
> *½ cup olive oil*
> *½ cup orange juice*
> *2 tablespoons lemon juice*
> *1 teaspoon salt*
> *Generous pinch of rosemary*

Peel the oranges and cut into sections, removing all of the white inner peel. Peel and slice the onions very thin. Wash and dry the greens. Blend the oil, juices and seasonings, and combine with the oranges and onions. When ready to serve, add the crisped greens, and toss well.

A SHORE DINNER ON THE GRILL FOR 8 TO 10

Drink a brisk Pouilly-Fuissé or a Muscadet with the fish. Either choice is refreshing and delicious.

GRILLED SHRIMP

TOASTED FRENCH BREAD

CUCUMBER FINGERS

BROILED WHOLE LOBSTER WITH

HERBED BUTTER

COLE SLAW

BLUEBERRY DEEP-DISH PIE   ICE CREAM

Grilled Shrimp

The large (7 to 10 to a pound) are the best for this type of grilling. Estimate 6 to 8 per person for large appetites; 4 to 5 for lesser ones.

Split the shrimp down the back with a pair of sharp scissors and remove the vein. Marinate the shrimp in white wine, olive oil, chopped fresh dill, and salt and pepper for several hours.

Broil the shrimp in a basket grill or on skewers for 4 to 5 minutes. Serve for a first course along with drinks or with wine, and also serve cucumber fingers and toasted French loaves split in half and buttered (with or without garlic).

Broiled Whole Lobster with Herbed Butter

I prefer to use 2- to 3-pound lobsters for this treatment. Broil the lobsters whole over medium heat for 13 to 16 minutes, turning several times during the cooking. Remove from the grill, split, remove the stomach. Serve with herbed butter.

For the Herbed Butter:

> ½ pound butter
> 1 tablespoon chopped shallots or green onions
> 2 tablespoons chopped parsley
> Chopped fresh tarragon to taste

Combine and melt over low heat. Sometimes a little lemon juice is a pleasant addition.

Cole Slaw

> 1½ large heads of cabbage, shredded
> 1 tablespoon celery seed
> 1½ cups well-flavored mayonnaise
> 1 cup sour cream

Combine the ingredients and marinate for 2 to 3 hours in the refrigerator. Correct the seasoning, and toss well. Serve in a chilled glass or pottery bowl.

Blueberry Deep-Dish Pie

For the pastry :

> *2¼ cups flour*
> *½ cup butter*
> *¼ cup vegetable shortening*
> *Ice water*
> *Salt*

Sift flour and salt into a mound on a mixing board or marble slab. Add shortening, and quickly rub into flour with the fingers. Then add just enough ice water to hold pastry together (3 or 4 tablespoons). Pull off small bits, flatten with the heel of your hand, and form into a ball. Chill in refrigerator for 1 hour.

For the filling :

> *2 to 2½ quarts blueberries*
> *Flour*
> *Sugar to taste (about 1 cup)*
> *6 tablespoons butter*
> *1 egg yolk*

Butter a pie dish lightly. Pour in blueberries, keeping them higher in the center. Dust with flour, then add sugar and dot with butter. Brush with beaten egg yolk.

Roll out crust, and cover berries. Flute edges, and cut a vent in the top. Bake at 450° for 10 minutes, then reduce heat to 350° and continue to bake till crust is browned. Serve warm with maple or vanilla ice cream, or with whipped cream.

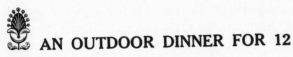 AN OUTDOOR DINNER FOR 12

Serve carafes of California Mountain Red with this meal. With coffee offer a fine old bourbon or cognac.

FIGS OR MELON

WITH PROSCIUTTO AND SALAMI

BREAD STICKS

SPITTED ROAST BEEF   POTATOES ANNA

ROMAINE QUARTERS

FRENCH BREAD   BUTTER

PEACH SHORTCAKE WITH

SHERRIED WHIPPED CREAM

Figs or Melon with Prosciutto and Salami

Select the best melon or figs available. If prosciutto is not available, use a Westphalian or a Virginia ham. Use a good imported salami. Serve the figs or melon on individual plates, and place a few slices of the ham and salami around the fruit. Pass the pepper grinder and plenty of breadsticks.

Spitted Roast Beef

You will need a 5- to 7-rib roast, according to the grill you are using. The roast should be rubbed with salt and pepper and then balanced on the spit. Roast over coals (without very much heat) allowing about 12 minutes per pound for rare or until your meat thermometer registers 125°. Catch the drippings in a pan, unless you have a specially designed grill that drains off the fat. Allow to rest for about 10 to 15 minutes before carving, and it should carve magnificently.

Potatoes Anna

See p. 369.

Romaine Quarters

Remove the coarse outer leaves of 3 heads of romaine lettuce, crisp in cold water, and cut into quarters. One quarter makes a serving. Offer your guests a choice of Vinaigrette Sauce (*see* p. 350), anchovy mayonnaise (*see* p. 349), or salt and pepper.

Peach Shortcake with Sherried Whipped Cream

6 to 8 ripe peaches, peeled and sliced
Sugar
2 cups flour
4 teaspoons baking powder
½ teaspoon salt
3 tablespoons sugar
4 tablespoons butter
¾ to 1 cup heavy cream
Melted butter

Sugar peaches to taste, and set aside. Sift flour, baking powder, salt and sugar together, then work butter and cream into the dry ingredients, using fingers or fork, to make a light dough. Roll or pat out ⅔ of the dough on a floured board to ½ inch in thickness and about 9 inches in diameter. Brush with melted butter, and place on a buttered baking sheet. Dot center with additional butter. Roll out the remaining dough a little thinner and to about 7 inches in diameter. Place the smaller round on the larger, and brush with butter. For 12 guests, you had better make 2 shortcakes.

Bake at 425° for 15 to 18 minutes, or until nicely browned.

Remove from oven. Separate layers. Arrange sugared peaches on lower layer, top with remaining layer, and decorate with more peaches. Serve at once with heavy cream or whipped cream flavored with sherry.

 ## OUTDOOR CHEF'S SUPPER FOR 6

Make old-fashioneds with Jamaica rum, and skip the orange and cherry. Serve a good Provençal rosé, chilled, with the supper, and mirabelle with the coffee.

BROCHETTE OF GIBLETS

GRILLED PIQUANT CHICKENS

EGGPLANT PROVENÇALE

RAW VEGETABLE PLATE

WITH TAPENADE

HOMEMADE CASSIS ICE CREAM

Brochette of Giblets

> *1 pound chicken hearts*
> *1 pound chicken livers*
> *1 pound chicken gizzards*
> *Water*
> *1 onion*
> *Salt and pepper*

1 cup red wine
½ cup soy sauce
½ cup oil
3 cloves garlic, finely chopped

Add the hearts, livers and gizzards from the chickens for the main course to the 3 pounds required here. Poach all the gizzards for 1 hour in water to cover with the onion, salt and pepper. Drain and cut in bite-size pieces. Trim and halve the livers. Combine the wine, soy sauce, oil, garlic, 1 teaspoon salt and ½ teaspoon freshly ground black pepper. Add the gizzards, livers and hearts, and marinate 1 or 2 hours. Drain, and dry on paper towels. String on small skewers, alternating the three kinds of giblets. Brush with the marinade and additional oil, and broil over charcoal. Serve with drinks. Toast or Armenian bread makes a good accompaniment.

Grilled Piquant Chickens

1 cup ground walnuts
6 shallots, or 1 medium onion, finely chopped
4 tablespoons butter
1 teaspoon salt
¼ cup chopped parsley
1 teaspoon dry mustard
Tabasco
6 chicken halves
⅔ cup melted butter
1 teaspoon paprika

Blend the nuts, shallots, 4 tablespoons butter, salt, parsley, mustard and ½ teaspoon Tabasco to a smooth paste. Loosen the skin on the chicken breasts, and stuff the paste under the skin. Brush the bone sides of the chicken halves with a mixture of the melted butter, paprika and 3 dashes of Tabasco. Broil, bone side to the fire, for 12 to 14 minutes over medium coals. Turn and brush the skin sides with the mixture, and continue broiling until the chickens are tender. Season with salt and pepper, and serve piping hot.

Eggplant Provençale

2 eggplants, peeled
Ice water
¼ cup olive oil
6 ripe tomatoes, peeled, seeded and chopped
1 teaspoon salt
1 teaspoon freshly ground black pepper
Oregano
3 cloves garlic, chopped
Buttered crumbs
Chopped parsley

Cut the eggplants into 3-inch slices. Soak for a few minutes in ice water. Drain, dry and brown quickly in the olive oil. Transfer the slices to a baking dish. Add more oil or butter to the pan, and cook the chopped tomatoes. Season with salt, pepper and oregano. Add to the baking dish with the chopped garlic. Top with buttered crumbs and chopped parsley, and bake in a 350° oven for 35 to 40 minutes.

You can prepare this in advance. It can stand in the warming oven while the chickens broil.

Raw Vegetable Plate

In place of a salad, arrange sliced cucumbers, sliced onions and rings or strips of green pepper on a serving plate. Add cherry tomatoes if you wish. Small raw artichokes, sliced raw turnips and carrot strips are nice additions. Serve with a bowl of tapenade for dunking.

Tapenade

1 cup bland mayonnaise (made with 1 egg and 1 cup
*   oil, no seasonings)*
½ cup finely chopped capers
Juice and finely chopped rind of 1 lemon
1 clove garlic, crushed
Chopped parsley
6 anchovy fillets, chopped

Blend all together thoroughly and chill in the refrigerator.

Homemade Cassis Ice Cream

2 cups black currant preserves
1 cup crème de cassis
Juice of 1 lemon
½ teaspoon vanilla
2 cups light cream
2 cups heavy cream
⅛ teaspoon salt

Put the preserves through a fine sieve, or puree in an electric blender with some of the cassis. Add lemon juice, the rest of the cassis and the vanilla. Mix the light and heavy cream with the salt and stir in the currant mixture. Pour into an ice cream freezer and freeze. Serve with currant preserves blended with cassis if you wish.

A BEER SUPPER PARTY FOR THE TERRACE
OR BEACH—SERVES 12

Since the theme of this gathering is beer, provide every kind
of foreign and domestic beer you can find. Chill in a large tub
of ice.

SAUSAGE TREE   HARD ROLLS

COQUILLAGE   RYE BREAD AND BUTTER

GRILLED HERBED DRUMSTICKS

GRILLED FLANK-STEAK SANDWICHES

SLICED TOMATOES   SCALLIONS

PICKLES   MUSTARD   SALTED PEANUTS

CHEESE BOARD WITH FRENCH AND RYE BREAD

FRUIT

Sausage Tree

Make a metal tree with hooks for hanging the sausages, or use
a real tree—a small potted one.

Buy as many different kinds of sausages as you can find. Look
for salami, teawurst, cervelat, summer sausage, blutwurst, liverwurst, Braunschweiger, kielbasy, bolgna, peperoni and mortadella. Buy a quarter, half or whole of each, depending on the
amount you will need. Tie the sausages to hooks and hang them
on the tree.

Coquillage

If you have ever been to a fine seafood bar in Europe, you undoubtedly remember the beautifully colorful displays of different kinds of shellfish arranged on seaweed or ice—the delicate pink of small shrimp, the orange and white of langoustines, the bright lobsters and langoustes, the blue-black of mussels, the pinky beige of clams, and the pale ivory of scallops.

Few foods are more tempting in summer than an assortment of seafoods served cooled, but not icy, with a choice of sauces such as plain or flavored mayonnaise, tartar sauce, or rémoulade sauce.

If you cook shrimp, remember that a white-wine court bouillon is best for these tender morsels, and that they must never be cooked for more than 4 or 5 minutes. A spicy red wine bouillon brings out the best in crawfish; and for lobster you need nothing more than plain salt and water.

Grilled Herbed Drumsticks

¾ cup melted butter (or more if needed)
1 teaspoon tarragon
2 teaspoons chopped chives
2 tablespoons chopped parsley
Salt and freshly ground black pepper
1 dozen chicken drumsticks

Melt the butter and stir in the herbs. Dip each drumstick in the herbed butter and grill them over charcoal until done to your satisfaction. Brush the drumsticks with more of the herbed butter as they cook and turn them to brown evenly. Season to taste with salt and freshly ground black pepper.

Grilled Flank-Steak Sandwiches

2 flank steaks
1 cup dry red wine
1 clove garlic, chopped
1 onion, sliced
1 handful chopped parsley

Salt and freshly ground black pepper
2 medium size loaves French bread
Thyme
1 clove garlic, crushed
Butter

Remove the tough outer membrane from the meat. Put the wine, chopped garlic, onion and parsley in a shallow bowl and let the meat marinate in this mixture for 2 or 3 hours. Keep it in the refrigerator and turn several times to be sure the steak is evenly bathed.

Flank steak should be at refrigerator temperature when grilled, so leave it in marinade until the last minute. Grill it quickly over charcoal, allowing only about 4 minutes to each side. It should be crusty brown on the outside but red rare in the center. Brush with the marinade as it cooks and season to taste with salt and pepper.

Split the loaves of bread the long way and spread the halves with butter mixed with crushed garlic and a little thyme. Press the loaves together again and roll in foil. Heat these on the grill as the steak is cooking.

With a very sharp knife, slice through the steak diagonally from top to bottom, cutting it into thin strips. Remove the bread from the foil, and take off the top half of each loaf. Arrange the steak slices on the bottom halves of the loaves and replace the tops. Cut the loaves into thick slices to make tasty hot and hearty steak sandwiches.

 AN INDOOR-OUTDOOR BUFFET FOR 20

Serve summer drinks before the meal—collinses, mint juleps, vodka and tonic, gin and tonic, and the like—and beer with the meal. With the drinks provide bowls of unshelled peanuts, pretzels, scallions, radishes, olives, pickles, and a board of various sausages, together with pumpernickel bread and several mustards.

CHUCK WAGON STEAK

LENTIL SALAD

CRISP GARLIC BUTTERED FRENCH BREAD

SLICED TOMATOES AND RED ITALIAN ONIONS

CANTALOUPE AND WATERMELON WITH

RASPBERRIES AND ICE CREAM

Chuck Wagon Steak

1 cup salad oil	*1 teaspoon pepper*
2 cups beer or ale	*1 teaspoon dry mustard*
¼ cup lemon juice	*1 teaspoon basil*
2 cloves garlic, crushed	*1 teaspoon oregano*
1½ teaspoons salt	*1 teaspoon thyme*
2 bay leaves	*1 10-pound chuck steak**

Combine oil, beer, lemon juice and seasonings; pour over chuck steak. Refrigerate several hours or overnight. Place steak in roasting pan; brush with marinade. Roast in hot oven (425°) 2½ hours for rare steak.

* You may tenderize the steak if you wish. Follow directions on the bottle of tenderizer.

Lentil Salad

2 to 3 pounds lentils	*1 cup olive oil*
Water	*¾ cup finely chopped onion*
1 tablespoon salt	*2 garlic cloves, finely chopped*
1 onion, stuck with cloves	*½ cup chopped parsley*
1 bay leaf	*1 cup crumbled crisp bacon*
2 whole cloves garlic	*Wine vinegar to taste*

¼ teaspoon Tabasco
1 teaspoon freshly ground black pepper
Additional olive oil, if needed

Soak lentils overnight. Drain, and cover with fresh water. Add salt, onion stuck with cloves, bay leaf and whole cloves garlic. Bring to a boil, and simmer till just tender. Drain, and while still hot add olive oil. Cool, then add remaining ingredients. Toss well, and correct the seasoning. This salad improves if it is allowed to stand for several hours. Garnish with chopped parsley and thinly sliced scallions before serving.

Sliced Tomatoes and Red Italian Onions

On a large platter arrange alternately peeled and thinly sliced tomatoes and thinly sliced red onion. Sprinkle with chopped fresh basil. Pass oil and vinegar, salt and pepper separately.

Cantaloupe and Watermelon with Raspberries and Ice Cream

Arrange halves of cantaloupe in ice, along with wedges of watermelon. Have a bowl of raspberries and powdered sugar near at hand, as well as vanilla ice cream. Your guests may fill their cantaloupe with berries alone or with both berries and ice cream —a dazzling mixture.

For added variety, have a chilled bottle of kirsch on hand, and, if you can find it, a bottle of framboise, for guests who prefer to have their fruit flavored with brandy.

 A TERRACE LUNCHEON FOR 8

Luncheon on a terrace or in a patio is ideal on a lazy summer day when the temperature is not too warm. First, you may have apéritifs indoors or out. Light potions like white wine cassis and Americanos are recommended, except for those who are incurable Scotch or martini drinkers. With luncheon serve Muscadet or a similar light white wine; and after luncheon, kirsch, framboise or port—the first two chilled. Bring out your gayest linens and china. Place a serving table near the host or hostess to cut down on trips to the kitchen.

DOUBLE CHICKEN CONSOMMÉ, JELLIED

COLD TROUT À LA TURQUE

SAUCE VERTE AND GREEN MAYONNAISE

MELBAED ENGLISH MUFFINS

SALADE RACHEL

FROZEN RASPBERRY AND MACAROON MOUSSE

Double Chicken Consommé, Jellied

2 pounds chicken necks	*6 tomatoes, peeled, seeded*
5 pounds chicken backs	*and chopped*
4 quarts water	*Freshly ground black*
Salt	*pepper*
1 onion, stuck with	*1 tablespoon chopped*
2 cloves	*fresh basil*
1 or 2 sprigs parsley	*2 tablespoons chopped*
1 pound chicken gizzards	*parsley*
1 egg white and shell	*Sour cream*
	Chopped chives

Place chicken necks and 2 pounds of the backs in a kettle with the water, 1½ tablespoons salt, onion, and parsley. Bring to a boil, lower the heat, and simmer 2 hours. Taste for seasoning, and simmer another ½ hour. Remove from heat and strain. Return broth to kettle and add remaining backs and the gizzards. Simmer 2 hours. Strain the broth and cool. Skim off all the fat, and clarify. To do this, strain the broth through a fine linen towel. Beat an egg white until frothy, and add the white and egg shell to the broth. Return to the heat, and cook a few minutes, beating with a rotary beater. Strain again through the towel, which has first been wrung out in cold water. The egg white and shell gather all loose particles together and leave the soup perfectly clear. Pour the soup into serving cups, and chill.

Combine the tomatoes with 1 teaspoon salt, freshly ground pepper to taste, basil and chopped parsley. Spoon this mixture over the chilled soup just before serving. Pass sour cream and chopped chives.

Cold Trout à la Turque

> *8 good-sized trout, cleaned*
> *White-wine Court Bouillon* (see *Poached Salmon,*
> *p. 51*)
> *1 tablespoon gelatin, soaked in ¼ cup cold water*
> *Dill, tarragon, or parsley*
> *Fresh-cooked asparagus tips*

Poach the trout in the court bouillon for 10 to 12 minutes or until they flake but are still firm. Cool. Trim the tails, and remove the skin. Arrange on a serving platter or platters. You may, if you wish, clarify the court bouillon. Prepare an aspic: Add gelatin to the court bouillon and chill until on point of setting. Coat the trout with it, adding any desired garnish, such as dill, tarragon or parsley. Surround with chopped, fully set aspic, tiny cooked asparagus tips. Serve with bowls of sauce verte and green mayonnaise.

Sauce Verte

> *1½ cups walnuts*
> *½ cup chopped chives*
> *¼ cup chopped parsley*
> *2 tablespoons chopped tarragon*
> *½ cup olive oil*
> *Salt*
> *Freshly ground black pepper*
> *1 tablespoon lime or lemon juice*

Grind the walnuts or chop them in an electric blender. Mix with the chives, parsley, tarragon, and add the oil. Season to taste with salt and pepper, and blend in the lime or lemon juice. If all the oil is absorbed by the nuts, add a little more—enough to make a smooth paste.

Green Mayonnaise

> *1 cup homemade Mayonnaise* (see *p. 348*)
> ½ *cup mixed finely chopped herbs and greens* (*parsley,*
> *tarragon, watercress, spinach*)

Mix the mayonnaise with the desired selection of chopped fresh herbs, which will lend a delicate green color and a good flavor.

Melbaed English Muffins

Slice 8 English muffins thin, as for Melba toast. Toast them, butter lavishly, and put in a warm oven to dry out and crisp a little. These make a nice change from hot bread or rolls.

Salade Rachel

> *1 celery root or 1 tin sliced celery root*
> *2 good-sized black truffles*
> *6 artichokes, cooked*
> *6 small new potatoes, boiled*
> *3 pounds asparagus, cooked but still crisp*
> *Romaine or Bibb lettuce*
> *Homemade Mayonnaise* (see *p. 348*)

Peel the celery root and cut into fine julienne strips. It may be used raw or blanched for 5 minutes in boiling water and then drained.

Cut the truffles in slices and then into julienne strips. Cut the artichoke bottoms away and trim them neatly. (You may use frozen artichoke hearts and cook according to directions on the package.)

Peel and slice the potatoes; cool. Trim the stalks of the asparagus neatly; cool.

Place a bed of romaine or Bibb lettuce on a large decorative salad server, and arrange bouquets of the celery root, asparagus, sliced potatoes and artichoke bottoms or hearts on top of the greens. Garnish with the truffles, and serve with a good home-made mayonnaise.

Frozen Raspberry and Macaroon Mousse

1 quart fresh raspberries
1 cup sugar
1 cup macaroon crumbs
Pinch salt
⅓ cup framboise
1 quart heavy cream, whipped

Puree the raspberries, and blend with the sugar. Add the macaroon crumbs, salt and framboise. Blend with the cream, pour into a mold and freeze until mushy. Mix well, and freeze until solid.

PICNICS

The English are the greatest of picnickers and have led the field for hundreds of years. They have hampers for the races, outdoor teas for the amusement of children, and all sorts of occasions for sitting and eating in the countryside. In France along the roads one sees families seated in collapsible chairs around a collapsible table eating and drinking with gusto. In Japan elaborate picnic boxes may be purchased to be taken to the football field or to a spot beside a placid pool. Here in America there are picnic tables along the roadside where one may set up a simple meal of sandwiches or do a barbecue.

Wherever it is done, picnicking can be one of the supreme pleasures of outdoor life. At its most elegant, it calls for the accompaniment of the best linens and crystal and china; at its simplest it needs only a bottle of wine and items purchased from the local delicatessen as one passes through town. I recall a recent picnic in France where we bought rillettes de Tours (in Tours), and elsewhere some excellent salade de museau, good bread, ripe tomatoes and cheese. A bottle of local wine and glasses and plates from the Monoprix helped to make this picnic in a heather field near Le Mans a particularly memorable one.

The color and charm of the countryside can make the most modest meal taste superb. Have a picnic at the slightest excuse. It is even fun to have a box lunch and a hot drink in the car on a wintry day, while you look out at a dazzling stretch of landscape.

A FESTIVE COUNTRY OR BEACH PICNIC— WITHOUT SANDWICHES—FOR 8

Serve either martinis or Americanos for cocktails, accompanied by salted nuts. With the food have some lightly cooled Beaujolais or California Mountain Red. Also take along cognac or kirsch to go with the cake, and, of course, fill a great vacuum bottle of hot or iced coffee. To use nice crystal, attractive plates and good cutlery goes without saying.

STUFFED TOMATOES

VEAL AND PORK TERRINE

BEEF À LA MODE EN GELÉE

POTATO SALAD OR GREEN SALAD

FRENCH BREAD   BUTTER

CHEESE   FRUIT

ANGEL FOOD CAKE

Stuffed Tomatoes

8 large ripe tomatoes
2   7-ounce tins tuna in olive oil
2   4-ounce tins anchovy fillets in olive oil
2 medium onions, finely chopped
8 hard-boiled eggs
Black olives
Basil-flavored Vinaigrette Sauce (see p. 350)

Cut off tops of the tomatoes evenly (reserve them), and scoop out the seeds and meat, leaving only the shell. Add pieces of tuna, a few anchovy fillets, some onion, and an egg. Top with another anchovy fillet and 2 or 3 black olives. Replace the tops of the tomatoes, and wrap each one in foil. Chill. Serve with the vinaigrette sauce and additional olives.

Veal and Pork Terrine

½ cup Madeira or sherry
½ cup cognac
4 cloves garlic (2 cloves finely chopped)
½ teaspoon Quatre Épices or Spice Parisienne
1 teaspoon sage
1½ pounds veal scallopine
Bacon
1 pound good sausage meat
Salt and pepper
1 pound ground pork and veal

Make a marinade of the Madeira, cognac, 2 whole garlic cloves, Quatre Épices and sage. Place the veal scallopine in this and soak for several hours, then pour off the marinade and reserve.

Cover the bottom of a 2½-quart terrine or casserole with bacon. Add a layer of the sausage meat, then a bit of the chopped garlic, a layer of veal scallopine and salt and pepper to taste. Continue with a layer of the ground pork and veal mixture, and repeat till the terrine is filled. Pour marinade over the meat, and cover with bacon. Top with chopped garlic. Place a piece of foil over the terrine, and cover. Set in a pan of hot water, and bake at 375° for 2 hours, adding additional hot water to pan if necessary. Cool.

Beef à la Mode en Gelée

4 pounds brisket of beef trimmed of fat	*2 cups white wine*
	1 bay leaf
1 cup chopped beef suet	*1 teaspoon thyme*
⅓ cup cognac	*1 pig's foot, split*
Salt and pepper	*½ teaspoon sugar*

1 cup canned beef bouil-
lon or consommé
6 young carrots

18 small white onions,
peeled

Brown the beef very well on all sides in the melted suet. Blaze with the cognac. Salt and pepper to taste, then add the white wine, bay leaf, thyme, pig's foot, sugar and bouillon. Cover and simmer for 2 hours. Add the carrots and cook another 1½ hours. Finally add the onions, which have been first sautéed in butter and sprinkled with sugar to glaze them. Continue cooking till meat is tender.

Remove the meat after it has cooled slightly, and cut into thinnish slices. Strip the meat from the pig's foot, and slice the carrots. Place meat and vegetables in a terrine or casserole, and pour pan sauces over all. When it is quite cool, remove the fat that has risen to the surface. Wrap the terrine in foil and chill. Carry to the picnic in a portable ice chest.

Serve with Dijon mustard and either a good potato salad or a tossed green salad. Also have crisp French bread or rolls and butter.

Potato Salad

See p. 370.

Cheese

For this picnic you might take along a piece of good aged cheddar and a piece of aged Switzerland Gruyère or Emmenthal. Serve with French bread and butter. Ripe pears or apples would be a good accompaniment also.

Angel Food Cake

1¼ cups egg whites
¼ teaspoon salt
1 teaspoon cream of tartar
1½ cups sugar
1 cup sifted flour
1 tablespoon cognac
½ teaspoon either vanilla or almond

Beat the egg whites with a large whisk or a rotary beater until they form soft peaks. Add salt and cream of tartar and beat till stiff but not dry—firm peaks and glossy surface. Add sugar, a few tablespoons at a time, and fold in gently.

Sprinkle thrice-sifted flour over the surface and fold very carefully but well. Add seasonings and fold lightly. Pour into a 10-inch unbuttered tube pan or into 2 loaf pans or 1 large loaf tin. Bake at 375° about 40 minutes or until cake will spring back when tested with finger.

Invert on a cooling rack. If there are no legs on your tube pan, rest the tube on a bottle or funnel till cool.

A CHAMPAGNE PICNIC FOR 4 OR 6

Here, champagne is the apéritif and the wine. This should be a well-appointed picnic: take good colorful china dinner plates, cups for the soup, additional plates for the fruit and cream cheese, cups for the coffee, and beautiful flutes or all-purpose glasses for the champagne. Also bring a portable ice box or cooler for the wine. Estimate at least half a bottle per person and perhaps some in reserve. That means 4 to 6 bottles.

MACADAMIA NUTS

POTAGE GERMINY

ROAST FILLET OF BEEF

POTATO AND HEARTS OF PALM SALAD

CHERRY TOMATOES

FRENCH OR ITALIAN BREAD

SWEET BUTTER

FRESH FRUIT

CREAM CHEESE OR ROQUEFORT

PETITS FOURS SQUARES

Macadamia Nuts

Take along a large jar of these deliciously flavored nuts to munch with your champagne as you prepare the *déjeuner sur l'herbe*.

Potage Germiny

This is a cold version of the soup.

> *1 cup rich chicken broth*
> *1 can condensed cream of chicken soup*
> *1 can condensed potato soup*
> *1 cup or more finely cut sorrel*
> *3 tablespoons butter*
> *1 cup heavy cream*
> *Salt and pepper*

Combine the chicken broth with the cream of chicken and potato soups. Add the sorrel, first wilting it in a skillet with the butter. Heat the soup just to the boiling point. Cool slightly and add the cream. Add salt and pepper if necessary. Chill for at least 12 hours. Garnish with finely chopped sorrel and parsley, and serve with homemade Melba Toast (*see* p. 329). Carry to the picnic in a vacuum jug.

Roast Fillet of Beef

If your picnic spot is not too far away, roast the fillet just before you depart, and it will be cooled to the perfect state by the time you are ready to eat.

> *1 fillet of beef, 5 to 6 pounds, trimmed*
> *4 to 5 garlic cloves*
> *1 teaspoon salt*
> *1 teaspoon freshly ground black pepper*
> *½ teaspoon Tabasco*
> *1 cup soy sauce (Kikkoman, preferably)*
> *½ cup olive oil*
> *1 cup port wine*
> *1 teaspoon thyme*
> *1 bay leaf*
> *Bacon strips*

Make small gashes in the roast, and fill with the garlic cloves, cut in thin slivers. Rub well with salt, pepper and Tabasco. Marinate in the soy, olive oil, port, and herbs, turning several times.

Place on a rack in a shallow roasting pan, top with a few strips of bacon, and roast at 425° for 30 to 35 minutes. Baste with the marinade several times. A meat thermometer inserted into the heaviest part of the roast should register 125° for rare, or 120° for very rare.

Potato and Hearts of Palm Salad

> *12 small new potatoes*
> *Salted water*
> *¾ cup olive oil*
> *Vinegar to taste*
> *Salt and pepper*
> *1 large Italian red onion*
> *Chopped parsley*
> *1 can hearts of palm, sliced*
> *4 hard-boiled eggs, sliced*

Boil the potatoes in salted water. Drain, and slip off the skins as soon as you can handle the potatoes. Slice fairly thin, and dress with oil, vinegar, salt and pepper to taste. Cool and chill. Just before packing the picnic, add the red onion, thinly sliced, the chopped parsley, and additional oil, vinegar and seasonings, if needed. Garnish at the picnic with hearts of palm and hard-boiled eggs.

Cherry Tomatoes

Fill a large bowl with cherry tomatoes, with some watercress as a garnish. No dressing is necessary. A little salt, possibly, is the only addition required.

Petits Fours Squares

> *2 cups sifted flour*
> *½ teaspoon baking powder*
> *⅛ teaspoon salt*

1 cup butter
2 teaspoons vanilla
1 cup light brown sugar, firmly packed
1¾ cups semisweet chocolate bits
½ cup finely chopped toasted almonds

Preheat the oven to 350°. Sift together the flour, baking powder and salt. Set aside. Blend the butter and vanilla, and gradually beat in the brown sugar. Add the flour mixture, chocolate bits and almonds, and blend well. Spread evenly in an ungreased 13-by 9-inch pan. Bake for 30 minutes. Remove from the oven and cool.

For frosting: Combine 1½ cups sifted confectioners' sugar, 3 tablespoons light corn syrup, 2 tablespoons milk, and ¼ teaspoon vanilla. Spread over cake. Decorate with chocolate glaze.

Chocolate Glaze: Melt over hot (not boiling) water ¼ cup semisweet chocolate bits and 1½ teaspoons vegetable shortening. Stir till blended. Drizzle or apply with a pastry tube in thin lines, lengthwise, about 1 inch apart. Then draw the tip of a knife or a toothpick across the lines of Chocolate Glaze, again about 1 inch apart, starting from one side of the pan and returning from the opposite side. This will pull the glaze along slightly and give the decoration a "feathered" look. Let stand till the frosting is set, then cut in 1-inch squares. This will yield 8 dozen petits fours.

AN ELEGANT PICNIC FOR THE BEACH

Bring along quantities of chilled Almaden rosé, but if you want to be truly elegant, nothing will do but iced champagne!

ROQUEFORT LOAF

SPECIAL STUFFED EGGS

CHICKEN SANDWICHES

FOIE GRAS SANDWICHES

CHERRY TOMATOES

FRESH PEACH ICE CREAM

SAND TARTS

Roquefort Loaf

1½ pounds Roquefort cheese
1 pound (or more) cream cheese
½ pound butter
Cognac
Crushed pecans

Blend the Roquefort, cream cheese and butter thoroughly and flavor with a little cognac. Add more cream cheese if necessary. The mixture should be quite stiff. Roll it out into a long sausage shape and then roll in crushed (not chopped) pecans. Chill the cheese roll in the refrigerator until very firm. Slice and serve with rounds of hot toast.

Special Stuffed Eggs

> *24 eggs*
> *1 tin mousse de foie gras*
> *1 tablespoon sour cream*
> *2 tablespoons chopped parsley*
> *1 truffle, finely chopped*
> *Salt and freshly ground black pepper*
> *Cognac*
> *24 truffle slices*

These are not the usual picnic eggs. They are very elegant, decorative and tasty.

Cook the eggs until just hard; remove the shells and cool. Cut a thin slice from the broad end of each egg to enable the eggs to stand upright on the serving dish.

Slice off the small ends of the eggs so that you can scoop out the yolks. Mash the yolks well and mix with the mousse de foie gras, sour cream, parsley, chopped truffle and salt and pepper to taste. Add enough cognac to make a good paste. Using the rosette tube of a pastry bag, force the yolk mixture back into the eggs and finish off the top of each egg with a decorative swirl. Top each with a slice of truffle and chill well. You may also glaze the eggs with aspic.

VARIATION: Mash the egg yolks and blend them with 3 tablespoons mayonnaise. Add 1 tin boneless and skinless sardines mashed, ½ cup finely chopped chives, ¼ teaspoon Tabasco, 1 teaspoon lemon juice and salt and freshly ground pepper to taste. Mix thoroughly and pipe this filling into the eggs, using directions above. Top with chopped chives or parsley.

Chicken Sandwiches

There is no substitute for really good chicken sandwiches. The only trick is to make certain that you use the very best ingredients.

Personally, I believe that chicken sandwiches should always be made with good homemade bread sliced very thin. If you freeze the bread and slice it as it is thawing, you can get nice even slices. Butter well with softened sweet butter and top with plenty of thinly sliced cold chicken. Season to taste with salt and freshly ground pepper and cover with a second slice of well-buttered bread.

Trim the crusts from the sandwiches and cut them into fingersized pieces. Wrap these in foil and cover them with a damp cloth or store them in the refrigerator.

VARIATION: Spread the bread with mustard-flavored or tarragon-flavored butter.

Foie Gras Sandwiches

Spread thin slices of homemade bread with a puree of foie gras and softened buttter. Remove the crusts and cut into finger-sized pieces.

Fresh Peach Ice Cream

Make the ice cream in a freezer ahead of time, pack the freezer with salt and ice (as directed for mellowing), and bring the whole freezer along. Serve directly from the freezer.

Sand Tarts

> 2½ sticks (10 ounces) butter
> 2 cups sugar
> 3 egg yolks
> 3 egg whites, beaten stiff but not dry
> 4¼ cups flour
> Cinnamon and sugar
> Almonds (optional)

Cream the butter and sugar together, and add egg yolks. Beat well and add the egg whites. Then blend in the flour, and beat well. Chill dough several hours.

Roll out a little at a time (keep the rest of the dough refrigerated) as thin as possible, and cut into rounds with a cookie cutter. Place on lightly buttered baking sheets, and brush with white of egg. Sprinkle with sugar and cinnamon. Bake at 425° for 8 to 10 minutes. Place half a blanched almond on each cookie, if you wish.

A BEER PICNIC FOR A LARGE GATHERING

This is easy to prepare, for the most part. The essential thing is to provide for thorough cooling of the beer. Take along a few bottles of wine for those who don't happen to like beer. Of course, there should be an ample amount of coffee in thermos jugs to go with the dessert—a huge apple kuchen.

SAUSAGE BOARD

WESTPHALIAN HAM

BOILED OR BAKED HAM

COLD MEAT LOAF

DEVILED EGGS   CAVIAR EGGS

PUNGENT EGGS

COLE SLAW

SENFGURKEN   DILL PICKLES

EMMENTHAL CHEESE

RYE BREAD, PUMPERNICKEL AND BUTTER

APPLE KUCHEN

Sausage Board

Get as wide a selection of sausage as you can find, and take knives and a cutting board to the picnic. Here are some possibilities:

Summer Sausage	*Teawurst*
Blutwurst	*Yachtwurst*
Lebanon Bologna	*Cooked Bratwurst*
Lachschinken	*Goose Liverwurst*
Kielbasy	*Tongue Sausage*
Leberwurst	*Mettwurst*
Cervelat	*Beer Sausage*

Cold Meat Loaf

Make your favorite meat loaf. Weight it down while it cools. Refrigerate. Serve sliced thin.

Deviled Eggs

Combine the hard-boiled yolks of 8 eggs with 1 small tin of boneless and skinless sardines, 1 small onion finely chopped, and ¼ cup of parsley. Bind with mayonnaise, and fill the egg halves.

Caviar Eggs

Combine the yolks of 8 hard-boiled eggs with 3 tablespoons caviar and 3 tablespoons onion juice. Bind with sour cream. Fill egg halves and decorate with caviar.

Pungent Eggs

2 garlic cloves, finely minced
1 tablespoon curry powder
1 tablespoon butter
8 hard-boiled eggs
1 tablespoon finely chopped chutney
Sour cream or mayonnaise
Chopped peanuts

Cook the garlic and curry powder in butter for 3 minutes. Combine with the egg yolks and chutney, and bind with sour cream or mayonnaise. Fill the egg halves, and garnish with chopped peanuts.

Cole Slaw

> *1 white cabbage, finely shredded*
> *1 red cabbage, finely shredded*
> *1 small onion, finely chopped*
> *1 tablespoon celery seed*
> *1½ cups mayonnaise*
> *1 cup sour cream*
> *1 teaspoon finely chopped fresh dill*
> *Salt and pepper*

Combine all ingredients, and toss well. Allow to stand for at least 2 hours in the refrigerator before serving. Garnish with additional mayonnaise and dill.

Apple Kuchen

> *Sweet Dough* (see p. 354)
> *6 to 8 green apples, peeled and thinly sliced*
> *1 cup sugar*
> *¾ cup butter* (approximately)

Prepare a sweet dough. After the first rising, roll out, and fit into an 11- by 14-inch buttered pan. Cover with the apples, which should be pressed lightly into the dough and placed close together. Sprinkle with sugar, and dot heavily with the butter. Let rise 10 minutes. Bake at 375° till the apples are fairly soft and the dough pleasantly brown and crisp. Serve with whipped cream, if you wish; or you may spread an Apricot Glaze (*see* p. 38) on this after it cools.

☙ AN ANTIPASTO PICNIC

This is eminently easy to prepare. In fact, the whole picnic may be assembled by shopping at the Italian delicatessens and the vegetable market. Bring along a thermos or vacuum jug of cocktails, or bring a cooler of ice and make Campari and soda or Americanos. Drink a well-chilled Soave with your food. You might also have a thermos jug of espresso coffee to finish off the meal, or make coffee on the spot, if you have the type of coffee pot which is heated by an alcohol burner.

Use paper plates and paper napkins, but have real glasses for the drinks!

For the Picnic

Loaves of good bread and plenty of sweet butter.

Sardines—Buy several different varieties, and serve them with lemon, hard-boiled eggs and perhaps mayonnaise.

Tuna Fish—Look for fillets of tuna packed in olive oil.

Anchovies—A large tin of fillets in olive oil. Scallions, capers and additional oil should accompany both the tuna and the anchovies.

Shrimp—Poached in a spiced bouillon and cooled in the shell.

Mortadella—Large Italian-style bologna.

Salami—Have it cut thin.

Prosciutto—Also cut thin. Serve with breadsticks.

Capocollo—This is hot Italian ham, and delicious it is.

Peperoni—This is a small dried sausage.

Caponata—Available in tins, an eggplant relish delicious with this type of meal.

Cherry Tomatoes.

Fennel—If in season.

Black and green olives.

Watercress.

Provolone and Gorgonzola cheese.

Also pack a large basket of fresh fruit—peaches, pears, cherries, melons, and whatever else the market offers.

CELEBRATIONS

Holiday dinners used to be staggering affairs with an over-whelming number of courses and many extra items that had been especially prepared for the occasion—cakes and pies of many flavors, all kinds of relishes, and a profusion of vegetables accompanying the main dish. It was as if one had ordered every-thing on the menu of a great, old-fashioned American-plan hotel!

Nowadays, save for communities far from the rush of modern life, there is not the same leisure or desire for a meal of such proportions. And the economic and sociological conditions are no longer the same. No longer available are the "hired girls" and "the generals" who cooked and cleaned and spent thirteen or fourteen hours a day attending the needs of a family. Also, fami-lies are smaller. The holiday dinner is no longer the conference table for great family conclaves. And no longer does the hostess try to outdo her relatives and friends in the production of a holi-day menu.

The emphasis today is on less work in the kitchen, but we are more particular about what we eat than our forebears—many of us are calorie-conscious—and we eat considerably less. Nowa-days it is a small group, usually, who sits down to a somewhat streamlined holiday dinner with good friends, good food and good wine. It is a satisfying compromise with tradition.

A NEW YEAR'S EVE PARTY FOR 20

New Year's Eve can be deadly if you let it get out of hand. The secret is to start off with drinks and rather substantial snacking at about 9:30. Toward 11:30 have supper ready and timed so the pièce de résistance and wine come along at the right moment to toast the old year out and the new in. With your guests thus fortified with food, you won't have nearly the number of cas-ualties on your hands that might be expected at the usual New Year's party. After dessert, coffee and a couple of drinks, people will be ready to go home—or on to their own merrymaking.

For the drinking period have a bar setup, with the addition of a good red and white wine, and champagne, of course. Here are suggestions for snacking:

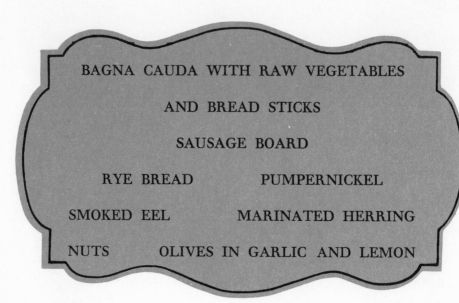

BAGNA CAUDA WITH RAW VEGETABLES

AND BREAD STICKS

SAUSAGE BOARD

RYE BREAD   PUMPERNICKEL

SMOKED EEL   MARINATED HERRING

NUTS   OLIVES IN GARLIC AND LEMON

The main part of the following supper may be assembled well in advance. In fact, the oxtail ragout improves with sitting. Only the noodles need be cooked at the last moment.

It is possible to do this party with absolutely no help. Even use paper plates—there are many attractive ones on the market—if you want to begin the New Year without dishwashing.

With the ragout and the cheese drink a good vin ordinaire, such as the California Mountain Red of Louis Martini, or a good French Beaujolais. Cognac, kirsch and mirabelle should be offered with coffee.

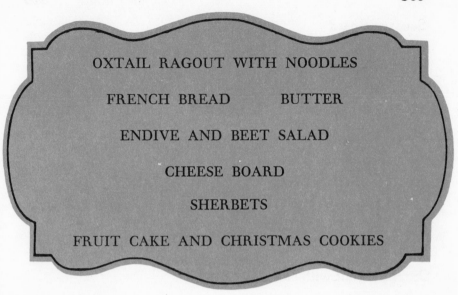

OXTAIL RAGOUT WITH NOODLES

FRENCH BREAD   BUTTER

ENDIVE AND BEET SALAD

CHEESE BOARD

SHERBETS

FRUIT CAKE AND CHRISTMAS COOKIES

Bagna Cauda

This "hot bath," literally, is made in a fondue or chafing dish and kept warm over low heat. Surround it with bowls of raw vegetables in ice and with plenty of bread sticks. Let people dunk to their heart's content. For 20 persons I would have two dishes going and enough mixture in the kitchen for replenishments.

For each dish :

> *1 quart olive oil*
> *8 garlic cloves, finely cut*
> *14 to 16 anchovy fillets, finely chopped*
> *Salt and freshly ground pepper*
> *1 teaspoon rosemary or oregano, or 1 of each*

Combine ingredients, and heat gently over low flame. Transfer to fondue or chafing dish, and keep warm.

The vegetables for dunking might include celery, fennel, carrot sticks, turnip slices, radishes, scallions, and cauliflower buds. The crisp, cold vegetables make an unusual contrast with the bagna cauda.

It would be a good idea to have plenty of small plates and paper napkins on hand near the dunking.

Sausage Board

Provide a large cutting board, good knives and forks, and a selection of sausages—kielbasy, bologna, mortadella, salami, Thuringer, ham salami, Lebanon bologna, Braunschweiger, Yachtwurst, etc. Thinly sliced rye and pumpernickel and plenty of sweet butter go with this, and also have several types of mustard and some really good pickles—dill, sour and sweet.

Smoked Eel and Marinated Herring

For 20 persons you will need about 3 pounds of smoked eel and about 12 fillets of herring (with sour cream and onions). You might also have some smoked herring if you are fond of it.

Oxtail Ragout with Noodles

15 to 16 pounds oxtail, cut into small joints	*3 bay leaves*
Flour	*1 tablespoon thyme*
1 cup chopped beef suet	*2 tablespoons salt*
½ cup butter	*1 tablespoon freshly*
6 large onions, peeled and sliced	*ground black pepper*
10 cloves garlic, finely chopped	*3 cloves*
	Dash nutmeg
18 carrots, cut in rounds	*Stock*
6 turnips, thinly sliced	*Red wine*
	Chopped parsley

Flour the joints lightly, and brown a few at a time in melted suet and butter, adding more fat if needed. When the joints are browned, transfer to one or two large kettles. Brown the onions and garlic lightly in the same fat. Add to the kettles, along with the carrots, turnips and seasonings. Just barely cover with 2 parts stock to 1 part red wine, bring to a boil, and boil for 5 minutes. Remove any scum that forms. Reduce the heat and simmer for 3 hours or until tender. Cool thoroughly and remove fat. Chill till ready to use.

Reheat over low flame, and thicken to taste with flour and butter kneaded together. Correct the seasoning. Just before serving, sprinkle with chopped parsley. Serve with noodles. For this party you will need about 5 pounds of noodles. Cook them in boiling salted water, adding a generous dash of oil, till just tender. Toss well with butter and grated Parmesan cheese.

Endive and Beet Salad

Use either Belgian endive cut into 1-inch lengths or chicory (curly endive, as it is called in some places). For 20 persons, you will need 5 pounds of Belgian endive or three or four heads of chicory. Combine with 5 beets, peeled and coarsely chopped.

For the dressing: 1½ cups wine vinegar, 1 tablespoon salt, and freshly ground black pepper to taste.

You will have to toss this salad in three or more bowls, unless you have an outsized bowl and a giant pair of tools.

Cheese Board

Buy half a Roquefort cheese, a good piece of Canadian or Vermont cheddar, and a Brie, if they are available, and perhaps a large piece of Switzerland Emmenthal. Serve bread and butter with the cheese, and plenty of red wine.

Sherbets

Buy good commercial sherbets and store in your freezer. Raspberry, lemon and pineapple would make a nice selection. Serve with all your leftover Christmas fruitcakes and cookies.

 # NEW YEAR'S DAY DINNER FOR 6

This used to be a more important meal than it is nowadays. Perhaps everyone attends a number of open-house parties and has neither time nor appetite for a big holiday meal. At any rate, this is a modestly festive menu and one easy to do.

Serve whatever drinks you fancy before dinner. With dinner

I suggest a nice light Bordeaux—a Prieuré Lichine or a Château Beychevelle. With coffee—Grand Marnier and cognac. May you never have a worse meal!

PÂTÉ DE CAMPAGNE   BUTTERED TOAST

STUFFED SQUAB CHICKENS

PUREED POTATOES   TINY PEAS

FRESH PEARS AND CHEESE

Pàté de Campagne

See p. 245–246.

Stuffed Squab Chickens

> *6 squab chickens*
> *3 cups finely cut scallions*
> *Butter*
> *1½ pounds sausage meat*
> *4 cups crumbs*
> *2 eggs*
> *½ cup chopped parsley*
> *1 tablespoon tarragon*
> *½ cup cognac*
> *Salt and pepper*

Sauté the scallions lightly in butter. Remove and, in the same pan, sauté the sausage meat, breaking it up with a fork. Combine the scallions and sausage meat with the remaining ingredients, seasoning to taste with salt and pepper.

Stuff the chickens, truss them, and butter well. Place on a rack in a shallow pan. Roast on one side for 15 minutes. Baste and turn to other side for 15 minutes more. Then place on backs and continue roasting till tender and nicely browned. Remove to a hot platter, and rinse the pan with additional cognac—about ⅓ cup. Pour this over the birds. Garnish with parsley and water-cress.

Pureed Potatoes

> *6 to 8 large potatoes, peeled and quartered*
> *½ pound butter*
> *½ cup heavy cream or more*
> *1½ teaspoons salt*
> *Freshly ground black pepper*

Cook potatoes in boiling salted water till just tender. Do not let them get watersoaked and soggy. Drain, and return to heat for 2 or 3 minutes, shaking the pan. Mash or put through a food mill. Blend with butter and cream, using a whisk. Add salt, freshly ground pepper to taste, transfer to a hot dish, and top with an additional dollop of butter.

NOTE: Some chefs say that potatoes should never be whipped —only mashed, in an up and down motion! Use your own judgment.

Tiny Peas

Use the boil-in-the-bag variety that come in a butter sauce.

Fresh Pears and Cheese

The delicious Oregon pears are at their peak at the beginning of the year. Most of us seem to get them as early as Christmas. Look for them at a good fruiterer's.

Serve ripe with Roquefort, a fine Camembert, or even with cream cheese and preserves.

A NEW YEAR'S DAY OPEN HOUSE

This is a day to cater to all different tastes. Some are nursing heads—for them we nominate cognac milk punch; some can't take a drink because of New Year's resolutions—for them tomato juice or milk; the others will drink as usual—for them champagne, Scotch, vodka, martinis or bourbon.

TINY PIZZAS BRIOCHE SANDWICHES

HORS D'OEUVRE STRUDEL

HOT KIELBASY WITH MUSTARDS

KATHARINE SMITH'S TINY NEW POTATOES

CHICKEN SANDWICHES

Tiny Pizzas

For the dough :

> *1 cake or 1 package of dry yeast*
> *1 cup warm water*
> *1 teaspoon sugar*
> *1 tablespoon salt*
> *2 tablespoons olive oil*
> *4 cups sifted flour (approximately)*

Dissolve yeastcake or dry yeast in warm water. Add sugar, salt, olive oil, and 2 cups flour. Beat until smooth. Gradually add additional sifted flour (1½ to 2 cups) to make a firm dough. Toss on a lightly floured board, and knead until smooth and elastic. Rub with olive oil and place in a bowl in a warm place to rise until double in bulk. When dough has risen, punch down, and

cut in half. Roll out to about ⅜ inch in thickness. Cut into small rounds with a cookie or biscuit cutter, and arrange on a buttered baking sheet. I suggest you bake a half at a time.
For Tomato Sauce:

> *1 No. 303 can Italian plum tomatoes*
> *2 cloves garlic*
> *1½ teaspoons basil*
> *1 can Italian tomato paste*
> *2 tablespoons olive oil*
> *Salt and pepper*

Cook the plum tomatoes, garlic and basil over medium heat for 20 minutes. Add the tomato paste and the oil. Cook down until thick and smooth. Season to taste. Strain, if you wish.
For the topping:

> *Mozzarella or Swiss Gruyère, grated*
> *Anchovy fillets*
> *Black olives*
> *Salami or coteghino*
> *Sardines*
> *Mushrooms*
> *Grated Parmesan*

Place a layer of grated mozzarella or Gruyère on the pizza, brush with tomato sauce, and sprinkle with freshly ground pepper and basil. On some pizzas place anchovy fillets and black olives; on others place thin slices of salami or coteghino; on the remaining ones place sardines or sliced cooked mushrooms. Sprinkle with grated Parmesan cheese. Brush lightly with oil. Bake at 400° until puffy and crisp on the edges.

Brioche Sandwiches

Cut brioche or chalah (or in a pinch, good white bread) into thin slices, and cut these into rounds with a cutter. Peel and slice thinly about 6 or 8 small white onions. Chop finely 1 large bunch of parsley or more. Have a bowl of mayonnaise at hand. Spread the rounds of bread with mayonnaise, top half of them with slices of onion and salt them well. Top these with the remaining rounds, and press them together firmly. Roll the edges in mayonnaise and then chopped parsley. Chill in the refrigerator several hours before serving.

Hors d'Oeuvre Strudel

> *Strudel leaves or fila sheet*
> *½ cup butter*
> *1½ cups filling (duxelle, cheese, liver, etc. Leftovers may be used, or a combination of cheese, and nuts, poppy seeds, etc.)*
> *More melted butter*

Thaw strudel leaves. Unroll on baking sheet or board. Brush well with melted butter. Spread filling. Roll and brush with additional butter. Place on buttered baking-sheet. Bake in a 375° oven for 10 to 20 minutes, depending upon filling. Cut in 1-inch slices. Serve hot.

Hot Kielbasy with Mustards

Various forms of Polish sausage may be found in almost any city in the country. Poach a large sausage for 25 to 35 minutes in a bouillon of half wine, half water, to which an onion has been added. Cut in slices, and serve hot with a variety of mustards and sliced pumpernickel.

Katharine Smith's New Potatoes

Choose the smallest new potatoes you can find. Scrub well, and boil with jackets on in salted water till just tender. With a small ball cutter, scoop out a hole in each potato, and fill with sour cream mixed with fresh dill or chives. Serve hot with coarse salt. These are to be eaten with the fingers. They are incredibly delicious.

Chicken Sandwiches

And I mean *chicken!* Too many people make turkey sandwiches, which are all right too, but there is an incomparable flavor to the fine white meat of chicken, thinly sliced and placed between slices of well-buttered bread with only the addition of a bit of salt and mayonnaise.

For this party poach four large roasting chickens. Reserve the dark meat for a chicken salad or chicken crêpes later on in the week. Allow the white meat to cool—do not refrigerate—and slice thin. Spread good white or whole wheat bread, preferably homemade, with sweet butter, and add slices of chicken. Salt lightly, and brush with mayonnaise. Trim sandwiches and pack in foil, waxed paper, or plastic till ready to cut and use. Keep cool with a wet towel rather than refrigerate.

 AN EASTER BREAKFAST FOR 10 OR 12

I feel that a festive event calls for good strong drinks. Nothing is better in the morning than the enlivening vodka drinks—Bloody Marys and Screwdrivers. With the drinks serve a plate of thinly sliced prosciutto and another of good bread sticks. Those with sesame seeds are superb. Let your guests roll their own—a slice of prosciutto around each bread stick. Also, colored Easter eggs help to set the theme and make excellent snacks. Have radishes, too—the harbinger of spring.

Drink a delicious rosé with this breakfast. A California rosé, properly chilled, would be ideal.

BREAD STICKS WITH PROSCIUTTO

EASTER EGGS   RADISHES

SHENANDOAH FRIED CHICKEN   CREAM GRAVY

BOILED NEW POTATOES

ASPARAGUS, VINAIGRETTE

HOT FRENCH BREAD   SWEET BUTTER

STRAWBERRY PRESERVES   BUCKWHEAT HONEY

FRUIT BASKET

Shenandoah Fried Chicken

> *12 chicken legs and thighs*
> *12 gizzards*
> *Hearts*
> *Flour*
> *2 eggs, beaten with 3 tablespoons water*
> *Coarsely rolled cracker crumbs, seasoned with salt and*
>   *pepper*
> *¼ pound butter*
> *2 cups vegetable shortening or 1½ cups olive oil*
> *4 tablespoons flour*
> *2 cups cream*
> *Salt and pepper*

I prefer the legs and thighs for this dish, for they are so much more juicy. The gizzards and hearts are for those who love them as much as I. Flour all parts well, dip into beaten egg, and then roll in cracker crumbs. Chill for 30 minutes to 1 hour, being careful to press the seasoned crumbs firmly into the chicken.

Melt the butter and vegetable shortening or olive oil in a heavy skillet or two. The fat should be about 1 inch deep. Add pieces of chicken, gizzards and hearts, and be sure to begin the thighs and legs skin-side down. Cook over fairly brisk heat till nicely browned, then turn and brown on other side. Reduce the heat, and continue cooking for about 15 to 18 minutes. Cover the pan for some of the cooking. Remove chicken pieces to absorbent paper placed on a baking sheet, and heat in a 250° oven for a few minutes while you make the cream gravy.

Cream Gravy

Pour off all the fat from the skillet, save 3 tablespoons. Add flour and blend well. Scrape in all bits of delicious crumbs that stick to the pan. Finally stir in cream, and continue stirring until the sauce thickens nicely. Season with salt and freshly ground black pepper, and allow to simmer for a few minutes. Pour into a sauceboat, and serve with chicken.

Boiled New Potatoes

See p. 365.

Asparagus, Vinaigrette

Cook 4 pounds or more of asparagus in boiling salted water till just tender and still crisp. (I find a large skillet works perfectly for this.) Drain and serve warm with Vinaigrette Sauce (*see* p. 350).

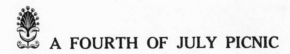 **A FOURTH OF JULY PICNIC**

This is a far cry from the old-time picnics with the traditional fried chicken, homemade potato salad and all the provender of the early 1910's and '20's. Here, we are going to be unorthodox and elegant.

If you begin with chilled champagne, continue with it

throughout the meal. Or serve a white wine cassis followed with a very young Beaujolais, lightly chilled. With the drinks serve small frankfurters (if you have a means of heating them) and crisp rolls. Or serve a fine bologna and liverwurst and crisp rolls. Pass hot mustard and salad mustard.

TINY FRANKFURTERS AND CRISP ROLLS

COLD LOBSTER WITH SPICY MAYONNAISE

GLAZED FILLET OF BEEF

RICE SALAD   VEGETABLE SALAD

CHERRY TOMATOES

PUMPERNICKEL BREAD AND BUTTER SANDWICHES

HOMEMADE BREAD WITH GARLIC BUTTER

GLENNA McGINNIS LANE CAKE

FRESH STRAWBERRIES OR RASPBERRIES

WITH KIRSCH

Cold Lobster

Poach a 1- to 1½-pound lobster for each person. Cool, and pack in a portable ice box. At the picnic, split each lobster with a large knife. Provide nutcrackers for the claws.

Spicy Mayonnaise

> 1 pint homemade Mayonnaise (see p. 348)
> ½ cup sour cream
> 1 cup chopped green onions

> 1 tablespoon tomato paste
> 1 tablespoon Worcestershire sauce
> 1 teaspoon Tabasco
> ¼ cup chopped parsley

Blend together and let stand for an hour or two before using.

Glazed Fillet of Beef

Marinate for several hours or overnight a whole fillet, well trimmed and fat removed, in 1 cup Japanese soy sauce, ⅓ cup olive oil, 4 finely chopped garlic cloves, ½ cup sherry. Turn several times.

Roast on a rack in a 425° oven, basting with the marinade from time to time, for about 28 to 30 minutes. Cool, and tote to picnic in foil. If you are not driving too far, do not even chill it.

Rice Salad

Combine 4 cups cooked rice with ½ cup olive oil, 2 tablespoons wine vinegar, and salt and freshly ground pepper to taste. Toss well and garnish with ⅓ cup finely chopped pimiento and a tablespoon chopped basil. Keep in portable ice box.

Vegetable Salad

Wrap up peeled and sliced beefsteak tomatoes, peeled and sliced cucumbers, crisp cooked whole green beans, sliced cooked beets, grated raw carrot, raw sweet peas and greens of your choice. Arrange on a plate or in a bowl at picnic spot, and toss with a jar of Vinaigrette Sauce (*see* p. 350) at the last minute. Or arrange on a platter, and serve the sauce separately. This is the preferred way.

Glenna McGinnis Lane Cake

> 1¾ cups butter
> 3¾ cups granulated sugar
> 1 teaspoon vanilla
> 3¼ cups sifted all-purpose flour
>
> 3½ teaspoons double-acting baking powder
> 1¼ teaspoons salt
> 1 cup milk
> 8 egg whites, beaten till stiff but not dry

12 egg yolks
½ cup rye or bourbon
whiskey
1½ cups coarsely chopped
pecans

1½ cups chopped seeded
raisins
1½ cups shredded fresh
coconut
1½ cups quartered
candied cherries

Grease four round layer pans (1 inch deep, 9 inches in diameter) with a little butter, and line bottoms with waxed paper cut to fit. If you have only 2 pans, simply bake 2 layers at a time.

With an electric mixer or a large spoon beat 1 cup butter in a large bowl until fluffy. Gradually add 2 cups sugar, beating after each addition until fluffy. Add vanilla, and beat until mixture is as light as whipped cream.

Sift, then lightly spoon 3¼ cups flour in a measuring cup. Level top with spatula. Put into a sifter, add baking powder and ¾ teaspoon salt. Sift onto a large piece of waxed paper. Add to butter mixture, alternating with the milk, beating in small amounts at a time. Fold in beaten egg whites carefully, and distribute evenly.

Divide batter among 4 pans and spread to sides with a spatula. Place on two oven racks so that one pan is not directly beneath another—one rack set in the middle of the oven, the other about 2 inches below. Bake about 15 minutes or until the cake shrinks from the sides of pan and springs back to light pressure of the finger. Let pans stand on cake racks 5 minutes. Carefully loosen edges and turn out upside down on racks. Slowly peel off waxed paper. Cool before frosting.

Put egg yolks in top part of a double boiler, and beat slightly with rotary beater. Add 1¾ cups sugar, ½ teaspoon salt, and ¾ cup butter. Cook over simmering water, stirring constantly until sugar is dissolved, butter melts, and mixture is slightly thickened. Do not overcook or eggs will become scrambled. Remove from heat, and add rye or bourbon, beating for 1 minute with rotary beater. Add nuts, raisins, coconut and cherries. Mix, and cool.

Spread frosting between layers and on top and sides. After an hour, if any has dripped off, spread it back on sides. Repeat if necessary. Cover with cake cover or loosely with foil, and store to ripen in a cool place for several days. The cake will keep well in storage for several weeks. If it is to be frozen, wrap in vapor-proof wrapping, and store. It will keep indefinitely.

MY OWN VERSION OF THANKSGIVING DINNER

I bow to tradition inasmuch as I usually have a turkey, but the meal is relatively simple. I always serve champagne, accompanied by nuts and celery or other raw vegetables, or perhaps olives flavored with olive oil and finely chopped garlic.

You may serve champagne or your favorite cocktails, as you wish. With the caviar or smoked salmon, serve either chilled vodka or champagne; and with the turkey and cheese courses, a fine Bordeaux—a Lascombes or a Château Haut Brion. You may also offer a sweet sauterne for the dessert. If you are so steeped in tradition that you must have cranberries with your turkey, have them, but be warned that they will impair the taste of wine! Drink kirsch, framboise or cognac.

CAVIAR OR SMOKED SALMON

BUTTERED PUMPERNICKEL OR RYE

TURKEY WITH TARRAGON CRUMB AND

SPICED SAUSAGE STUFFING

PAN SAUCE WITH GIBLETS

MASHED YELLOW TURNIPS WITH BUTTER

SALAD

CHEESE

RICH PUMPKIN PIE

Tarragon Crumb Stuffing for a 12-Pound Turkey

2½ quarts (10 cups) freshly made bread crumbs
2 cups finely chopped scallions or shallots
¾ pound butter
1 tablespoon or more tarragon, to taste
½ cup chopped parsley
2 teaspoons salt
1 teaspoon freshly ground black pepper

Make the crumbs in an electric blender, or grate them. French or Italian bread is recommended, and you may use part whole wheat if you wish. Place the scallions or shallots in a pan with the butter, and heat just enough to melt the butter. Mix with the crumbs, add the seasonings, and toss well. Taste for salt. If the stuffing is too dry, add a little sherry, cognac or turkey broth.

Stuff the larger cavity, place a piece of folded foil in the vent, and secure the vent with skewers or sew it.

Spiced Sausage Stuffing (for the neck vent)

First remove the neck, leaving the skin intact.

2½ pounds lean ground pork
1 clove garlic, finely chopped
¼ cup finely chopped parsley
1 teaspoon or more of salt
½ teaspoon Tabasco
¼ teaspoon nutmeg
1 teaspoon freshly ground black pepper
1 teaspoon thyme
1 tablespoon cognac

Combine ingredients, blend well, and fill the neck cavity. Mold into shape, and sew or skewer the skin to the bird.

To Roast the Turkey

I like to use a rack placed in a shallow pan. Tie the legs securely or run a larding needle through the thighs with string attached and then tie this around the legs. Rub turkey well with butter, and sprinkle with salt and pepper. Place breast side down on the rack, and cover lightly with a piece of foil. Roast at 325° for 1 hour. Turn on one side, baste, and continue roasting another 45 minutes. Turn on opposite side, and repeat. Remove foil, turn turkey breast side up, and baste well. Continue roasting till done—45 minutes to 1 hour. Baste 2 or 3 times more during this last period. If there are not enough pan juices for basting, combine ¼ pound melted butter with ½ cup white wine.

It is difficult to tell when a turkey is perfectly done, because turkeys vary so in structure and tenderness. A standard test is to see if the legs and thighs move up and down freely. For a more accurate test insert a meat thermometer into the thickest part of one thigh without touching the bone. The interior temperature should be about 170°.

Allow the turkey to settle in a warm place for 15 to 20 minutes before carving.

To Serve: Remove the strings and skewers from the turkey, and place on a hot platter large enough to allow for carving. Garnish discreetly with watercress; the carver needs all the space he can find. The carver's implements should include a sharp carving knife; a small, sharp boning knife for the legs, thighs, and wings; spoons for the stuffing; a large fork for holding the bird; and a serving fork. A small extra platter for the legs, thighs, and wings is valuable also.

Pan Sauce with Giblets

You may either use the pan drippings in reasonable quantity, or you may pour off all but 2 tablespoons, adding 1½ cups giblet broth, together with the giblets, chopped. If you do the latter, cook down for 4 minutes, correct the seasoning and thicken with butter and flour kneaded together. Add 2 tablespoons Madeira or cognac.

Mashed Yellow Turnips with Butter

For 6 persons peel and slice 2 medium or one very large yellow turnip—or rutabaga or swedes, according to the part of the country in which you live. Cook in boiling salted water till tender.

Drain and mash with ¼ pound butter. Add salt and freshly ground pepper to taste.

NOTE: If you must have mashed potatoes, that is your privilege. For my starch, I prefer the dressing!

Salad

Serve a simple romaine or Bibb lettuce salad with a basic Vinaigrette Sauce (*see* p. 350).

Cheese

Select 2 or 3 good cheeses of varying types and serve with toasted French bread or rolls.

Rich Pumpkin Pie

Plain Pastry for 2 9-inch shells (*see* p. 359–360)

> *2 cups mashed pumpkin—canned is ideal*
> *6 eggs*
> *2 cups heavy cream*
> *¼ teaspoon salt*
> *⅔ cup sugar*
> *1 teaspoon cinnamon*
> *¼ teaspoon ground cloves*
> *½ cup finely cut preserved or candied ginger*
> *½ cup cognac*
> *¼ teaspoon mace*

Fill shells with foil and beans and bake at 425° for 12 minutes. Remove foil and beans.

Place pumpkin in a bowl and make a well in center. Add lightly beaten eggs combined with heavy cream, seasonings and chopped ginger. Blend thoroughly. Correct the seasoning—you may want a spicier pie. Pour into the partially baked pie shells, and bake at 375° till custard is just set.

I prefer to serve this pie on the warm side with cognac-flavored and sweetened whipped cream.

A CHRISTMAS EVE SUPPER

This can be a delightfully informal meal to be partaken of by the family, invited guests, and close friends who drop in unannounced to leave a gift or to say Merry Christmas. Provide a selection of favorite drinks, including champagne. Eschew if you can Tom and Jerries and eggnogs, which to me are unpalatable concoctions that ruin the appetite! For the food, I like a rather international menu.

With the food serve chilled champagne and white wine (perhaps a Pouilly-Fumé) or a California Mountain Red or Pinot Chardonnay. Also offer beer and soft drinks.

SMOKED-FISH PLATTER

SMITHFIELD HAM

ROAST TURKEY

FRENCH BREAD   SWEET BUTTER

MUSTARD   MUSTARD MAYONNAISE

ENDIVE   CELERY   RADISHES   OLIVES

CHEESE BOARD   CRACKERS   FRENCH ROLLS

FRESH FRUIT   FRUIT CAKE

Smoked-Fish Platter

This might include: smoked salmon, sturgeon, whitefish, eel, one or two types of herring (with sour cream and onions or maatjes herring, or both), kippered tuna, and any other smoked or cured fish you can find in your neighborhood.

Serve with thinly sliced pumpernickel, rye bread, sweet butter, thinly sliced onions, capers, olive oil, and a bowl of thinly sliced cucumbers dressed with oil, vinegar and dill weed or fresh dill.

Smithfield Ham

This may be bought ready to eat. Be sure to carve in very thin slices.

Roast Turkey

See p. 324–325.

The fish should be kept coolish, the coffee hot, and the rest of the food can be at room temperature. This will make it easy for you to keep platters replenished through the evening.

 CHRISTMAS BREAKFAST FOR 12

This is a pleasant custom that takes the place of the more usual Christmas Eve supper. Serve fruit juice or Bloody Marys before eating and white wine throughout the meal.

FRUIT JUICES

CHEESED MELBA TOAST

CODFISH IN CREAM WITH EGGS

CRISP BACON

ITALIAN SAUSAGES, HOT AND SWEET

RAW MUSHROOM AND BIBB LETTUCE SALAD

BRIOCHE   STOLLEN   TOASTED MUFFINS

PRESERVES   CREAM CHEESE

FRESH FRUIT

Fruit Juices

The juices should be freshly squeezed or done to order and should include grapefruit and orange, with perhaps one reconstituted frozen juice, such as pineapple or tangerine. The wine, which is, after all, fermented grape juice, counts as a juice. And those in need will be grateful for tomato juice in the form of a Bloody Mary.

Cheesed Melba Toast

Make your own Melba toast by slicing bread quite thin and drying it out in a 250° oven. When it is crisp, brush with butter and sprinkle with grated Parmesan mixed with a little black pepper and paprika. Add a dash or two of Tabasco, and reheat for a few minutes to blend the cheese. Serve crisp and warm.

Codfish in Cream with Eggs

4 pounds filleted salt codfish
Water
6 tablespoons butter
5 tablespoons flour
2 cups milk
1 teaspoon salt
⅛ teaspoon nutmeg

¼ teaspoon Tabasco
¾ cup heavy cream
4 egg yolks
12 hard-boiled eggs,
    peeled and sliced
Chopped parsley
14 pieces fried toast

Soak codfish overnight, changing the water once. Add fresh water, and bring to a boil. Simmer for 6 to 8 minutes or until fish will flake easily. Taste for salt. Break fish up into bite-size sections.

Prepare the cream sauce by melting the butter over low heat, blending in the flour and slowly adding heated milk. When sauce has thickened and is smooth, season with salt, nutmeg and Tabasco. Add the cream and egg yolks. Stir until well blended and thickened over medium heat. Do not let sauce boil. Just before serving add codfish, sliced eggs and parsley. Serve with fried toast.

Crisp Bacon

Arrange 1½ pounds bacon on a broiling pan and bake in 350° oven till desired state of doneness is reached.

Italian Sausages, Hot and Sweet

Poach 2 pounds or more small sausages for 10 minutes in white wine to cover, allowing the wine to cook down a bit. Remove sausages to a broiling pan rack and brown in the oven or under the broiler.

Raw Mushroom and Bibb Lettuce Salad

1½ pounds firm mushrooms, sliced in rounds
8 to 10 heads Bibb lettuce
Vinaigrette sauce (see p. 350)
Freshly ground black pepper

Wash Bibb well, and dry it. Nothing is worse than wet salad greens unless it be sandy and gravelly Bibb lettuce! Cut the heads in quarters (Bibb is the only lettuce that takes cutting, it seems to me). Add the sliced raw mushrooms, add a few grinds of fresh pepper, and toss with a basic vinaigrette sauce made with 4 parts good olive oil to 1 part wine vinegar.

Brioche, Stollen, Muffins

To make Brioche, see recipe on page 356.

Unless you are an ambitious baker, buy your stollen from a good bakery that specializes in this holiday delicacy. Slice it very thin.

Toast the muffins to order, or keep a toaster on the buffet table so guests may help themselves.

With these items serve plenty of sweet butter and interesting preserves. Cream cheese is especially pleasant when combined with the preserves.

For a pleasant ending, produce lots of hot coffee and a large, decorative bowl of fruit to which you have added dried raisins and nuts.

 MY OWN CHRISTMAS DINNER FOR 8

This is the Christmas dinner I am apt to serve these days. My feeling for tradition has changed, and thus the holiday dinner is considerably simplified. It is much more to my taste and it seems to find general approval among my guests, who favor it over yesteryear's feast.

I prefer to begin the festivities with champagne. You may want to serve Scotch, dry martinis, Lillet, or any number of other drinks. With the apéritifs I produce the first course and it is usually a foie gras with good toast—not a great deal of it, but enough to be thoroughly savored. If it is a large party, sometimes I make tiny baking-powder biscuits, and sandwich a piece of foie gras in them. They are light and short and make a nice setting for this delicacy. If foie gras is not your dish, you might substitute prosciutto and melon or a bit of smoked sturgeon or some caviar. At any rate, be festive!

Serve a Burgundy of a good year—a Vosne Romanée or a red Chassagne Montrachet—with the meat, vegetable and cheese; after dinner, cognac and eau de vie de Framboise.

FOIE GRAS   TOAST

ROAST SIRLOIN STRIP

BROWNED POTATOES

BRAISED BRUSSELS SPROUTS

CHEESE

APPLE AND MINCE FLAN

Roast Sirloin Strip

The sirloin roast is a particular favorite of mine. You may buy the loin with the T-bone and a bit of the tenderloin and the sirloin together. Or ask your butcher to give you boneless shells or strips, which roast perfectly, carve easily and look elegant when served.

You will want 10 or 11 pounds at least—or more, if you like cold beef as well as I do.

Rub the roast with salt and freshly ground pepper, place on a rack in a shallow pan, and roast at 325°, allowing about 10 minutes per pound, or until the roast reaches an inner temperature of 120°. Remove to a hot platter and allow to rest for 12 to 14 minutes. Garnish the platter with watercress and freshly grated horseradish.

For Sauce: When you remove the roast from the rack, spoon off most of the fat from the drippings, add 1½ cups beef broth to the drippings, and bring to a boil. Then add ¼ cup Madeira and salt and pepper to taste. Serve in a sauce boat with the roast.

Browned Potatoes

> *12 good-sized potatoes*
> *2 cups finely chopped beef suet*
> *Salt and pepper*

Peel the potatoes and cut in half lengthwise. Boil for just 8 minutes in salted water. Drain. An hour before the potatoes go in, place the beef suet in a roasting pan, and melt in the oven. Add the potatoes and roast them for 1 hour or till tender, turning them once or twice to color them nicely.

Braised Brussels Sprouts

> *3 pints Brussels sprouts*
> *Boiling salted water*
> *¾ cup butter*
> *Salt and pepper*
> *Sliced lemon*

Trim the sprouts well, and blanch them in boiling salted water for 4 minutes. Drain. Melt butter in a heavy saucepan, and add the sprouts. Cover tightly and cook over low heat till they are just tender when pierced with a fork. Correct the seasoning, and serve at once with thin slices of lemon.

Cheese

Choose several varieties of the best cheeses, and leave them at room temperature for several hours before serving. Toasted rolls or crisp French bread are best with cheese. Continue with the red wine which you served with the beef.

Apple and Mince Flan or Tart

Rich Pastry (see *p. 359–360*).

> *6 apples*
> *¼ pound butter*
> *Vanilla*
> *¼ cup sugar*
> *2 cups mincemeat (approximately)*
> *Apricot Glaze* (see *p. 38*)

Make a double recipe of Rich Pastry. Cool for 1 hour. Roll out and fit into 2   9-inch flan rings, a large baking dish, or 2 9-inch pie tins. Chill again.

Peel the apples and cut into eighths. Melt butter in a heavy skillet and add apples and a dash of vanilla. Cover, and steam apples over medium heat till soft but not mushy. Sugar to taste. Cool.

Fill pie shells or flan shells with a layer of apples and a layer of mincemeat. Bake at 450° for 10 minutes. Reduce heat to 350° and continue baking till nicely set and crust is browned. Cool slightly. Glaze with apricot glaze. Serve warm. Some people like to serve mince pie with sweetened whipped cream flavored with additional cognac!

VARIATION: You may make strips of pastry for the top and make a lattice over the mincemeat. In this case brush the pastry with 1 beaten egg blended with 2 tablespoons cream.

 CHRISTMAS DINNER FOR 6

This dinner is more difficult but should be delicious whether you serve it in the country or the city. It also would be suitable for a New Year's dinner. Start with your favorite potables, pass some good salted almonds and olives, then move on to the table with a fine Madeira for the soup course. A really great Hermitage should accompany the goose and the cheese. Try to find a rare old one of a fine year. Cognac and coffee are musts after this dinner.

TURTLE SOUP WITH MADEIRA

BUTTERED TOAST

ROAST STUFFED GOOSE WITH PRUNES

AND APPLES

WATERCRESS

BRAISED SAUERKRAUT   PUREE OF CHESTNUTS

COGNAC AND COFFEE ICE CREAM

MACAROONS   SAND TARTS

RAISINS, NUTS, DATES, PRUNES, GLACÉ FRUITS

Turtle Soup with Madeira

Purchase a fine brand of turtle soup and a can of turtle meat. For 6 persons buy 3 large cans of soup and a can of meat. Cut the meat into small dice, and combine with the soup. Cook for 30 minutes or until the soup has reduced one-fourth. It should be rich and gelatinous. Flavor to taste with Madeira, and correct the seasoning. Serve very hot with buttered toast and a fine Madeira.

Roast Stuffed Goose with Prunes and Apples

1 goose
18 pitted prunes that have been soaked in sherry or
Madeira for 4 days

6 to 8 apples, peeled, cored and halved
Nutmeg and lemon slices
Salt and pepper
6 potatoes, peeled and quartered lengthwise

There is a great deal of fat on a goose. Therefore it should be roasted slowly and on a rack so that the bird will crispen while the fat drips down into the roasting pan. I like to roast potatoes in the goose fat, for they become rather crisp and thoroughly saturated with flavor. Reserve the fat for future cooking. It can be used for many dishes.

Stuff the goose with the prunes and the apples, which have been lightly salted and dusted with a bit of nutmeg. Here and there add a lemon slice. Place the goose on a rack in rather a deep pan, and cover lightly with foil. Roast at 325°. At the end of 2½ hours remove the foil and baste with the drippings. Continue roasting till browned and tender. A large goose should take about 3 or 3½ hours to cook.

If the potatoes are added to the bottom of the pan 1 hour after the goose is placed in the oven, they will be ready with the goose delicious, crisp, and rich as can be!

I always like to serve a large bowl of watercress with goose. It is so refreshing and seems somehow to offer an appropriate contrast of flavor as well as color.

Braised Sauerkraut

Goose fat
4 pounds sauerkraut, washed and drained
1 clove garlic, finely chopped
1 teaspoon freshly ground black pepper
White wine
Juniper berries (optional)

Heat 4 tablespoons goose fat in a heavy kettle. Add the sauerkraut, the chopped garlic and the pepper. Cover with a good dry white wine and bring to a boil. Place a lid on the pan and simmer for 2½ hours, adding more white wine if necessary. A few juniper berries may be added.

Puree of Chestnuts

> *2 cans chestnuts in brine*
> *¼ pound butter*
> *Salt*
> *Pepper or nutmeg*
> *3 tablespoons cream*

Wash the chestnuts and either mash them or put them through a food mill. Melt the butter in a heavy pan, stir in the puree, and heat gently. Season with salt and a few grains of pepper or a dash of nutmeg. Just before serving stir in the cream, and heat again.

Cognac and Coffee Ice Cream

I love real old-fashioned ice cream turned in a freezer. (You can get a freezer attachment for your Kitchen Aid that will save a lot of muscle!) This is a favorite.

> *1 quart heavy cream*
> *1 cup light cream*
> *1 cup sugar*
> *1 teaspoon vanilla*
> *½ cup cognac*
> *2 tablespoons instant coffee, or to taste*

Combine ingredients and stir. Add a dash of salt, place in refrigerator, and chill well. Freeze in freezer packed with salt and ice. Follow directions for your particular freezer. If using hand freezer, turn until it will turn no more. Wipe the cover carefully, remove the dasher, and repack with ice and salt until ready to use. Serve with Macaroons (*see* below) and Sand Tarts (*see* p. 299).

Macaroons

> *1 cup almond paste*
> *1 cup confectioners' sugar*
> *3 to 4 egg whites*
> *Granulated sugar*

Blend together the almond paste and the confectioners' sugar, being certain that it is well mixed. Add the egg whites, one at a time, until the texture is soft enough to flow through a pastry tube yet firm enough to hold its shape. You may not need all the egg whites.

Force through a pastry bag fitted with a plain tube onto baking paper arranged on a baking sheet. Sprinkle with granulated sugar, and bake at 300° for 12 to 16 minutes.

 PARTY FOR A TEEN-AGE CROWD

INDIVIDUAL HEROES

GRILLED CHEESEBURGERS   BUTTERED BUNS

FRENCH FRANKFURTERS

HOT POTATO SALAD

ICE CREAM SUNDAES

COLD DRINKS

Individual Heroes

You'll need a sizable stack of split hero loaves and a mound of butter. Next to the loaves place platters of sliced salami, ham and bologna, sliced cheeses, sliced onions, tomatoes and pickles, hot peppers, and greens. Keep cooked Italian sausages hot in a chafing dish. Let each guest make his own hero.

Grilled Cheeseburgers

> *3 pounds ground beef*
> *1 pound grated Cheddar cheese*
> *3 tablespoons catsup*

½ *cup chopped onion*
1 tablespoon salt
1 teaspoon freshly ground black pepper
Buttered buns

Mix meat and seasonings, and form into 4-ounce patties. Pile them between sheets of waxed paper or foil and place on a platter or board next to the grill. Have an equal amount of buttered buns. Appoint a grill monitor.

French Frankfurters

These French franks should be prepared in the kitchen and sent out to the party in relays.

With an apple corer make a hole through the length of individual French rolls. In each one put a good dab of butter. Place the rolls in a 350° oven to heat for 12 minutes. Meanwhile, heat frankfurters. Brush each frank with mustard, and slip it into a hot roll. Serve at once. A tray of assorted relishes is a nice addition.

Hot Potato Salad

See p. 371.

Ice Cream Sundaes

Provision a bar with large containers of ice cream, ice cream dippers, and the following assortment of toppings: fresh raspberries and strawberries, crushed and sugared; a variety of jams and preserves in bowls; bananas; chopped pecans; chopped almonds; chopped peanuts; chocolate syrup; whipped cream; and cherries, both maraschino and candied.

Serve brownies and sugar cookies, too.

Cold Drinks

Arrange tubs of ice (washtubs are good for this job) filled with cold bottled drinks. Fill large insulated jugs—the type with spigots—with lemonade made from lemonade mix, with a few drops of raspberry syrup added for color. Fill more jugs with orange juice made from orange concentrate.

APPENDIX

BASIC RECIPES

 SAUCES

Béchamel Sauce

3 tablespoons butter
3 tablespoons flour
1¼ cups liquid (light cream, milk, chicken, fish or
    vegetable broth)
Salt
Pepper
Nutmeg
Tabasco (optional)

Combine butter and flour and cook over low heat for 2 or 3 minutes, stirring gently with a spatula, wooden spoon or wire whisk. Gradually pour in heated liquid while stirring, and continue to stir until mixture thickens. Season to taste with salt, freshly ground pepper and a dash of nutmeg. A dash of Tabasco will give this sauce an added lift.

MORNAY SAUCE: To the above Béchamel sauce, add ½ cup grated Parmesan cheese and blend thoroughly.

CHEESE SAUCE: Add ½ to ¾ cup grated Gruyère, Emmenthal, or cheddar cheese to the Béchamel sauce and stir until melted. Add a good dash of Tabasco.

SAUCE SUPRÈME: To recipe of Béchamel made with chicken or veal stock, add 1 cup heavy cream and three egg yolks. If you are using French cream add only 1 cup heavy cream—crème fraiche.

VELOUTÉ SAUCE: To 1 cup of Béchamel, made with milk or with 1 cup of meat, poultry, fish or vegetable stock, add ½ cup heavy cream that has been blended with 2 egg yolks. Stir until thickened but be careful that it does not boil.

Basic Brown Sauce (or Sauce Espagnole)

½ pound butter or clarified butter
2½ cups flour (approximately)
4 cups strong beef broth or bouillon
2 tablespoons heavy tomato paste
½ teaspoon thyme
Sprig of parsley
Onion stuck with two cloves
Salt
3 or 4 mushrooms, sliced
2 tablespoons glace de viande or beef extract

Prepare a brown roux, which you may keep in a jar or a tin in the refrigerator for several weeks. Melt butter or clarified butter in a heavy skillet and combine it with an equal amount—in weight—of flour. This would be a little over 2¼ cups. Blend and cook slowly over a very low heat until the roux turns a delicate brown.

For the sauce, 1 cup of the roux is combined with beef broth or bouillon, tomato paste, thyme, parsley, an onion stuck with cloves and salt to taste. Bring to a boil, add mushrooms or some mushroom stems, coarsely chopped, and simmer for 45 minutes. Cool and put through a fine sieve. Add glace de viande or beef extract if you have it.

This is a basic sauce espagnole or brown sauce, which is used as a base for many of the famous brown sauces. It will keep for some time under refrigeration and may be used for the following:

SAUCE BORDELAISE:

6 shallots or 12 small green onions, peeled and chopped
1½ cups good red wine
1 tablespoon chopped parsley
1 cup sauce espagnole
Pat of butter

Poached marrow

Combine shallots or onions with wine and chopped parsley. Reduce over a brisk flame to ¾ cup. Strain and combine with sauce espagnole. Bring to a boil and simmer for 1 or 2 minutes. Add a pat of butter and correct the seasoning. Add some poached marrow to the steak or roast with which you are using the sauce.

SAUCE MADÈRE :

> 6 shallots or 12 small onions, peeled and chopped
> 1 cup sauce espagnole
> ⅓ cup Madeira

Sauté shallots or small onions. Combine sauce espagnole with Madeira and bring to a boil. Add shallots, simmer 5 to 6 minutes and correct seasoning.

SAUCE PERIGOURDINE : To sauce madère above, add 2 tablespoons finely chopped truffles.

SAUCE DUXELLES : To 1½ cups of the basic sauce madère, add ¾ cup Duxelles (*see* p. 353) and simmer for 5 minutes. Add a dash of lemon sauce. Correct the seasoning.

SAUCE DIABLE :

> ¼ cup tarragon vinegar
> ¾ cup white wine
> 1 shallot, finely chopped
> 1 teaspoon tarragon
> 1¼ cups sauce espagnole
> Dash Tabasco
> 2 teaspoons dry mustard
> Pepper
> Parsley, finely chopped
> Fresh tarragon, finely chopped

Combine tarragon vinegar and wine with chopped shallot and tarragon. Reduce to one half and add to sauce espagnole with a good dash of Tabasco and dry mustard. Bring to a boil and simmer 3 minutes. Add several grinds from the pepper grinder and strain. Serve with a dusting of parsley and fresh tarragon, both finely chopped.

SAUCE POIVRADE: Reduce 1 cup port to ½ cup and blend with 1½ cups sauce espagnole. Bring to a boil and simmer for 4 minutes. Add 1½ teaspoons freshly ground black pepper and correct the seasoning.

SAUCE PIQUANTE:

2 cloves garlic, finely chopped
4 shallots, finely chopped
½ cup wine vinegar
1 cup red wine
1 teaspoon oregano
1½ cups sauce espagnole
3 tablespoons concentrated tomato paste
1 tablespoon Dijon mustard
Dash Tabasco

Combine chopped garlic and shallots with wine vinegar, red wine and oregano. Reduce to ½ cup over brisk heat. Strain and add to sauce espagnole along with tomato paste, Dijon mustard and a hearty dash of Tabasco. Blend and simmer for 5 minutes.

Basic Hollandaise Sauce

¼ pound butter
3 egg yolks
½ teaspoon salt
1 tablespoon lemon juice
Dash Tabasco

Cut the butter into three equal parts. Beat egg yolks slightly and add seasonings. Place in an enamel, glass or pottery container over hot water. Using a wire whisk or spatula beat in ⅓ of the butter, then the second piece and then the third. Do not let the water boil.

If the hollandaise should curdle, add a touch of boiling water and continue stirring till it emulsifies again.

BLENDER HOLLANDAISE:

4 egg yolks
2 tablespoons lemon juice
½ teaspoon salt

Dash Tabasco
½ cup butter, melted

Place egg yolks, lemon juice, salt and Tabasco in the blender jar. Turn on and off very quickly. Heat butter until it is hot and bubbly. Turn blender to high and dribble butter into egg mixture steadily until mixture emulsifies and thickens. This will hold over warm water for several hours.

SAUCE MOUSSELINE: To 1 cup hollandaise add ½ cup heavy cream, whipped.

SAUCE BÉARNAISE:

> *3 shallots or scallions, finely chopped*
> *1 teaspoon tarragon or 1 tablespoon chopped fresh*
> *   tarragon*
> *¼ cup wine vinegar*
> *¼ cup white wine*
> *1 teaspoon chopped parsley*
> *Basic hollandaise recipe*

Add to shallots or scallions the tarragon, wine vinegar, white wine and chopped parsley. Bring to a boil and reduce to practically a glaze. Add this to basic hollandaise and correct seasoning.

If tarragon is fresh, it is sometimes pleasant to stir in an extra amount.

ANCHOVY SAUCE: To basic hollandaise, add 4 finely chopped anchovy fillets, a clove of crushed or chopped garlic and a few capers; or if you are making a blender hollandaise, place 4 egg yolks, no salt, the chopped anchovy fillets, a clove of garlic and 1 tablespoon lemon juice in the blender. Turn on and off. Gradually pour in, with the blender at high speed, ⅔ cup bubbling melted butter.

Beurre Blanc

> *¼ cup white wine*
> *¼ cup wine vinegar*
> *1 tablespoon chopped shallots or onions*
> *¼ teaspoon salt*

1 dash freshly ground black pepper
12 ounces chilled butter (3 sticks cut into 24 squares)
Salt and pepper

Boil liquid and onions (in Pyrex or enamel) until they are reduced to 2 tablespoons. Add salt and pepper. Remove the pan from the fire; and with a wire whisk, beat in two pieces of butter. When it begins to cream, beat in another piece; when this begins to cream, beat in another; and continue in this manner, holding the pan over low heat or warm water until all the butter is added. The resulting sauce will be creamy and light amber in color. Do not let it get too hot or it will break.

Basic Mayonnaise

2 egg yolks
About 1 pint oil
1 teaspoon vinegar
1 teaspoon salt
Dash of Tabasco
1 teaspoon dry mustard

Mayonnaise is an emulsion of egg yolk and oil. It may be mixed with a fork, an egg beater, or an electric mixer. Beat yolks well in a soup plate, if you use a fork; a bowl, if you use an egg beater; or in the mixer bowl, if you use an electric mixer. Add oil slowly till the emulsion begins to thicken. Begin with a teaspoon or a thin dribble if you are using the electric mixer. Gradually increase the amount added. When the mixture becomes very thick add vinegar, salt, and Tabasco. Finally add dry mustard and continue beating. Taste and add additional vinegar if needed.

BLENDER MAYONNAISE:

1 whole egg
2 teaspoons wine vinegar
½ teaspoon salt
1 teaspoon dry mustard
1 cup oil

Place egg, wine vinegar, salt, and dry mustard in the blender container.

Turn blender to high and dribble oil through the top till mixture emulsifies and thickens. Takes about 1 minute.

MUSTARD MAYONNAISE : Add Dijon mustard to taste and a little dry mustard. About 1 tablespoon Dijon and 1 teaspoon dry mustard makes a good, brisk mustard sauce.

ANCHOVY MAYONNAISE : Add 2 teaspoons Dijon mustard and 2 tablespoons finely chopped anchovy fillets. Omit salt in this mayonnaise.

Sauces with a Mayonnaise Base

RÉMOULADE : To 1 cup of mayonnaise add 1 minced clove of garlic, 1 teaspoon of dry or 1 tablespoon fresh chopped tarragon, ½ teaspoon dry mustard, a finely chopped hard-boiled egg, 1 teaspoon of capers, 1 tablespoon chopped parsley, and a dab of anchovy paste.

GREEN GODDESS : To 1 cup mayonnaise add ½ cup mixed, chopped green herbs—parsley, chives, tarragon—and 3 chopped anchovy fillets.

RUSSIAN : Blend together and allow to stand for 2 hours, 2 cups of mayonnaise, 1 teaspoon dry mustard, 2 tablespoons finely chopped onion, 1 tablespoon Worcestershire sauce, and 2 ounces of caviar.

TARTAR : Blend 2 cups of mayonnaise, 3 tablespoons finely chopped onion, 2 teaspoons finely chopped parsley, 2 teaspoons lemon juice, and 2 tablespoons finely chopped dill pickle—or fresh dill, if you prefer.

THOUSAND ISLAND DRESSING : To 1 cup of mayonnaise add 1 tablespoon of finely chopped onion, 3 tablespoons of chili sauce, 1 chopped hard-cooked egg, and a touch of dry mustard.

Sauce Vinaigrette or French Dressing

> *6 tablespoons olive or vegetable oil*
> *2 tablespoons wine vinegar*
> *½ to 1 teaspoon salt*
> *12 grinds of the pepper mill*

Blend the oil and vinegar and the salt and pepper. You may adjust the vinegar content to suit the salads or the individual palate. Also salt and pepper to taste.

Variations

These are endless.

1) Mustard, either dry or Dijon, may be added—a dash of dry and up to a tablespoonful of Dijon for certain salads.

2) Garlic is delicious in many dressings and can be added to your taste. Crush the clove and rub well into the salt before adding oil to the bowl.

3) Add chopped or crushed fresh or dried herbs to the salad. Tarragon is a perfect salad herb. Basil is superb with tomatoes. Dill goes with cucumbers. Rosemary goes with salads that have a little orange or grapefruit in them.

4) Finely sliced onion or chopped green onion or chives make a superb flavoring for salad.

The important thing is to make your dressing fresh each time and adjust it to suit the salad ingredients.

Sauce for Vegetables à la Grecque

> *⅔ cup olive oil or peanut oil*
> *1 cup white wine or vermouth*
> *1 teaspoon salt*
> *½ teaspoon freshly ground pepper*
> *1 or 2 sprigs parsley*
> *Thyme, rosemary or tarragon*

With this base one can experiment and add various flavors—such things as coriander seeds, mustard seed, celery seed, cummin, garlic or Tabasco, allspice or tomato puree.)

Poach vegetables in this sauce until crisply tender and then cool and serve in the sauce. Among the vegetables to be served this way are celery, small artichokes, zucchini, cucumbers, celery root, small onions, fennel and leeks.

Dress with chopped parsley before serving.

Sauce Italienne

> *1 clove garlic, finely chopped*
> *1 small onion, finely chopped*
> *2 tablespoons olive oil*
> *1½ cups solid-pack tomatoes*
> *½ teaspoon basil*
> *1 can (6 ounces) tomato paste*

Sauté garlic and onion in olive oil. Add tomatoes and basil. Simmer 30 to 40 minutes. Add tomato paste and allow to simmer 15 minutes.

Strain. If not thick enough, cook over brisk heat several minutes to reduce it, stirring often and being careful that the sauce is not scorched.

Tabasco Cocktail Sauce

> *1 cup catsup or chili sauce*
> *2 tablespoons lemon juice*
> *½ teaspoon salt*
> *¼ teaspoon Tabasco*
> *1 tablespoon horseradish*

Mix ingredients thoroughly. Chill well before serving. Serve with shrimp, crab or lobster. Makes approximately 1¼ cups.

Barbecue Sauce

> *2 medium onions, quartered*
> *¼ cup salad oil*
> *1 teaspoon dry mustard*
> *1 tablespoon Worcestershire sauce*
> *¼ cup lemon juice*
> *½ cup chili sauce*
> *1 small hot chili pepper (peeled green chilies)*
> *¼ cup brown sugar*

1 teaspoon salt
6 peppercorns

Put all ingredients into container of electric blender. Cover and blend on high speed for 20 seconds. Pour into saucepan and heat until boiling. Makes 1½ cups sauce.

Oriental Sauce

1 large onion, coarsely cut
1 clove garlic
4 tablespoons butter
1 tablespoon curry powder
4 tablespoons flour
1 cup hot chicken broth
1 cup hot water

Into container of electric blender put onion and garlic. Add water to cover, cover container, and flick motor on and off high several times until vegetables are finely chopped. Drain.

In saucepan melt half the butter and in it sauté the chopped vegetables with the curry powder for 5 minutes.

Into container put flour, remaining butter, and chicken stock. Cover and blend on high speed for 20 seconds. Remove cover and, with motor on, pour in hot water. Add to vegetables in saucepan and cook over low heat for 10 minutes, stirring occasionally. Makes 2 cups sauce.

Mushroom Sauce

1 3-ounce can cooked mushrooms or ½ cup Duxelles
    (see below)
2 tablespoons flour
2 tablespoons soft butter
½ cup hot chicken broth
½ cup heavy cream

Into container of electric blender put mushrooms, flour, butter, and chicken broth. Cover container and blend on high speed for 15 seconds. Remove cover and, with motor on, pour in cream. Pour sauce into saucepan and cook over simmering water for 15 minutes, stirring occasionally. Makes 1½ cups.

Duxelles

Chop 1½ pounds of mushrooms very finely. Melt 4 ounces of butter in a heavy skillet. Add 1 clove of garlic finely chopped and 2 finely chopped shallots. Add the mushrooms and let them sauté very slightly. Add more butter if necessary until they cook down and turn dark. Sprinkle with 2 tablespoons flour and let them cook down more. Store in refrigerator.

 # BREADS AND PASTRIES

Basic Homemade Bread

2 cups milk
3 tablespoons butter
1 tablespoon salt (approximately)
2 tablespoons sugar
1 cake or package of yeast
6 cups sifted flour (approximately)

Scald milk. Combine 1 cup with butter, salt, and sugar. Dissolve 1 cake or package active dry yeast in remaining cup of milk. Combine the 2 cups and work in 3 cups sifted flour. Blend well, gradually beat in remaining 3 cups, or more, flour and knead on a floured board until smooth and springy and tiny blisters form.

Place dough in a buttered bowl and daub top with butter. Cover and place in a warm spot without drafts to rise to double its bulk. Turn out on floured board, punch down and work slightly. Let dough rest for a few minutes, then shape into loaves and place in buttered bread pans. Cover and allow to rise again till almost doubled in bulk. Center of loaf will probably be higher.

Bake at 400° about 45 to 50 minutes.

NOTE: If you are in a hurry, use twice the amount of yeast, knead more vigorously and pound the bread dough a bit.

Sweet Dough

> ½ *cup scalded milk*
> ½ *cup sugar*
> 1 *tablespoon salt*
> 4 *tablespoons butter*
> 2 *cakes or packages of yeast*
> ½ *cup warm water*
> 2 *eggs, well beaten*
> 5 *to 6 cups all-purpose flour*

Combine scalded milk, sugar, salt, and butter and cool to luke-warm. Dissolve yeast in warm water. Combine with the milk and butter mixture and add eggs, and 3 cups all-purpose flour. Work in 2 to 3 more cups flour till you have a soft dough. Knead on a lightly floured board until dough is springy and blisters slightly. Place in a buttered bowl, brush with melted butter and put to rise in a warm, draft-free place. When doubled in bulk, punch down and work slightly.

Use this dough for coffee cakes, kuchen and sweet rolls.

KUCHEN: Roll out sweet dough ¾ inch thick and arrange in an 11- by 14-inch pan that has been buttered. Let rise 5 minutes. Arrange fresh fruit on top, sprinkle with sugar, and, if you wish, dust with cinnamon. Dot with butter and bake at 375° until nicely risen and the fruit is cooked. Apples, plums, peaches, prunes, all lend themselves to kuchen.

CINNAMON ROLLS: Roll out sweet dough ¾ inch thick. Spread or brush well with melted butter. Dust with cinnamon and sprinkle with 1 cup granulated sugar. Brush with butter again and sprinkle with ½ cup each broken walnut or pecan meats and sultana raisins. Roll and cut into 2-inch sections. Arrange on a buttered baking sheet, brush with melted butter and sprinkle with sugar. Let rise for 15 minutes.

Bake at 375° until the rolls are nicely browned and cooked through—about 20 minutes. Brush with sugar and milk icing if you wish.

Sponge Cake

> *1¼ cups flour*
> *1¼ cups sugar*
> *¼ teaspoon salt*
> *6 eggs*
> *2 tablespoons lemon juice*
> *1 tablespoon grated lemon rind*
> *2 tablespoons water*
> *½ teaspoon cream of tartar*

Sift together the flour, salt and 1 cup sugar; separate the eggs. To the yolks, after they have been lightly beaten, add the flour mixture, the lemon juice and rind, and the water and beat well with the electric beater or with a heavy whisk till thick and ribbony. This will require about 4 minutes of beating or 3 or so in the electric beater.

Beat egg whites till they hold soft peaks. Sprinkle cream of tartar over them and add half the sugar and beat until well blended. Add remaining sugar and beat till the mixture holds firm peaks and is glossy.

Fold yolk mixture into whites and pour into a 10-inch tube pan or into a 13- by 9-inch pan or into a loaf pan.

Bake at 350° until cake springs back when tested with finger and is nicely browned, about 30 to 40 minutes.

Pizza Dough

> *1 cake or package of yeast*
> *1 cup lukewarm water*
> *1 teaspoon sugar*
> *2 teaspoons salt*
> *3 tablespoons olive oil*
> *3½ to 4 cups all-purpose flour*

Dissolve yeast in lukewarm water. Stir in sugar, salt and olive oil. Gradually add flour and beat until smooth. Turn out on a floured board and knead until smooth, satiny and springy. Cover and let rise in a buttered bowl for about 1 hour or until double in bulk.

Divide dough into two pieces and knead a few minutes. Roll out into rounds to fit pizza pans. Use any pizza filling you wish. Bake in a hot (400°) oven for about 25 minutes.

Brioche

> ½ *cup milk*
> ½ *cup margarine or butter*
> ⅓ *cup sugar*
> ½ *teaspoon salt*
> ¼ *cup warm water*
> *1 cake or package of yeast*
> *1 egg yolk, beaten*
> *3 whole eggs, beaten*
> *3¼ cups sifted enriched flour*
> *1 egg white beaten with 1 tablespoon sugar*

Scald milk. Cool to lukewarm. Cream thoroughly margarine or butter. Add gradually and cream together sugar and salt. Measure into bowl warm (not hot) water (cool to lukewarm for compressed yeast) and sprinkle or crumble in active dry or compressed yeast and stir until dissolved. Stir in lukewarm milk and creamed mixture. Add beaten egg yolk, beaten whole eggs, and flour. Beat for 10 minutes. Cover. Let rise in warm place, free from draft, about 2 hours or until more than doubled in bulk. Stir down and beat thoroughly. Cover tightly with waxed paper or aluminum foil and store in refrigerator overnight. Stir down and turn out soft dough on floured board. Divide into 2 pieces, one about ¾ and the other about ¼ of dough. Cut larger piece into 16 equal pieces and form into smooth balls. Place in well-greased muffin pans 2¾ inches in diameter by 1¾ inches deep. Cut smaller piece into 16 equal pieces. Form into smooth balls. Make a deep indentation in center of each large ball and dampen slightly with cold water. Press a small ball into each indentation. Cover and let rise in warm place, free from draft, about 1 hour, or until more than doubled in bulk. Brush with egg white and sugar mixture. Bake in moderate oven (375°) about 20 minutes.

Croissants

3 ounces fresh yeast
1 tablespoon sugar
2 teaspoons salt
1 cup cold milk
1 pound bread flour (or 4 cups unsifted flour)
¾ pound sweet butter

Cream yeast with sugar and salt to make a syrup. Add cold milk. Add about three cups of flour, or enough to make a medium firm dough. Work in ⅛ pound (half a stick) of soft butter. Knead dough till it is very smooth and elastic—at least 15 minutes. Let dough rest 20 to 30 minutes covered with bowl.

While dough is resting, cream medium-firm butter with remaining flour. Roll butter-flour mixture between sheets of floured wax paper into a rectangle less than ½ inch thick. If butter becomes very soft and sticky, place in refrigerator till it becomes firm but not hard.

After dough has rested, roll it on a floured cloth into a rectangle three times as long as it is wide. Cut butter rectangle in half and place half in center of dough. Fold one end of dough over butter. Place remaining butter on folded end of dough. Cover butter with remaining dough, sealing ends as well as possible.

Turn dough so that open ends face you. Roll out again into a rectangle. Bring both ends of rectangle to meet in center of dough. Fold in half, making four layers. Wrap in floured cloth or aluminum foil and refrigerate for one hour, or more if desired.

After one hour, place dough on floured cloth, open ends facing you. Roll and fold again, as before. Place in refrigerator for at least six hours, preferably overnight, before shaping into croissants.

To shape, roll dough out, using half at a time, into a sheet less than ¼ inch thick. Cut into triangles that are 4 inches wide at the base. Chill triangles briefly. Roll up tightly into croissants. Place on well-greased (or paper-lined) cookie sheets. Chill very well. Brush with beaten egg yolk mixed with a tablespoon of cream. Bake in a 450° oven for 5 minutes, or till croissants are well puffed. Reduce heat to 350° and continue baking till golden brown. Cool slightly before serving. These may be frozen.

Pâte à Choux

> ¼ *cup butter*
> ½ *cup hot water*
> ½ *cup flour*
> ¼ *teaspoon salt*
> ¼ *teaspoon sugar*
> 2 *eggs*

Combine the butter and the hot water and place them over the flame. When the butter is melted and the water boiling, add the flour, salt and sugar and stir with a wooden spoon until the mixture leaves the sides of the pan and forms a ball in the middle of the pan. Remove from the pan and continue beating or place in the electric beater. Add the eggs, one at a time, and continue beating until the dough is waxy and smooth. This may be forced through a tube or dropped by spoonfuls into a baking dish or into hot fat. If baked, these should be placed in a 450° oven for 10 minutes and then reduce the temperature to 350°. They should be baked until well browned and crisp.

Baking Powder Biscuit

> 2 *cups sifted flour*
> 2½ *teaspoons double acting baking powder*
> ¾ *teaspoon salt*
> 5 *tablespoons butter or other shortening*
> ¾ *cup milk* (*approximately*)
> *Melted butter*

Sift the flour, measure it, add baking powder and salt, and sift again into a mixing bowl. (Some people add sugar to biscuit, but I don't think it necessary. If you prefer it, add 2 teaspoons.) Work in the butter or other shortening with your fingers till it is the consistency of cornmeal. Add milk to make a soft dough. Turn onto a floured board. Knead for a minute, and roll or pat out to ¾-inch thickness. Melt butter in a baking pan or a small saucepan. Cut the biscuits according to your taste. Dip each one in melted butter and arrange on a baking sheet or pan. If you want them crisp all around, place them far apart. If you want them crisp on top and fluffy, place them close together.

Bake at 450° for 12 to 15 minutes. Makes 12 to 18 biscuits.

BUTTERMILK BISCUIT : Add ¼ teaspoon soda to the recipe above, and use buttermilk instead of sweet milk.

Shortcake Dough

Increase butter content of Baking Powder Biscuit recipe to ¼ pound and use heavy cream for mixing. Add 2 tablespoons sugar.

Divide dough into two portions, one twice the size of the other. Use the larger portion for bottom piece. Arrange on a baking sheet and brush with melted butter. Roll out remaining portion. It should, of course, be smaller than the first piece. Dot lower piece with additional butter where the upper piece will rest. Brush top with butter. Bake as for biscuits.

Plain Pastry

> *2 cups flour*
> *½ teaspoon salt*
> *⅔ cup butter or ⅓ cup butter and ⅓ cup vegetable*
> *   shortening*
> *Ice water*

Sift the flour and salt onto a pastry board. Make a well in the flour and add the butter and shortening, cut into small pieces. Cut with two knives or blend with finger tips till flour is mealy and the size of small peas. Add just enough ice water to make the flour and shortening form a firm ball. Chill for at least 30 minutes before rolling. Makes 1 2-crust pie or 2 shells.

Rich Pastry

> *2 cups unsifted flour*
> *3 tablespoons sugar*
> *½ cup butter*
> *¼ cup vegetable shortening*

1½ teaspoons grated lemon rind
3 hard-cooked egg yolks or 2 raw egg yolks, or 2 egg
whites (see *Note*)
½ teaspoon salt

Make a well in the center of the flour. Add sugar; butter, not too hard, not too soft, cut in small pieces; vegetable shortening cut in small pieces; lemon rind; hard-cooked yolks crushed with a fork; and salt. Work quickly with finger tips to make a firm, smooth pastry. Dough should form a ball and leave table top or bowl fairly clean. Chill pastry for at least 30 minutes before rolling. Makes 1 2-crust pie or 2 shells.

NOTE: If a very rich pastry is desired, use raw yolks of eggs. The whites will make a more brittle and less fragile pastry. If you are making flans or shells you may roll out and fit pastry and freeze till ready to use. Use the pastry frozen. If you are baking a shell, fit the inside of the pastry with foil and fill with dry beans or peas, then bake. Remove the foil and beans and reserve beans for future bakings. If you are baking tart shells you may place the tins one over the other, after having lined them with pastry, and turn them upside down on a baking sheet. Weight lightly and bake.

This pastry may be made in the Kitchen Aid mixer if desired. Use paddle attachment.

Cream Cheese Pastry

½ pound butter
½ pound cream cheese
¼ cup heavy cream
2½ cups flour
½ teaspoon salt

Cream the cheese and butter together well. Add the cream and whip for 3 minutes. Gradually add the flour and salt, and work into a firm ball. Chill before using.

Pound Cake

1 pound butter
2 cups sugar

10 eggs, separated
¼ teaspoon salt
4 cups sifted flour
½ teaspoon mace
2 tablespoons cognac

Cream butter until light and fluffy. Add sugar and continue creaming until light and very fluffy. Beat egg yolks till light and lemon-colored and add to the butter-sugar mixture. Fold in the stiffly beaten whites to which you have added salt. Add sifted flour, mace, and cognac. Beat well for 5 minutes. Pour into buttered loaf tins or tube pan and bake at 300° for 1¼ to 1½ hours.

Fruit or nuts may be added to this basic recipe. Mix with ¼ cup of the flour and add at the last. You may use about 1 cup fruit or nuts.

Corn Bread for Toasting

This is a simple bread, delicious when baked, split and toasted. It is not light and fluffy but corny, in the best sense of the word.

Combine 1 cup corn meal with 2 cups scalded milk, 2 teaspoons sugar, 1 teaspoon salt and 3 tablespoons melted butter. Spread in a 9-inch-square pan that has been well buttered, or drop by spoonfuls onto a buttered pan. Bake at 350° until brown. You may eat this hot from the oven; or cool, toast, and serve with plenty of butter.

Génoise

1 cup sugar
6 eggs
1 cup sifted cake flour
1 cup clarified butter

Place sugar and eggs in a double-boiler top. Place over hot water and beat for about 12 minutes with a wire whisk, or until the mixture is light and creamy. Place in the bowl of your electric mixer and beat at medium-high speed till it is thick and lemon-colored. If you do not have an electric mixer, a rotary beater is necessary.

Gradually fold in, a little at a time, sifted cake flour, using a wooden or rubber spatula.

Fold in by tablespoons clarified butter—butter that has been melted and siphoned off, leaving behind any water or solid residue. Pour into a 9-inch round or square cake pan that has been buttered and floured, or one that has been lined with silicon baking paper. Bake at 350° about 35 to 40 minutes. The cake will leave the sides of the pan when it is done.

Remove immediately to a rack to cool.

Sable Normande

> 1 cup (2 sticks) butter
> 1 cup sugar
> 1 teaspoon orange-flower water
> 3 cups all-purpose flour
> Pinch salt

Work butter, sugar and orange-flower water together with your hands. Little by little work in a mixture of flour and salt until dough feels sandy in texture. Chill in refrigerator until firm enough to handle. Divide dough in half and roll half at a time, on a lightly floured board, about ¼ inch thick. Cut with a 2-inch round cookie cutter and place on ungreased cookie sheets. Bake in a preheated 350° oven for about 15 minutes or until edges are rimmed with gold. Makes approximately 50 sables.

Crêpes (Unsweetened)

> ⅞ cup all-purpose flour
> ⅛ teaspoon salt
> 3 eggs
> 2 tablespoons melted butter
> 1½ cups milk

Sift flour and salt together and add eggs one at a time, mixing well, until there are no lumps (a mixer at low speed is excellent). Add melted butter. Gradually stir in milk and mix until the batter is the consistency of thin cream. Let batter rest an hour or two before baking.

Bake the crêpes in a 6-inch, well-buttered pan over a medium-high heat. Pour a little of the batter in pan and tip, so it runs over the entire surface. Turn and brown lightly on the other side. Keep hot in the oven.

DESSERT CRÊPES: Sift ¼ cup sugar with the dry ingredients; and after mixing in the eggs, add 2 tablespoons cognac or rum and 1 teaspoon vanilla or 1 teaspoon grated lemon rind. Continue as above.

 POTATOES

Baked Potatoes

The Idaho is surely the finest baking potato. It is said to be grown in a particular soil that has great lava content and that this greatly resembles soil in Peru, where the same type of potato abounds.

Allow 1 baking potato per person, or, if they are extra large, ½ potato will be ample. Preheat the oven to 375°. Scrub potatoes well and place them on a rack in the oven. Bake for approximately an hour or until the potatoes are soft to the touch.

Split at once and serve with freshly ground black pepper and salt. They are perfect this way, but you may want to add any of the following:

1) Butter
2) Cream, chives, bacon and parsley
3) Butter and paprika

VARIATION: Preheat oven to 375°. Scrub potatoes well and rub with oil or butter. Make a thin slit in each potato. Bake till just soft—approximately an hour. Split and serve as above.

Stuffed Baked Potatoes

Bake as above. Cut about ¾ inch off the potato with a sharp knife. Scoop contents into a bowl or saucepan. For 6 potatoes add:

¼ pound (1 stick) butter	1½ teaspoons freshly
1½ teaspoons salt	ground black pepper

1 teaspoon paprika
¾ cup heavy cream

¾ cup grated Swiss
Gruyère or cheddar

Beat in the butter, seasonings and cream. Add ½ cup of the cheese and beat well. Return the potatoes to the shells and top with remaining cheese. Return to the oven to melt cheese and reheat potatoes.

Disgustingly Rich Potatoes

For 6 persons, bake 6 large Idaho potatoes as directed above. When soft, split and scoop out each potato into a mixing bowl. Scrape out the shells.

Add to the potatoes ¾ cup butter, 2 teaspoons salt, 1 cup heavy cream and 1 teaspoon freshly ground black pepper. Mix lightly and transfer to a flat baking dish. Dot heavily with butter and sprinkle with shredded Gruyère or cheddar cheese. Bake at 375° for 15 minutes.

NOTE: Spread the skins with butter and place them on a rack in a 500° oven or under a broiler to crisp. Serve for a cocktail accompaniment—an idea I gleaned from Mildred Knopf.

Sautéed Baked Potatoes

Peel cold baked potatoes and sauté in butter or bacon fat. Add a little cream and let it cook down.

Sweet Potatoes Baked

After baking, peel and slice. Sauté in butter and add a touch of nutmeg and a sprinkling of brown sugar. Then mash and combine with a great deal of butter and a dash of Madeira. Spoon into a baking dish and top with toasted sliced almonds. Dot with butter and brown in a 375° oven.

Sweet potatoes are really best when they are baked and served simply—with butter, salt and pepper.

Browned Potatoes

These are peeled and halved potatoes, preferably Idaho or similar potatoes. Drop them into the fat in a roasting pan when roasting beef or pork or lamb, and allow them an hour. Turn once or twice during the cooking time so that they brown on all sides.

NOTE: You may parboil these potatoes before tossing them into the fat. They will cook more quickly.

Roast Potatoes without a Roast

You may roast potatoes, peeled and halved (or scraped new potatoes or small whole potatoes) in beef drippings, butter, oil or pork drippings. You will want enough dripping to cover the pan to a depth of 1 inch. Peel the potatoes and preheat the oven and the pan to 350°. Add potatoes and roast, turning twice or three times till they are just pierceable and nicely browned. Salt and pepper.

Boiled Potatoes

Estimate ½ pound per person or slightly more for larger appetites. At least 1 potato per person should be the rule. Peel potatoes and boil in salted water till just soft to the fork. Drain and return to the stove for a moment or two to dry. Serve very hot with:
  1) *butter*
  2) *parsley butter*
  3) *chive butter*
  4) *fines herbes butter*
  5) *plain, with parsley*

These are served with fish, stews and ragouts and often with sautéed chicken or other sautés.

Boiled New Potatoes

Estimate 4 to 8 potatoes per person, depending on size. Tiny ones are by far the best. Cook them in their jackets, with a "belly band" cut around them, or scrape them if they are freshly dug. Boil quickly in salted water. Drain and dress with butter and salt and pepper.

NOTE: You may use chopped fresh parsley, fresh chervil, fresh chives or fresh mint with these delicious little potatoes.

Mashed Potatoes

Alexander Dumaine was once quoted as saying that "the mashing process should only be an up and down one." Thus he would eliminate that pleasant American term "whipped potatoes." For 6 persons peel and boil 8 medium potatoes. Drain and dry for a second over the heat. Mash the potatoes with a masher. Add ¾ stick butter (6 tablespoons) and salt to taste. Mash again. Add ½ cup heavy cream that has been heated and whip potatoes with a spatula or a whisk. Serve very hot in a hot dish with an extra pat of butter in the center and a dusting of freshly ground black pepper.

If potatoes are exceptionally dry you may add more cream.

VARIATIONS:

1) Whip in a little chopped parsley or chopped chives, or both.

2) Whip together equal quantities of potatoes and yellow turnips that have been mashed with butter.

3) Combine potatoes and mashed celery root.

Duchesse Potatoes

Prepare the same as whipped potatoes, but add 2 or 3 egg yolks before whipping vigorously. Force through a pastry bag fitted with a rosette tube. Form small medallions on a buttered baking sheet or use for a border on made dishes or planked dishes. Brown in a 375° oven.

Sautéed Mashed Potatoes

These may be formed into flat cakes and sautéed quickly in hot butter, beef fat or bacon fat and turned once or twice to give them a lovely golden color. Delicious with almost any dish, hot or cold. Perfect with cold turkey after that holiday dinner.

Home Fried Potatoes

Allow 1 to 1½ potatoes per person. Peel and slice potatoes. Sauté them in a heavy skillet, using butter, olive oil, beef fat or pork fat. Cook slowly, turning them occasionally till they are brown and nicely crisp on both sides. Salt and pepper to taste.

German Fried Potatoes

Peel potatoes (allowing 1 to 1½ potatoes per person) and cut into ⅛-inch slices. Heat 5 tablespoons butter in a skillet (for 4 medium-sized potatoes). Sauté potatoes over fairly intense heat. Turn often with a spatula and salt and pepper to taste. Potatoes should be crisp and brown.

Galette Potatoes

Peel and slice thinly 4 Idaho potatoes. Melt 6 tablespoons butter in a heavy skillet. Arrange potato slices in rosette fashion in pan. Start with a large slice in center and overlap other slices. Salt and pepper each layer and dot with butter. Cover and cook over fairly low heat for 20 to 25 minutes. Increase the heat and shake the pan lightly. Invert on a hot platter. Serves 4.

NOTE: You may also invert potatoes and return to pan to brown other side.

Hash Brown Potatoes

Allow 1 to 1½ potatoes per person. Peel and slice potatoes and then chop them rather coarsely. Melt butter (1 tablespoon for each potato) or beef fat in a heavy skillet and get the pan quite hot. Add potatoes and press down. Cook till they form a crisp brown crust on the bottom. Invert on a hot plate. If you wish, you may slide the potatoes back in the pan to brown on the other side. Salt and pepper to taste.

Lyonnaise Potatoes

Peel and slice 6 to 8 potatoes. Peel and slice thinly 2 medium onions. Melt 6 tablespoons butter in a skillet. Add the onions and sauté lightly. Add potatoes and turn well till they begin to brown nicely. It may be necessary to add more butter. Just before serving, add salt and pepper to taste and ¼ cup chopped parsley. Turn well and serve very hot. Serves 6 to 8.

O'Brien Potatoes

Peel and cut in ¾-inch dice 6 to 8 precooked potatoes. Peel and slice 1 medium onion. Clean and dice ½ green pepper, and dice 1 pimiento. Melt 6 tablespoons butter or bacon fat in a skillet, add onions and pepper, and cook for 4 minutes. Add diced potatoes and sauté gently, shaking the pan and turning them from time to time. Add salt and pepper to taste and, just before serving, the chopped pimiento and ¼ cup chopped parsley. Serves 6 to 8.

Deep Fried Potatoes

Use any vegetable oil, vegetable fat or even beef fat. Strain through a cheesecloth after frying, for reuse.

Various potatoes require different frying times. Try soaking them in ice water and drying them before frying or frying them without any preparation. Experiment till you find the perfect potato for frying.

For all potatoes of this kind one needs a deep-frying pan with a basket to lower and raise the potatoes. The temperature for deep-frying should be from 350° to 370°. The lower temperature is for blanching potatoes that you will later recook at a higher temperature. Fry a few potatoes at a time. Be sure your temperature control goes back to the original temperature each time. Keep potatoes hot in the oven or warming drawer.

The following are the styles of potatoes most often deep fried:

CHIPS: These are small new potatoes cut into halves or quarters and cooked in deep fat till crisp and brown.

FRENCH FRIES: Potatoes cut in ¼- to ½-inch square strips or into dice. These are either fried in fat at 370° or blanched at 350° and refried at 370° later. Salt them well and serve very crisp. Nothing is worse than a soggy French fried potato.

JULIENNE POTATOES: These are cut into ¼- or ⅛-inch strips and fried.

SHOESTRINGS: For these you need an appliance called a "mandoline," which cuts vegetables into various shapes and sizes. Shoestrings are exceedingly narrow cut strings of potatoes that are fried crisp at about 355° to 360°.

SARATOGA OR POTATO CHIPS: These are cut very thin on the mandoline and deep fried till golden and crisp.

WAFFLE POTATOES: These are cut on the mandoline in a latticed pattern and cooked crisp at 360°. Delicious hot or cold.

DAUPHINE POTATOES: Combine 1 cup each Pâte à Choux (see p. 358) and mashed potatoes and beat well. Drop by spoonfuls into fat at 370° and fry till golden brown and puffy.

Potatoes Anna

For 6 persons peel and thinly slice 6 medium potatoes. Butter a heavy iron skillet or a baking dish and arrange the potatoes in overlapping layers, dotting each layer lightly with butter and salting. Top with butter and bake in a 400° oven until potatoes are soft in the centers and crisp at the edges and those at the bottom are browned. You may cover the pan for part or all of the cooking time, if you wish. It is impossible to say how long the potatoes will take. I have had them cook in 45 minutes and again have had them take 1¼ hours. Invert the dish on a hot platter.

Boulangère Potatoes

Butter a baking dish and arrange freshly sliced potatoes in layers, dotting each layer with butter. You will need about 1 largish potato per person. Salt and pepper to taste, and, just before putting the potatoes in a 350° oven, add 1 cup or more beef broth or consomme. Cover for 30 minutes. Remove cover and continue baking till potatoes are tender and well soaked with broth. Add additional broth if potatoes cook dry.

Pommes Dauphinoise

Butter a deep baking dish and arrange layers of thinly sliced potatoes. Dot each layer with butter and sprinkle with grated Gruyère cheese or Parmesan cheese. Salt and pepper to taste. Cover and bake at 350° until potatoes are tender.

VARIATION: Arrange layers of sliced potatoes dotted with butter and sprinkled with salt and pepper. Add ½ cup heavy cream, cover and bake at 325° till potatoes are barely tender. Add another ½ cup cream and sprinkle top lavishly with grated Gruyère cheese. Return to oven uncovered and cook till cheese has melted and browned.

Cheddar cheese may be used instead of Gruyère; and thin slices of sausage meat may be placed on top before the cheese is added.

Sweet Potatoes Boiled

Sweet potatoes may be boiled and mashed; boiled, sliced and glazed with butter and sugar; or mashed, blended with butter and pecans, rolled in chopped pecans, brushed with butter and baked in the oven for 20 minutes at 350°.

Potato Salad I

Boil 6 to 8 potatoes and as soon as they are cooked run under cold water. Peel and slice while still hot. Transfer to a bowl. Add ½ cup olive oil, 2 tablespoons wine vinegar, and salt and pepper to taste. Cool and let stand in refrigerator overnight. When ready to serve add seasonings to taste, such as:

> ½ cup finely chopped onion or scallion
> ¼ cup finely cut celery
> ¼ cup chopped chives
> ½ cup chopped parsley
> ¼ cup grated carrot
> ¼ cup chopped green pepper

You may use any of these or all of them if you wish. Correct the seasoning and add more oil and vinegar if necessary. Garnish with hard-cooked eggs and cherry tomatoes.

Potato Salad II

Boil 6 to 8 potatoes and chill. Peel and cut into ¾-inch dice.

Combine with ¾ cup each chopped onion and celery, ¼ cup chopped parsley, ½ teaspoon freshly ground pepper, and salt to taste. Bind well with mayonnaise or boiled dressing. Spoon into a bed of greens and decorate with sliced hard-boiled eggs and ripe olives.

Hot Potato Salad I

Boil 6 to 8 potatoes in their jackets and peel while still hot. Try out 8 rashers bacon cut in small pieces. Add ½ cup chopped onion and ¼ cup wine vinegar to the pan. Toss with the potatoes and add ¼ cup chopped green onions and ¼ cup chopped parsley. Correct seasoning.

Hot Potato Salad II

This one should be made with new potatoes. Boil in their jackets and peel while still hot. Cut in halves or quarters. Add ⅔ cup hot olive oil, 3 tablespoons wine vinegar, and salt and freshly ground pepper to taste. Add finely chopped onion if desired. Serve with sausages, sauerkraut dishes, etc.

A GUIDE TO
WINES, APÉRITIFS,
AND LIQUEURS

A GUIDE TO WINES

Wine	Source	Characteristics	Serve with
BEAUJOLAIS (almost always red)	France, from the district of the same name in Burgundy.	Fruity and lively, with a spicy bouquet. Should be full-bodied and is best drunk quite young. Though red wines are normally served at room temperature, this one can (and should) be lightly chilled during the summer months.	Simpler versions of beef, and lamb. Macaroni parisienne. Terrine. Some veal dishes. Chicken, roasted or braised. A good picnic wine.
BEAUNE (both red and white)	France, from the Côte d'Or in Burgundy.	A light, soft wine. Drink young.	Salmon braised in red wine. Beef bourguignon. Estofat of beef. Lamb. Game.
BORDEAUX Regionals (red)	France.	*Médoc:* Home of the greatest Bordeaux or clarets. These are slow to mature and shouldn't be drunk in the first flush of youth.	Turkey. Chicken. Lamb. Duck. Steaks.
		St. Emilion: Big wines, somewhat similar to burgundies. Should not be drunk too young.	Fowl with distinctive flavor. Game. Spiced braised dishes. Leg of lamb.
CABERNET SAUVIGNON (red)	A California varietal wine.	This is the grape from which most of the great French Bordeaux are made. Superior California clarets are produced in Napa, Sonoma and Santa Clara counties.	Kidneys. Beef. Stews. Roast fowl. Tomato dishes.
CHABLIS	France, from Burgundy.	The best are a pale straw color, delicate in bouquet and flinty dry. Drink young.	Apéritif with crème de cassis. Delicate fish dishes, such as cold lobster, shad roe, oysters on the half shell. Clams.

Wine	Source	Characteristics	Serve with
CHAMBERTIN (red)	France, from the vineyards of the same name, near the Côte d'Or in Burgundy.	These are big, fine wines that should have five years or more to develop before they are drunk.	Baby Lamb. Coq au Vin de Chambertin. Beef. Game.
CHAMPAGNE (white)	Strictly speaking, these are French wines produced in the Champagne district of France. However, some very fine ones, such as Almaden, Korbel and Beaulieu, are made in California.	Traditionally *the* wine for festive occasions. Serve chilled, of course.	Apéritif with cassis. Caviar. Smoked salmon. Chicken. Ham. Turkey. Seafood. Almost any food.
CHASSAGNE-MONTRACHET (red)	France, from the Côte d'Or in Burgundy.	These soft, well-balanced wines are little known in comparison to their white counterparts. They reach perfection in about five years.	Beef roasts. Fish cooked with red wine. Veal roasts. Small game. Cheese.
CHÂTEAU AUSONE (red)	France; a Bordeaux from St. Emilion.	A big, full wine that matures slowly.	Roast fowl. Game. Beef. Squab. Guinea hen. Cheese.
CHÂTEAU BEYCHEVELLE (red)	France; a Bordeaux from St. Julien.	This is one of the light Médocs that can be drunk young quite successfully.	Fowl. Stuffed squab chickens. Lamb. Kidneys. Cheese.
CHÂTEAU CHEVAL BLANC (red)	France; a Bordeaux from St. Emilion.	Another exceptionally full wine that develops slowly.	Roast chicken (formal dinner). Game fowl. Beef. Great cheese.
CHÂTEAU HAUT-BRION (red)	France, from Pessac-Graves.	One of the greatest of Bordeaux. Ready to drink as young as five years old.	Holiday turkey. Great game dishes. Exceptional beef and lamb dishes. Cheese.

Wine	Source	Characteristics	Serve with
CHÂTEAU DE LASCOMBES (red)	France; a Bordeaux from Margaux.	Shares in the bigness and fullness characteristic of wines from the Médoc. Matures more rapidly than some of its cousins.	Holiday birds. Roast beef. Game birds. Venison.
CHÂTEAU PRIEURÉ LICHINE (red)	France; a Bordeaux from Margaux.	This is one of the light Bordeaux that can be drunk young.	Fowl. Game such as partridge. Steaks. Squab.
CHÂTEAUNEUF-DU-PAPE (red)	France, from the Rhone Valley.	Stout and robust with a full flavor. Should be at least five years old.	Hearty dishes such as cassoulets and stews. Game. Venison. Duck. Goose.
CHIANTI (most often red)	Italy, though some is produced in California.	Agreeable, though not what one would call distinguished. Should be drunk young.	Classic for Italian dishes. Pasta with red sauces. Stews and ragouts.
FLEURIE (red)	France, from the Beaujolais district of Burgundy.	Fruity and lively, and best drunk young. Delicious chilled in summer.	Informal meals. Terrines. Deviled chicken. Chops. Roast lamb.
GEWURZTRAMINER (white)	A native of Alsace; quite creditable versions are also produced in California.	A full-flavored, spicy wine with pronounced bouquet. Should be drunk in its youth.	Pig's feet. Sauerkraut. Poached chicken. Fruits. Some fish dishes.
GREY RIESLING	A California varietal wine.	A delicate, delicious wine. The one produced by Charles Krug is particularly good.	Hors d'oeuvres. Sautéed fish. White chicken dishes. Veal. Sweetbreads.
MOUNTAIN RED	California.	A delightful wine that submits gracefully to light chilling in the warmer months. Louis Martini has an outstanding one, which is also available in bulk.	Beef. Turkey. Ragouts. Perfect picnic wine. General use.

Wine	Source	Characteristics	Serve with
MOUNTAIN WHITE	California.	Another case where the Louis Martini vineyards rate special marks.	Shellfish such as lobster. Picnics. General use.
MUSCADET (white)	France, from the Loire.	Very light and dry, this should be drunk quite young. It is a lovely "summer wine" that is excellent when chilled.	Cold trout. Grilled shellfish. Veal. Sweetbreads. Brains. Any fish dish.
HERMITAGE (red; also white)	France, from the Rhone Valley.	A big, full-bodied wine that is long lived.	Lamb. Hearty dishes such as roast beef or goose.
JULIÉNAS (red)	France, from the Beaujolais district of Burgundy.	Has the fruitiness and freshness characteristic of Beaujolais. It, too, should be drunk young.	Beef. Red meats in informal dishes. Chops. Picnics.
MADEIRA	Portugal, from the island of Madeira.	A fortified wine and one of the longest lived. It ranges from the light and dry Rainwater through Sercial and Verdelho, to rich, sweet Bual and heavy Malmsey. Can be put to most of the uses of the corresponding sherries.	Apéritif. Turtle soup. After a fine dinner.
NEUCHÂTEL (white)	Switzerland.	A light, dry wine that is at its best young.	Swiss tarte à l'oignon. Fondue. Veal dishes. Trout.
NUITS ST. GEORGES (red; also white)	France, from the Côte de Nuits.	A full, rich wine that should be at least three or four years old.	Lamb. Chicken and fowl. Game. (White.) Veal and fish.
PINOT CHARDONNAY	A California varietal wine.	A light, delightful wine.	Ham. Roast turkey. Fish. Light chicken dishes. For summer drinking.

Wine	Source	Characteristics	Serve with
PINOT NOIR (red)	A California varietal wine.	This is quite similar to French Burgundy.	Roast kid. Beef. Lamb. Cheese.
PORT	The original and finest come from Portugal, though many other countries make ports.	A fortified wine.	Fruits. Cheeses. Dessert wine.
POUILLY-FUISSÉ	France, from Burgundy.	A dry wine with a lovely bouquet. It should be drunk young.	Shrimp. Lobster. Crab. Veal. Light dishes.
POUILLY-FUMÉ (white)	France, from the Loire.	A light, agreeable wine that is best drunk young.	Smoked fish. Perfect luncheon wine. Cold dishes.
PULIGNY MONTRACHET	France, from the Côte d'Or in Burgundy.	One of the great Burgundies, dry and with deep flavor. Should not be too old.	Sweetbreads. Veal. White chicken dishes. Fish.
RIESLING (white)	Produced in Alsace, Germany, California and Chile.	This is a sharp, exceptionally dry wine.	Apéritif. Fish dishes. Pork.
ROSÉ	Produced in almost all wine-growing countries. Particularly good are the Tavels from France and the Almaden from California. The latter is available in bulk.	This is a light, refreshing wine that can be drunk with almost anything and, like Beaujolais, should be quite young.	Excellent picnic wine. Ham. Summer dishes. Cold dishes.
SANCERRE (white)	France, from the Loire.	Fresh, fruity and dry, it is best when drunk young.	Fish. Broiled chicken. Veal. Summer foods.
SAUTERNE (white)	Originally France; now also from New York and California.	A sweet wine.	Desserts. Sometimes with hors d'oeuvres.

Wine	Source	Characteristics	Serve with
SAUVIGNON BLANC (white)	A California varietal wine.	A charming wine, ranging from dry to sweet.	Hors d'oeuvres. Cold dishes. Veal. Light chicken dishes.
SHERRY	Spain; also produced in America.	Sherries, like ports, have a great range of flavor. They go from the pale, very dry Finos to the dark and sweet Creams.	Apéritif (drier ones). Soup. Occasionally, hors d'oeuvre.
SOAVE	Italy.	A dry wine that should be served well chilled. Drink young.	Antipasto. Fettucine. Veal dishes. Chicken.
TRAMINER (white)	Produced in Alsace, Germany, and California.	Especially noted for its marvelous bouquet.	Fish. Eggs. Light dishes.
VALPOLICELLA (red)	Italy.	A light wine that should be less than four or five years old. Can be lightly chilled with great success.	Chicken. Ragouts. Pasta.
VERDICCHIO (white)	Italy.	Light, dry, and faintly earthy. This should be drunk young.	Antipasto. Fettucine. Fish. Veal.
VOLNAY (red)	France, from the Côte d'Or in Burgundy.	A soft and rather delicate wine, pleasing to most palates.	Most meats. Fowl.
VOSNE-ROMANÉE (red)	France, from the Côte d'Or in Burgundy.	A big, full-bodied wine that is a wine lover's delight. Should be at least five years old.	Beef. Cheese. Game. Duck. Goose.
ZINFANDEL (red)	A California varietal wine.	A fresh, fruity wine similar to Beaujolais.	Red meats. Pasta. Ragouts. Informal meals.

A GUIDE TO APÉRITIFS

Wine Apéritifs, or Quinquinas, from France

These are the most common of the quinquinas. They were so called because they formerly contained quinine, which was especially beneficial to those living in the tropics who were exposed to malaria. Some of these are now made in America and sold under the same names, although in a few cases they are slightly altered to please the mythical thing called "the American palate."

DUBONNET: Probably the most famous of all apéritifs. Comes in dark and blond varieties. Sweet and rather cloying, it may be combined with gin or vodka and ice for a less sweet drink.

LILLET: A delicate, dryish wine-based drink from Bordeaux. Comes in dark and light varieties. Slightly orange in flavor. Best on the rocks with a strip of orange zest or with a bit of soda.

RAPHAEL OR ST. RAPHAEL: A quinquina with a somewhat overpowering bittersweet flavor. Good on the rocks, with soda or with a drop of gin.

BYRRH: (Pronounced "beer.") Similar to the other bittersweet drinks. It is a lovely color and is best served cold, although Europeans prefer it at room temperature.

LA SEINE: A drink that resembles French Dubonnet so closely that it is astonishing. Use like Dubonnet.

Aromatized Wines

DRY OR FRENCH VERMOUTH: In addition to being the element that changes straight gin into a martini, dry vermouth is, for many people, the ideal apéritif. It can be served on the rocks, frappéed, or mixed with ice and strained into a cocktail glass. Mixed with a few drops of crème de cassis, with the addition of a strip of lemon zest and a bit of soda, it becomes a Vermouth Cassis.

SWEET WHITE VERMOUTH: This is Italian in origin and is usually served straight, either chilled or not.

SWEET VERMOUTHS: The dark vermouth, familiar to most of us as the additive to whisky in a Manhattan, is perhaps the most popular apéritif in the world. It is especially a favorite in South America, in the Caribbean, and in Europe —served straight, chilled, or on the rocks. Combined with Campari bitters (3 parts vermouth, 1 part Campari) and soda, with a twist of lemon zest, it becomes an Americano. An ounce of sweet vermouth, one of gin and one of Campari, with ice and soda, make a Negroni.

BITTERS: Campari is perhaps the best known and is exceedingly popular throughout the Latin world. It is usually combined with soda or with sweet vermouth. Punt Y Mes is popular in Italy and Spanish-speaking countries, either straight or combined with vermouth.

Chilled Wines

WHITE WINE: Chilled white wine without embellishment is a delicious apéritif. It should be on the dry side. Mixed with a few drops of crème de cassis, it makes a most popular apéritif known as *Kir*—approximately 1 teaspoon of cassis to a glass, or to taste.

CHAMPAGNE: This, of course, is the greatest of all apéritifs. It may be served with a touch of cassis, but certainly do not use your finest brut.

Fortified Wines

DRY SHERRY: The dry and only the dry ones make good apéritifs. They should be chilled. These include the Montillas, Manzanillas, Finos and Dry Amontillados.

DRY MADEIRA: This may also be served as an apéritif and is best when chilled.

A GUIDE TO LIQUEURS

Liqueur	Flavor	As a Drink	Uses in Cooking
APRY (French) APRICOT LIQUEUR (French, American, Dutch)	Apricot	Straight. In punches.	To flavor soufflés, apricot glaze for fruit tarts, crêpes, apple tart or charlotte. On pineapple, fruits, ices.
CHERRY HEERING (Danish)	Cherry	Straight or with soda, or with fresh lime and tonic (quinine water). In lemonade, Rum Collins.	In cherry tart, soufflé, duck Montmorency. On fruit, ices.
GRAND MARNIER (French) AURUM (Italian) COINTREAU (American) CURAÇAO (Dutch) TRIPLE SEC (American) MANDARINE (French)	Orange, except for Mandarine, which has a tangerine flavor.	Straight, or in long and mixed drinks. Half and half with cognac. Aurum, in coffee.	To flavor orange sauces for duck, crêpes. In soufflés, butter creams, Bavarian cream, mousse, syrup for baba or savarin. On fruit, ice cream. To baste pork roasts.
PEACH LIQUEUR (French, American, Dutch)	Peach	Straight. In punches.	In sauces. On peaches, other fruits, especially raspberries, or ice cream.
FRAMBERRY (French)	Raspberry	Straight. In punches.	To flavor sauces, crêpes, soufflés. On fruit, ices.
CRÈME DE VIOLET (French, Dutch)	Violet	Straight.	In sauces. On parfaits, ice cream.
KUMMEL (French, American, Dutch)	Caraway	Straight. In punches.	In some sauces, soufflés.
TEA LIQUEUR (French)	Tea	Straight, chilled. In hot or iced tea, or lemonade.	On ice cream.
PIMIENTO DRAM (Jamaican)	Rum and spice	Straight. In punches.	On pineapple, rum baba.

Liqueur	Flavor	As a Drink	Uses in Cooking
LIQUEUR D'OR (French)	Aromatic herbs (contains bits of gold leaf)	Straight.	On ice cream. Combine with other liqueurs.
STREGA (Italian)	Herbs and citrus	Straight. In coffee.	In sauces, soufflés.
CHARTREUSE (French)	Herbs	Straight. With cognac, Scotch.	In pudding and ice cream sauces, hard sauce, Bavaroise. On lemon ice, ice cream.
BÉNÉDICTINE (French)	Aromatic herbs	Straight, with coffee. In cognac.	In hard sauce, apple pie, mincemeat, soufflés.
B & B or BÉNÉDICTINE AND BRANDY (French)	Aromatic herbs	Straight, with coffee.	
CRÈME DE CASSIS (French)	Black currant	With soda. In Vermouth Cassis, Cognac Cassis, White Wine Cassis.	With raspberry or black currant purée for sauces. In cassis sherbet. On fruit.
CRÈME DE CACAO (French, Dutch, American)	Cocoa	Straight. In Alexander, Grasshopper.	In chocolate soufflé, sauces. On ice cream.
TIA MARIA (Jamaican) KAHLUA (Mexican) ESPRESSO (Italian)	Coffee	Straight. In hot or iced coffee, or hot chocolate.	In coffee syrups, sauces, or soufflés. On parfaits, ice cream.
CRÈME DE VANILLE (French, American, Dutch)	Vanilla	Straight. In eggnog, iced chocolate.	In vanilla soufflé, mousse, Bavaroise, ice cream sauce. On ices.
CRÈME DE NOYAUX (French, Dutch)	Almond-hazelnut	Straight. As substitute for orgeat. In Pink Squirrel cocktail.	In sauces, soufflés, fruit coupes. Often combined with fruit liqueur.
CRÈME DE MENTHE, green (French, American, Dutch)	Mint	Straight, or frappé. With water or vodka. In Grasshopper.	With pears. On ices.

Liqueur	Flavor	As a Drink	Uses in Cooking
CRÈME DE MENTHE, green (French, American, Dutch)	Mint	Straight, or frappé. With water or vodka. In Grasshopper.	With pears. On ices.
CRÈME DE MENTHE, white (French, American, Dutch)	Mint	Straight or with water. With cognac in Stinger.	In chocolate or ice cream sauces. With pears.
FIOR DE ALPE (Italian)	Aromatic with rock candy base.	Straight, chilled. In punches.	Same as Chartreuse.
IZARRA (French)	Aromatic herbs	Straight.	On ice cream.
ANISETTE (French, American, Dutch) ANIS (French) OUZO (Greek)	Anise	Straight, on the rocks, or with soda or water.	In certain sauces.
DRAMBUIE (Scottish)	Scotch and honey	Straight. In punches.	In custard sauce for poached fruit, soufflés.
IRISH MIST (Irish)	Irish whisky and honey	Straight.	On sliced oranges.

INDEX

A

Aïoli, 33, 181
  accompaniments of, 181–182
Ala, nutted, 174
Almonds, warm salted, 251
Anchovied radishes, 238, 246
Anchovy butter, 259
Anchovy mayonnaise, 349
Anchovy sauce, 347
Anguilles au vert, 204
Antipasto, 122
  Picnic, 303
  Plate, 211
Apéritifs, A Guide to, 380–381
Appetizers, *see under* separate listings
Apples,
  Bonne femme, 59
  Charlotte, 36
  Kuchen, 302
  Steamed, 160
  with cheddar cheese, 43
Apricots,
  and pineapple flan with almonds, 163
  Glaze, 38
  Soufflé, 69
  Tarte, 38
  Bottoms with foie gras, 102
  Salad, 79
Artichoke,
Asparagus, 15
  Tips, 220
  Vinaigrette, 121, 152, 319
Avocado, *see* Guacamole, 268

B

Bacon,
  Crisp, 330
  -Wrapped dates, 236
  -Wrapped prunes, 236
Bagna cauda, 309
Baking powder biscuit, 358–359
Barbecue sauce, 351–352
Barley with mushrooms, 93
Basic brown sauce, 344
Bavarian cream, *see* Crème Patissière,
  213–214

Beans, black, with rice and cracklings,
  225–226
Beans, fava, 186
  Hot with fresh herbs, 192
Beans, green,
  Haricots verts, 106
  Salad, 84
  Vinaigrette, 133
Beans, pinto, with chili and sausage,
  269
Béarnaise sauce, 347
Béchamel sauce, 343
Beef,
  à la mode en gelée, 290–291
  and pork chili with eggs, 224–225
  Cold, en daube, 166
  Corned, hot, 243
  Daube provençale, 145–146
  Estofat de boeuf, 151
  Fillet,
    Cold, japonais, 197
    Glazed, 321
    Roast, 294
    Stuffed, 117
  Ground,
    Cheeseburger balls, 236–237
    Grilled cheeseburgers, 139
    Grilled hamburgers with garlic,
      268–269
    Steak tartare, 239
  Roasts,
    Cold, with mustard sauce, 55
    with mustards, 241–242
    Sirloin strip, 332–333
    Spitted, 273–274
  Salad parisienne, 37–38, 188
  Sandwiches,
    Grilled flank steak, 280–281
  Steaks,
    au poivre flambé, 120
    Broiled flank, 8
    Chuck wagon, 282
    Double entrecôte, mustard hollan-
      daise, 263–264
    Teriyaki strips, 236
    with anchovy butter, 259
  Tournedos au poivre flambé, 47–48

Beef (*Cont.*)
   Viennese goulash, 95
   Zratys nelson, 83
Beets, *see* salads
Beurre blanc, 347–348
Biscuits,
   Baking powder, 358–359
   Buttermilk, 359
Black beans and rice with cracklings,
      225–226
Black cod, steamed, smoked, 10
Blueberries with maple cream, 55
Bordelaise sauce, 344–345
Bourride, 32–33
Bread,
   Corn, 201
   Corn, for toasting, 361
   Croustades, 14
   Herb, 180
   Homemade, 353
   Homemade whole wheat, 184
Breakfasts,
   Early, 3–10
   Late, 11–28
Brioche, 356
   Cassonade, 182
   Sandwiches, 315
   Sausage en, 34
   with preserves and cream cheese, 24
Broccoli, beurre noir, 118
Broth, clam and tomato, 80
Brussel sprouts, 103–104, 333
Buffets,
   Dinner, 194–214
   Luncheon, 180–193
   Supper, 215–226
Buttermilk biscuit, 359

C

Cabbage,
   Champagne kraut, 155
   Perdreaux aux choux, 89–90
Caesar salad, 62–63
Cakes,
   Angel food, 291–292
   Apple kuchen, 302
   Coffee, 6
   Chocolate génoise roll, 40

Cakes (*Cont.*)
   Glenna McGinnis Lane cake, 321–322
   Linzer torte, 155–156
   Petits fours squares, 296
   Pound, 360–361
   Rehruecken, 96–97
   Sponge, 355–356
   Shortcakes,
      Dough for, 349
      Peach, with sherried whipped cream,
         274–275
      Quick raspberry, 130
   Zuppa inglese, 213–214
Calf's liver sautéed, 25
Canapé provençale, 70
Cannelloni with tomato sauce, 140
Carnitas, 148
Cassonade, 182
Cassoulet, quick, 44
Caviar,
   Black, 104, 252
   Red, 28
Cervelat salad, 190–191, 222
Champagne kraut, 155
Charcuterie, 21–22
Cheese, 121, 326
   Bel Paese, 158
   Board, 205, 242, 248, 311
   Cheddar, 43, 171
   Gorgonzola, 48, 123
   Gougère, 250–251
   with fruit, 43, 48, 171, 291, 313
Cheese sauce, 343
Cheeseburgers,
   Balls, 236–237
   Grilled, 338–339
Chestnuts,
   how to prepare, 72
   Puree of, 337
Chicken,
   Broiled with rosemary butter, 56
   Chili, 137–138
   Chili con queso, 247
   Coq au riesling, 201
   Coq au vin en brioche, 142–143
   Crêpes de volaille, 49
   Fried legs, 248
   Giblets, brochette of, 275–276

Chicken (*Cont.*)
  Gravy, cream, 319
  Grilled,
    Deviled with sauce béarnaise, 92–93
    Herbed drumsticks, 280
    Piquant, 276
  Hash superb, 14
  Kiev (kievski) 102
    variations, 103
  Livers, chopped, 244
  Mayonnaise with walnuts, 198–199
  Perfect roast chicken with tarragon, 114
  Sandwiches, 298–299, 317
  Shenandoah fried, 318–319
  Squab chickens, *see* Squab
  Swiss enchilada, 148–149
  Vol-au-vent with sweetbreads suprême, 67–68
  with madeira, 79
Chili,
  Chicken, 137–138
  Con queso, 247
  and sausage, with pinto beans, 269
Chipolatas, 15
Chocolate frosting,
  Helen Evans Brown's, 40
Chocolate génoise roll, 40
Chocolate glaze, 296
Choucroute garnie, 195–196
Cinnamon rolls, 354
Cocktail parties,
  Large, 230–244
  Small, 245–253
Codfish, *see* Fish
Coeur à la crème with strawberries, 57, 185
Coffee cake, 6
Coffee granita, 167
Cole slaw, 271, 302
Consommé, *see* Soups
Cookies,
  Cinnamon stars, 218–219
  Macaroons, 337–338
  Peanut crisps, 232
  Sables, 146–147
  Sand tarts, 299
Coquillage, 280

Corn bread, 201
  for toasting, 361
Corned beef, hot, 243
Cornmeal mush, fried, 9
Court bouillon, 51, 160
Crab,
  Soufflé, 65
  Soup, Margaret Jennings, 116–117
Crabmeat,
  Charentais, 82–83
  Orientale, 188
Crawfish, spiced, 183–184
Cream cheese pastry, 360
Cream gravy, 319
Crème patissière, 213–214
Crêpes, 362–363
  de volaille, 49–50
  Soufflés, 81–82
Croissants, 357
Croustades, tiny, 14
Crudités, 49, 145
  with anchovy mayonnaise, 187
  with sauce niçoise, 56
Cucumbers,
  Open faced sandwiches, 249–250
  Sandwiches, 18
  with cherry tomatoes, 71
Curry sauce, 26
Custard,
  Angel food, 262
  Cassonade, 182

D

Dates, bacon-wrapped, 236
Desserts, *see* Cakes, Custards, Ices, Pies, Puddings, *see also* Fruits, Omelets, and Soufflés
Diable sauce, 345
Dinners,
  Buffets, 194–214
  Easy to prepare, 120–135
  Formal, 100–119
  Informal, 76–99
  Summer, 164–175
  to prepare in advance, 136–163
Dressings, *see* Sauces
Drinks, cold, 339

Duck,
  Glazed with curry and honey, 86–87
  Terrine of duckling, 207–208
Duxelles, 48, 353
  Sauce, 345

E

Éclairs, coffee, 106–107
Eels,
  Anguilles au vert, 204
  Smoked, 310
Egg orangeade, 4
Eggplant,
  Gratin of, 81
  Provençale, 277
Eggs, *see also* Omelets
  Caviar, 301
  Caviar stuffed, 248
  Devilled, 301
  in jelly, 222
  and mushrooms in tarragon cream, 12
  Oeufs en cocotte, 37
  Pungent, 301
  Special stuffed, 298
  Stuffed, 265–266
  Table scrambled, 16
  with ratatouille, 22
  Woven, 60–61
Empanadas, 223–224
Endive,
  Braisées, 112
  and beet salad, 311
  with beet dressing, 68–69
English muffins, melbaed, 286
Espagnole sauce, 344

F

Fava beans, 186
  Hot with fresh herbs, 192
Fettucine Alfredo, 27
Figs,
  with bacon, 263
  with prosciutto, 27
  with prosciutto and salami, 273
Filberts, salted, 233

Fish,
  Black cod, steamed, smoked, 10
  Bourride, 32–33
  Codfish,
    in cream with eggs, 330
    Provençale, 20–21
  Herring salad, 194–195
  Red snapper, cold with shrimp and mustard sauce, 70–71
  Sablefish, steamed, smoked, 10
  Salmon,
    Braised in red wine, 124–125
    Dill paste, 238
    Kedgeree, 26
    Poached, beurre blanc, 51
    Smoked, 252–253
  Shad roe poached in butter, 131
  Sole,
    en escabeche, 224
    Paupiettes of, 161–162
  Smoked fish platter, 327–328
  Smoked and cured fish, 17–18
  Soupe de poisson, marseillaise, 193
  Striped bass with cream sauce, 171
  Trout,
    Cold, à la turque
    Sauté meunière
    Stuffed, pyramide, 94–95
Flageolets, 127
Flan, 149–150
Foie gras, 253
  Sandwiches, 238, 299
  with artichoke bottoms, 102
Frankfurters, French, 339
French dressing, 350
Fruit desserts,
  Apples,
    Bonne femme, 59
    Charlotte, 36
    Steamed, 160
  Apricots, tarte aux, 38
  Blueberries with maple cream, 55
  Cantaloupe and watermelon with raspberries and ice cream, 283
  Fruits rafraîchis with sables, 146
  Grapefruit with sherry, 66
  Oranges, sliced, with grand marnier, 129, 193
  Peaches,

Fruit desserts (*Cont.*)
  Peaches (*Cont.*)
    Broiled, flambé, 44–45
    with bourbon, 199
    with marsala, 141
    with raspberry puree, 33–34
  Pears conde, 84–85
  Pineapple,
    with kirsch, 74, 132
    with rum, 138
  Raspberries in red wine, 61
  Strawberries,
    Quick sherbet, 50
    Romanoff, 63
      in meringue shells, 174–175
Fruit, hot compote of, 5
Fruit juices, 329
Frutti di mare, 39

G

Génoise, 361–362
Génoise roll, 40
Giblets, brochette of, 275–276
Goose, roast stuffed with prunes and
    apples, 335–336
Gougère, 250–251
Goulash, Viennese, 95
Grapefruit,
  Sections, 8
  Sherried, 10
  with sherry, 66
Gravy, cream, for chicken, 319
Green Goddess dressing, 349
Green noodles bolognese, 211–212
Guacamole, 268

H

Ham,
  Beer-glazed, 205
  Country, 208
  Jambon persillé, 62
  Smithfield, 328
    Cold, 12
  Steaks, charcoal broiled, 23
  Virginia ham sandwiches, 251
Hare, *see* Hasenpfeffer
Hasenpfeffer, 154
Heavenly crown, 205–206

Heroes, individual, 338
Herring salad, 194–195
Hollandaise sauce,
  Basic, 346
  Blender, 346–347
  variations, 347
Homemade bread, 353
Hominy, whole, 138
Hors d'Oeuvre strudel, 316

I

Ices–Ice Creams,
  Apricot ice, 104
  Coffee granita, 167
  Cognac and coffee ice cream, 337
  Fraises Kate, 112
  Fresh peach ice cream, 299
  Fresh strawberry ice cream, 267
  Homemade cassis ice cream, 278
  Ice cream sundaes, 329
  Kumquat parfait, 88
  Lemon granita, 90
  Mocha parfait, 93
  Raspberry sherbet with peaches, 109
Irish stew, 42–43
Italienne sauce, 351

J

Jambon persillé, 62

K

Kedgeree with curry sauce, 26
Kid on a spit, 266
Kidneys,
  Broiled, 19
  on the half shell, flambé, 132–133
Kielbasy, *see* Sausages
Knockwurst with shallot mustard, 240
Kuchen,
  Apple, 302
  Dough, 354
Kumquat parfait, 88

L

Lamb,
  Baron of baby lamb, sauce niçoise, 105

Lamb (*Cont.*)
　Chops, tiny grilled, 73
　Fillets of lamb with cepes, 80
　Hindquarters of baby lamb, provençale, 126
　Irish stew, 42–43
　Marrakech, 216
　Saddle of lamb, Prince Orloff, 111
Leeks à la grecque, 189
Lemon granita, 90
Lentil salad, 282–283
Linzer torte, 155–156
Liqueurs, a guide to, 382–384
Liver,
　Calf's, 25–26
　Chopped chicken, 244
Lobster,
　à la nage, 97–98
　and zucchini, 47
　Broiled whole, 271
　Cold, 320
　Cold, sauce verte, 123–124
Luncheons,
　Buffets, 180–193
　Formal, 45–52
　Informal, 31–45
　Ladies', 64–74
　Summer, 53–63

M

Macaroni parisienne, 157–158
Macaroons, 337–338
Madère sauce, 345
Madrilene with chives and sour cream, 50
Mango macadamia syrup for ice cream, 219
Mantequilla de pobre, 148
Mayonnaise,
　Anchovy, 349
　Basic, 348
　Blender, 348–349
　Green, 286
　Mustard, 349
　Spicy, 320–321
Meat loaf, cold, 301
Melba toast, cheesed, 329
Melbaed English muffins, 22

Melon,
　Cantaloupe and watermelon with raspberries and ice cream, 283
　with port, 23
　with prosciutto, 4, 78
　Honeydew with port, 157
Mocha parfait, 93
Mornay sauce, 343
Mousse,
　Chocolate, 135
　Coffee, 116
　Frozen raspberry and macaroon, 287
Mousseline sauce, 347
Mushrooms,
　and eggs in tarragon cream, 12
　in madeira cream, 107–108
　Salad, *see* Salads
　Sauce, 352
　Sautéed on toast, 5
　Stuffed, 232
Mussels,
　Moules marinière, 134–135
Mustard,
　Burgundy, 241
　Butter, 241
　Shallot, 240

N

Nesselrode pudding, 71–72
Niçoise salade, 200
Nockerli, 95–96
Nuts,
　Almonds, salted warm, 251
　Filberts, salted, 233
　Macadamia, 294

O

Oeufs à la neige, 152–153
Olives, garlic flavored, 246
Omelets,
　Red caviar and sour cream, 28
　Soufflé, 125
Onions,
　French fried, 84
　Glazed, 152
　Monegasque, 220
　Salad, *see* Salads
　Sandwiches, 235

Onions (*Cont.*)
　Spiced, 234
　Swiss tarte, 41
Orange marmalade soufflé, 35
Orangeade with egg, 4
Oranges
　and onion salad, 59, 270
　Sliced Mexican, 20
　Sliced with grand marnier, 129, 193
Oriental sauce, 352
Oxtail ragout with noodles, 310

P

Pasta
　Cannelloni with tomato sauce, 146
　Fettucine Alfredo, 27
　Gnocchi
　　Semolina, 103
　　Spinach, 209
　Green noodles bolognese, 211–212
　Macaroni parisienne, 157–158
　Spaghetti alla carbonara, 122–123
　with white truffles, 78
Pastrami, 243
Pastry, *see also* Pies and Tarts
　Cream cheese, 360
　Plain, 359
　Rich, 359–360
Pâté à choux, 358
Pâté de champagne, provençale, 245–246
Peas,
　New, 51–52
　Petit pois grandmère, 163
　Petit pois with mint, 68, 109
　Salad, with mushrooms, 259–260
　Snow, with mushrooms, 57, 87–88
　Soup,
　　Cream of pea, 153–154
　　Curried, 89
Peaches,
　Broiled, flambé, 44–45
　Ice cream, 299
　with bourbon, 199
　with marsala, 141
　with raspberry puree, 33–34
Peanut crisps, 232
Pears,
　Condé, 84
　with gorgonzola, 48

Perdreaux aux choux, 89–90
Peppers, green,
　Salad, 220
　　with onions, 149
　Sauteed with onions, 262
　Stuffed, 139–140
　Stuffed with sausage, 16
Perigourdine sauce, 345
Petit fours squares, 296
Petit pois, *see* Peas
Picnics, 288–303
Pies, *see also* Pastry
　Apricot and pineapple flan with almonds, 163
　Blueberry deep dish, 272
　Rich pumpkin, 326
Pig's feet, grilled, sauce diable, 159–160
Pineapple,
　with kirsch, 74, 132
　with rum, 138
Pinto beans with chili and sausage, 269
Piquante sauce, 346
Pissaladière, 249
Pizza dough, 355
Pizzas, tiny, 314–315
Potatoes,
　Anglaise, 36
　Anna, 369
　Baked, 363
　　Disgustingly rich, 364
　　Sauteed, 364
　　Stuffed, 363–364
　Boiled, 365
　Boiled new, 25, 365
　Boiled new potatoes with herbs, 205
　Boulangère, 369
　Browned, 333, 364–365
　Butter steamed, 10
　Chips, 368
　Deep fried, 368
　　variations, 368–369
　Duchesse, 366
　Dumplings, 155
　Fluffy, 143
　Fondant, 118
　French fried, 368
　Galette, 19, 367

Potatoes (*Cont.*)
  German fried, 367
  Glazed, 151
  Gratin de pommes de terre à l'ail, 106
  Hash browns, 367
  Home fried, 366–367
  Katherine Smith's new potatoes, 316
  Lyonnaise, 367
  Mashed, 366
    Sautéed, 366
    variations, 366
  New potatoes with mint, 52
  O'Brien, 368
  Parisienne, 111
  Persillés, 162
  Pommes dauphinoise, 369–370
  Pureed, 313
  Roast potatoes without a roast, 365
  Roesti, 58–59
  Salad,
    Salad I, 370
    Salad II, 370–371
    Potato and hearts of palm salad, 295
    Hot, 35, 371
  Savoyarde, 115
  Sweet, *see* Sweet potatoes
Pork,
  Carnitas, 148
  Chinese ginger and pork balls, 232
  Cold barbecued loin of pork, 191
  Double roast loin of pork, chinese style, 261
  Hot roast loin of smoked pork, 234
  Rillettes, 231
  Spareribs, glazed, 240
  Terrine aux aromates, 91–92
Port wine with melon, 23
Pound cake, 360–361
Princess Charlotte pudding, 52
Prosciutto,
  and figs, 27, 273
  and melon, 4, 78, 273
Prunes,
  Alice B. Toklas, 210
  Bacon-wrapped, 236
  Compote of, 42
  in madeira, 24

Puddings,
  Les oeufs à la neige, 152–153
  Nesselrode, 71–72
  Princess Charlotte, 52
Pumpernickel sandwiches, 18

R

Radishes, 186
  Anchovied radishes, 238, 246
  Salad, 226
Raspberries,
  in Red wine, 61
  Puree, with peaches, 33–34
Ratatouille, 22
  Hot with grated cheese, 54–55
Rayte, 20–21
Red snapper, cold with shrimp and mustard mayonnaise, 70–71
Rehruecken, 96–97
Rémoulade sauce, 349
Rhubarb compote, 25
Rice,
  Pilaff, 87
  Risotto frutti di mare, 39
  Salad, 166–167, 198, 321
  sweet, 84–85
  with chopped chives and parsley, 133
  with pinenuts, 216–217
Rillettes, 231
Rillons, 231
Rolls,
  Cinnamon, 354
  Homemade, 43
Romaine,
  and onion salad, 43
  Quarters, 274
Roquefort loaf, 297
Russian dressing, 349

S

Sables, 146–147
  Normande, 362
Sablefish, steamed, smoked, 10
Salads,
  Artichoke, 79
  Asparagus tips, 220
  Bean, 84
  Beef salad parisienne, 37–38, 188

Salads (*Cont.*)
  Beet,
    and chicory, 158
    and egg with onion dressing, 40
    and endive, 311
    and onion, 143–144
    Vinaigrette, 96
  Bibb lettuce and cherry tomato, 266–267
  Caesar, 62–63
  Celery, 220
  Cervelat, 190–191, 222
  Cole slaw, 271
  Corn, 221
  Cucumber, 219
    and cherry tomato, 71
  Dandelion, 141
  Endive,
    and beet, 311
    with beet dressing, 68–69
  Fabulous, 209–210
  Green pepper, 220
    with onions, 149
  Green salad, vintners style, 115
  Herring, 194–195
  Lentil, 282–283
  Mushroom, 220
    and bibb lettuce, 330
    and pea, 259–260
    and romaine, 130
    with watercress, 66
  Niçoise, 200
  Onion,
    and beet, 143–144
    and orange, 59, 270
    and romaine, 43, 135
    and tomato with cucumbers, 184
    Monegasque, 220
  Orange and onion, 270
  Pea and mushroom, 259–260
  Potato,
    Cold, 370, 371
    and hearts of palm, 295
    Hot, 35, 371
  Rachel salade, 286
  Radish, 226
  Raw vegetable, *see* Vegetables, Raw
  Rice, 166–167, 198, 321

Salads (*Cont.*)
  Romaine quarters, 274
    and onions, 43, 135
  Summer, 174
  Tomato, 23–24, 159, 219
    Cherry, 10, 295
    in dill, 73
    Sliced
      Ripe, 7
      and red Italian onions, 283
      with basil, 264
      with cucumbers, 71
      with onions, 18
      thinly, 199
  Watercress and raw mushroom, 66
Salami, *see* Charcuterie, 21–22
Salmon, *see* Fish
Salsa fria, 226
Sand tarts, 299
Sandwiches,
  Cheeseburgers, grilled, 130, 338–339
  Chicken, 298–299, 317
  Foie gras, 238, 299
  Frankfurters, French, 339
  Grilled flank steak, 280–281
  Heroes, individual, 338
  Open-faced cucumber, 249–250
  Pumpernickel, 18
  Snitters, 230–231
  Thin onion, 235
  Virginia ham, 251
Sardine paste, 244
Sauces,
  Aillade, 142
  Aïoli, 33, 181
  Anchovy, 347
    Butter, 259
  Barbecue, 351–352
  Basic brown, 344
  Bèarnaise, 347
  Béchamel, 343
  Beet dressing, 68–69
  Beurre blanc, 51
  Bordelaise, 344–345
  Chablis cream sauce, 208–209
  Cheese, 343
  Curry, 26
  Diable, 345
  Dipping sauce for raw vegetable, 215

Sauces (*Cont.*)
  Duxelles, 345, 353
  Espagnole, 344
  Green Goddess, 349
  Hollandaise,
    Basic, 346
    Blender, 346–347
    variations, 347
  Horseradish applesauce, 192
  Horseradish cream, 166
  Italienne, 351
  Madère, 345
  Mayonnaise,
    Anchovy, 349
    Basic, 348
    Blender, 348–349
    Green, 237, 286
    Mustard, 71, 349
    Spicy, 320–321
  Mornay, 343
  Mousseline, 347
  Mushroom, 352
  Mustard, 55
    Burgundy, 241
    Mustard butter, 241
  Niçoise, 56, 105
  Oriental, 352
  Perigourdine, 345
  Piquante, 346
  Poivrade, 346
  Provençale, 259
  Raw vegetable dunk, 242
  Rèmoulade, 349
  Russian dressing, 349
  Soubise, 111
  Supreme, 343
  Tabasco, cocktail sauce, 351
  Tapenade, 277
  Tarragon cream, 12–13
  Tartar, 349
  Thousand island dressing, 349
  Tomato, 140–141, 315
  Vegetables a la grecque, sauce for,
    350–351
  Velouté, 344
  Verte, 285
  Vinaigrette, 350
    variations, 350

Sauerkraut, braised, 336
Sausage,
  Board, 301, 310
  Broiled, 19
  Chipolatas, 15
    Stuffing for peppers, 16
  en brioche, 34
  Hot kielbasy with mustards, 316
  Italian, hot and sweet, 330
  Stuffing for turkey, 324
  Tiny rolls, 251
  Tree, 279
Savarin with apricot glaze, 169–170
Scallops,
  en seviche, 168
  Sauté provençale, 36
Seafood plate, provençale, 258
Semolina gnocchi, 103
Seviche in avocado shells, 137
Shad Roe, poached in butter, 131
Shellfish, *see under* separate listings
Sherbet, raspberry with peaches, 109
Sherry jelly, 99
Shortcake, *see* Cake
Shrimp,
  Aillade, 142, 172
  Grilled, 271
  Liz Lucas shrimp, 198
  Pacific shrimp appetizer, 86
  Potted shrimp paste, 233–234
  with green mayonnaise, 237
Snitter, 230–231
Snow peas, 57
  and mushrooms, 87–88
Sole, *see* fish
Sorrel, 73
Soufflés,
  Apricot, 69
  Cold orange, 189–190
  Crab, 65
  Crêpes, 81–82
  Ginger, 133–134
  Glacé grand marnier, 260
  Gruyère, 127–128
  Omelet, 125
  Orange marmalade, 35
  Pets de nonne (beignets), 144
  Savarin with apricot glaze, 169–170

Soups,
  Clam and tomato broth, 80
  Consomme,
    aux profiteroles, 110
    Double chicken, 165–166
      Jellied, 284–285
  Crab soup, Margaret Jennings, 116–117
  Pea,
    Cream of, 153–154
    Curried, 89
    Split, with sausages, 218
  Madrilene with chives and sour cream, 50
  Potage, germiny, 294
  Soupe de poisson, marseillaise, 193
  Turtle,
    Clear, with madeira, 113
    with madeira, 335
Spaetzle, 95–96
Spaghetti alla carbonara, 122–123
Spareribs, glazed, 240
Spinach,
  Gnocchi, 209
  with cream and nutmeg, 128–129
  with oil and garlic, 171
Sponge cake, 355–356
Squab chickens,
  Sautéed, 8
  Stuffed, 312
  with forcemeat stuffing, 108
Stuffing for turkey,
  Spiced sausage, 324
  Tarragon crumb, 324
Stew,
  Irish, 42–43
  Viennese goulash, 95
Steaks, *see* Beef
Strawberries, 6
  Quick sherbet, 50
  Romanoff, 63
  Romanoff in meringue shells, 174–175
  with coeur a la crème, 57, 185
Striped bass with cream sauce, 171
Sweetbreads Albert, 173–174
Swiss enchiladas, 148
Swiss tarte à l'oignon, 41
Syrup, mango macadamia, 219

T

Tabasco cocktail sauce, 351
Tapenade, 277
Tarts,
  Apple, 196
  Apple and mince, 334
  Apricot, 38
  Blueberry tarts with whipped cream, 264
  Mincemeat, 118
  Strawberry, 202
  Swiss, a l'oignon, 41
Tartar sauce, 349
Tarte aux apricots, 38
Teriyaki strips, 236
Terrine aux aromatas, 91–92
Thousand island dressing, 349
Tian, 187
Tomatoes,
  Grilled with duxelles, 48
  Salad, *see* Salads
  Sautéed, 127
  Stuffed, 289–290
Tournedos au poivre flambé, 47–48
Tortillas, 138
Trout, *see* Fish
Truffles with Pasta, 78
Turkey,
  Boned and rolled, 204
  how to roast, 324–325
  Pan sauce, 325
  Stuffings for, 324
Turnips, mashed yellow with butter, 325–326
Turtle soups, *see* Soups

V

Veal,
  and pork terrine, 290
  Cutlets sicilienne, 169
  Paillard of, 128
  Scallopine with lemon, 58
  Tenderloin of veal with basil and black olives, 212
Vegetables, *see* individual vegetables
Vegetables, raw
  Bagna cauda, 309
  in ice, 242
  Plate, 49, 145, 277, 321

Velouté sauce, 344
Vinaigrette sauce, 350
Vol-au-vent with chicken and sweet-
    breads, suprême, 67–68

W

Watercress and raw mushroom salad,
    66
Wines,
  A Guide to, 375–380

Z

Zabaglione, frozen, 79
Zratys Nelson, 83
Zucchini,
  and lobster, 47
  Frittate, 23
  Sautéed with garlic, 131, 132
Zuppa inglese, 213–214